THE CHOICE

THE CHOICE

by

Sister Kirsty

HODDER AND STOUGHTON
LONDON SYDNEY AUCKLAND TORONTO

British Library Cataloguing in Publication Data

Kirsty Sister
  The Choice
  1. Community of St Mary the Virgin
  I. Title
255′.98′0924   BX5185.C/

ISBN 0 340 26345 8

Dedicated with much love to all my sisters.

ACKNOWLEDGEMENTS

Grateful acknowledgements are made to Messrs. Faber & Faber, and Collins; to the Reverend Mother General C.S.M.V., the Sisters and the Revd Basil T. Davies [one of our·Community Chaplains], who encouraged, supported and advised me in this venture; to Gwenda Hutchinson and Ann Morgan of Shefford Office Services for the expert and kindly help given in the typing of the manuscript; and very especially to Ann and Edward England, Directors of Edward England Books Ltd., without whom this book would never have been undertaken or completed.

CONTENTS

COMMUNITY OF ST MARY THE VIRGIN, WANTAGE

The Community of St Mary the Virgin was founded in 1848 by William John Butler, then Vicar of Wantage and later Dean of Lincoln. Although the Rule derives from St Augustine, the Founder was also greatly influenced by St Francis de Sales and his Sisters of the Visitation, so that from the beginning the community followed the 'mixed' life, a life that was both active and contemplative, the way of Mary and Martha. The Constitution states:

> The active work of the Community shall be the service of our Lord and Saviour Jesus Christ through sharing in his teaching and redemptive ministry, according to the words of the blessed Virgin Mary, "Whatsoever he saith unto you, do it." In consequence, the Community has never been restricted to any particular work or works, but has tried to meet the needs of the time in a variety of ways. The daily Eucharist is central to the life of the Community, and the Day Hours are recited in choir, in addition to a generous rule of personal prayer. In recent years, the Community has moved away from large residential works, and the newer branch houses are small and non-institutional. There are also increasing calls upon the sisters to preach and give talks, to take part in missions and to conduct retreats and schools of prayer. The spirit of the Community is summed up in the words engraved on the cross which each sister receives at profession: "Ecce ancilla Domini, fiat mihi secundum verbum tuum."

INTRODUCTION

The Choice is the story of God's call to me to become a sister of the Anglican Community of St Mary the Virgin, which has its Mother House at Wantage, near Oxford. But my name is not Kirsty. Nor are any of the names I have used those of sisters in the present community. I have not described actual or particular sisters, simply hiding their identity under pseudonyms, for although I accept, with eyes wide open, the possible pain of self-exposure, and do so in order to share very personally something of the particular joys and sorrows that went into the making of my life choice, I could not presume to involve other sisters in that exposure in a way that might crash the barriers of their 'hidden-ness'. So, with the exception of Sister Geraldine, who bears a remarkably close resemblance to my first novice mistress, Sister (later Mother) Harriet Ruth and Sister Zoe, all the characters in this book are representative. Readers of *The Choice* and visitors to the convent would not be able to identify any of them with actual sisters in the community . . . or, if they tried to do so, they would fail.

It is not because my story is exceptional or unusual that it is recounted here. There are others who would have more dramatic experiences to share. However, simply because it is fairly ordinary, I may be speaking for a wide section not only of my own community, but of all communities. It is my story, telling of first impressions and lessons through my eyes. Others would doubtless recall theirs differently, and yet I trust that fundamentally I am in tune with what we would all say in our different ways. But if what I have written leads to misunderstanding or misconceptions, I must claim complete and total responsibility.

It is a story of a religious vocation from its early beginnings through to profession in a community. It covers the period of training given in the Novitiate, the voyage of self-discovery, the gradual deepening in understanding of the Religious Life which finally leads to life commitment.

Do not look for the wisdom and insights of a long-professed sister in this book. At the request of the publishers I am writing now, as one recently professed, before the memories fade. I fully acknowledge that much of what I have learned and come to believe has yet to be lived over a long period of time, and that whilst the testing of the novitiate period is over, the far deeper testing of the professed life is only just beginning.

I have endeavoured to recall and reflect faithfully the impressions, shocks, discoveries and choices as I experienced them at the time. Already I feel differently about some things, but have tried to be honest in describing how they affected me then. It is a true story in almost all details with one or two exceptions where I have made adjustments in order to shield others. For example, although I have written in the singular, I had a companion at profession. All that I describe of the election, profession retreat and the profession day itself were shared experiences with my fellow novice and, obviously, the sharing of such joy produces special bonds that last throughout one's community life. Especially do we feel that link on the anniversaries of our profession. Other adjustments in the book are very minor.

One further point of elucidation should be made. The terms monk, nun, and monastic are strictly speaking reserved to those communities which are principally enclosed, contemplative orders, following a monastic form of life. Other communities, like our own, which combine the contemplative life of prayer with active works and mission, are usually referred to as religious communities. We are called either Religious or, in our case, sisters rather than nuns. But just as there is much overlap in our callings, so the distinctions of terminology between enclosed and mixed communities are blurred. By and large, I have attempted to use the correct terms in this book, but have been flexible where it seemed to aid clarity and have therefore sometimes used them interchangeably to cover the whole field of dedicated life.

1

POINT OF DEPARTURE

The very last thing I had wanted was any delay, any prolonging of the agony of this separation, and now I was snarled up in a traffic jam around Shepherd's Bush with Pompey, my blue Burmese, howling dismally in his basket on the passenger seat beside me. Animals are very sensitive to human vibes, and there was no doubt that he was picking up the pain that I was feeling at the approaching parting with him. I felt an absolute traitor handing him over to a new owner, he who had been my faithful companion for nearly eight years. I sat behind the wheel of my car feeling numb with misery. Finally the traffic began to clear a bit and slowly we crawled out of central London to our destination. I delivered Pompey safely and departed rapidly. This was just one part of the final packing up of my home and the settling of my temporal affairs; for I was about to enter a convent.

For three years I had known that this was where I was heading, but I and the community I was joining felt the sense of call to the religious life had to be tested slowly before I took any irrevocable steps. And, anyway, I had a commitment to my job which made resignation well nigh impossible for three years. Why was I doing it, what had started me on this crazy lunatic journey in which I seemed to be doing great violence to my nature? My mind went back to a certain bedroom in a friend's house. I could still

15

see the moonlight, shining in over the tops of the fir trees in the drive, there was an uncanny stillness and a profound silence. It was the middle of the night and nothing stirred, and I was still too, absolutely still, because even the smallest movement was agonisingly painful. As quite a young child I had had an accident which had damaged my spine and now all these years later some of the effects of that damage were beginning to be very evident, and I feared that it was the onset of a life of increasing inactivity. Indeed, I had actually been warned on good authority that I might be in a wheelchair by the time I was forty-five. Never had I expected this kind of interruption to my life. Other people were having to cover my work for me, correspondence was piling up and all sorts of engagements had to be broken. But it is always salutary to discover that one can be knocked out of action, and life does not actually grind to a halt in one's absence, and however inconvenient, God was clearly going to make good use of my inactivity. For once he had got me still. I certainly hadn't realised the extent to which my vast activism had held him at bay, and created an inner noise that was so great it drowned his voice at times. How could I? I was fully persuaded that the tremendous output of work and expenditure of time and energy were all on his behalf. It was my genuine and sincere belief that this was service that was well pleasing to him. God had been a reality to me since early childhood and deep down I had wanted to give him my all, but now I began to see that it had largely been on my own terms.

In the silence of those long sleepless nights and in the new inner stillness which had come with the physical stillness, God was able to say (don't ask me how I knew, but I knew with an awful clarity), "I know you want to give me your all, but are you prepared to listen and to hear from me how I would like that gift? I don't want just your works, I want you." Yes, the message came through clearly enough, and there in the moonlit room, with Pompey asleep in his basket, I chewed it over and I digested it, but what did it mean? Somehow, because God's presence in that silence and stillness was so real, I turned quite naturally to prayer.

16

Not in any formal prayerbook language. There wasn't any language at all really; I simply rested in God's presence, offered my pain on behalf of others and entered into silent and loving communion with him. The coming of daylight and breakfast did nothing to break it and it flowed on into each day; I had no inclination to read devotional books or study, it was enough just to stay in that presence.

It had long been my practice to make a retreat two or three times a year to punctuate my life with periods of stillness, but this was different. For one thing it was a much longer time of withdrawal, and then too, I really had been *forced* to let go and drop my work. So my nights became filled with God's presence and prayer flowed on through the day; it was like breathing in the clear mountain air of the Alps. I knew that I had experienced a new dimension of existence and of relationship with God, and life would and could never be the same again. There is a mixture of the Mary and the Martha in all of us, but this time had confirmed for me that, if I was to be true to my real self, I had got to give the Mary in me a far greater place. This insight meant that all my activism was thrown into new perspective which would be all right, so I thought, as long as I reviewed my life pattern and adjusted it accordingly in order to build into it more space. At all costs I would have to deal with my diary and timetable to make it a practical reality. This taste of 'being' prayer through stillness, silence, pain and emptiness had left me with an insatiable desire and I knew that I could never settle for anything less.

It was quite a long time before it dawned on me that it wasn't going to be a matter of simple adjustment of my programme. Something far more radical had happened in those weeks on my back, and it would require an essential change. I don't quite know how or when it dawned on me, but gradually I knew where God was leading me.

I had been an oblate (a lay member) of a religious community for some while, and valued the discipline and support that membership with its Rule of life gave me. But never had I thought of entering a community fully as a sister. God had seemed to be so clearly leading me to take

17

on extra responsibility in my professional life, surely he could not be back-pedalling on that? Yet the gnawing feeling that I was being called to the Religious Life grew stronger and stronger, and never left me. It all seemed too ridiculous for words. The very affliction which had felled me and made me a temporary invalid was enough reason for not joining a community. After all, everyone knows that the life of a nun is extremely tough and involves a lot of physical hard work – long hours and non-stop days. I would never qualify on medical grounds. Well that was a relief! But in that case, what was God doing? Why did he appear to be calling me to this, at the very time when it must be abundantly clear that I was quite unsuitable material for an aspiring nun? Still, recent promotion in my work made it impossible to do anything about it at once, so there was a merciful period of three years in which God could make it abundantly clear that I was reading him wrong. It seemed sudden, this upheaval with its new discovery, for my life seemed to have taken the direction of becoming more settled with my own home and place in professional, church and social life. But looking back through the years, I could see the thread weaving right back to my earliest experiences. Even as a very tiny child I had my contemplative moments. That's not at all unusual for small children, for they still live close to the wonder of life, and wonder is an essential ingredient of contemplation. Now I began to see how these childhood experiences had imperceptibly been marking out the direction that my life would take. I suppose most of us can look down through the years and see those moments which stand out rather like milestones along the road of our spiritual journey, when suddenly we encountered reality in a new way.

Life had always been full and, with the exception of a few periods, very joyful. I loved my work and was always fully involved in church life. As far as I could judge, I would just continue up the promotional ladder in my profession. I suppose no single person quite rules out the possibility of marriage, but I certainly wasn't consciously entertaining the idea, or hankering after it. It had been hard at a younger age and like most women I had hoped that one day I might meet the right man and settle down in my own home, but gradually as I had become more involved in my work and took on new responsibilities, I felt satisfied and fulfilled. I had my own house, a wide circle of friends, independence, financial security and reasonable prospects for the future. There came a time when I knew I might find it very hard indeed to give it up, even for love of a man.

At one point when I was doing some further study, I needed to do some research in a convent itself and the opportunity came through a friend to visit the Community of St Mary the Virgin at Wantage. So, much to the amusement of some of my friends, I found myself one bank holiday driving down to the little market town in Oxfordshire wondering what on earth I was letting myself in for, and armed with all sorts of good advice from people who knew little more than I did as to what to do and what not to do. That was the first time I had ever knocked on a convent door, and little did I suspect then that one day I would knock again, and ask for admittance – for good.

Far from the strict regime I had expected, I found the sisters disciplined but relaxed, very warm and welcoming, delighted that I actually enjoyed their milk puddings, and asked for second helpings, and more than willing to show me anything that would help with the study I was doing. No pressure was put on me to attend the Divine Office and Liturgy, but naturally I wanted to be there and even though some of it was incomprehensible to me, I was just happy to absorb what I could and leave the rest. Everyone seemed totally relaxed and unfussy. "What if I do the wrong thing or get in the wrong place?" I had asked a knowledgeable friend in panic beforehand. "Don't worry," she answered, "even if you prostrated yourself flat in the middle of the aisle they would quietly step over you. No one would worry or think it odd." That took a lot of the alarm out of this particular excursion. It was enthralling to share in the worship of chapel and look at old community publications and documents, but without any doubt the high spot was my encounter with Sister Zoe, my mentor and guide for the duration of the visit. I could scarcely believe that I was talking so freely and at such depth with someone who had been a stranger only a few days before. What's more – it was the first time I had ever conversed with a nun. But her twinkling blue eyes and warmth drew people out almost on contact. Behind the twinkle was a shrewd judge of character and an original and daring thinker. She made no effort to paint rosy pictures of the Religious Life and certainly there was no attempt to draw me in. I was treated with honour as a guest and left completely free in every way. Maybe Sister Zoe did not fully realise the impact that first visit was making on me. Silence pervaded the convent and there was a space to pray; I shared that gift hungrily. There was a rhythm in the day, it flowed on punctuated at regular intervals by services in chapel and one day was like another. That too was refreshing to one whose programme varied from day to day and for whom there was no routine and scarcely any rhythm. There was a simplicity about the life that moved me. It still mattered to do things well and carefully. Things were treated with reverence as well as people. The hens ranged freely and happily, the pigs and cows were friendly and docile, which clearly indicated the gentle and loving way in which they were handled, and I stood back in awe as Sister Zoe took me via the hives and in a very matter of fact way saw to the bees, who buzzed round her like friends. It intrigued me too that as she showed me round the complex of buildings, from the farm to the printing room, to the gatehouse and the studio (where I saw quite incredibly beautiful sculpture in the making), all the time as we walked she was sandpapering wood that later she would use for making icons. Time itself is regarded as a gift from God and none is wasted.

Even to this day I remember the very spot where I was suddenly hit by the curious feeling that I had come home. Shattered though I was by the inner homing device that had been triggered off, which I most certainly didn't reveal to anyone else at the time, I convinced myself that it was a perfectly normal reaction to a life that had so much of what sophisticated city life lacks. Silence, simplicity, manual work, harmony with nature, rhythm and reverence for life in general. It was merely an emotional response I persuaded myself. It would pass in time.

It didn't. I knew I would visit again; it was compulsive, and the sense of being at home got stronger each time. When finally after I had requested help with my Rule of life, I was asked if I would like to consider becoming an oblate of the community, I thought 'So this is what God is asking of me.' After looking carefully at the commitment it would involve in the light of all my other commitments, I decided that it was right and took the plunge. So I had one foot inside the life, but still I never dreamed of going any further. On the contrary, a friend and I would spend a wonderfully happy weekend at the convent, meet all our friends amongst the sisters, dive thankfully into the silence and peace and let the strains drop away, but when we arrived back home we would sink comfortably into our chairs, put our feet up and enjoy a glass of sherry. "It was gorgeous, and when can we go again?" we would say. "But isn't it lovely to be back in the comfort of our own homes." Invariably that's what we said . . . and meant.

God, it seemed, had other ideas. And over the four years since that first visit he had been at work. Step by step he had made his will clear, and so it was all fixed that I should start my life at Wantage in September.

Winding up one's affairs is always difficult, even if it is just a case of changing jobs. I had had that experience before, but this time it was very odd.

Firstly there was the hurdle to leap of breaking the news. The stunned looks and disbelief on the faces of my colleagues as one by one they were told was all that I had dreaded, and more. Only my closest friends had known that I even had links with the religious community, so it came to the others as a huge shock. Many of them seemed too embarrassed to comment or discuss it with me. "What would you like as a leaving present?" a senior colleague asked. Help! That was a problem. What indeed? I was busily trying to dispose of things, not add to them, but how grateful I was to them for their great sensitivity. At the farewell party with strawberries and cream (would this be the last time I had such a luxury?), I was handed some cosmetics for my immediate journey, ie to the Middle East, and a book token for that longer, more searching journey. Marvellous! This would mean an addition to the convent library that all could share.

So I came to the point of departure for a holiday. On board the plane some of the strains of the last weeks began to fall away. Everyone was in a holiday mood, we were heading for the sun and the sea and sights which I had longed to see. From Athens we were to board our ship and begin cruising, first stop Crete, then Egypt, the Lebanon and the Holy Land. There was a curious mixture of feelings. On the one hand wanting to fill every moment and do all the things one could do for the last time, and on the other hand already feeling almost adrift. When it came to it I didn't want a last fling because already I had lost the taste for many of the things that at one time would have given pleasure. I felt an alone-ness that was sharpened by the size of the ship's company, perhaps it can be compared to the isolation a deaf person must feel in a large company of people. It was very clear to me that having begun to cut loose from my moorings by resigning my job, clearing out so much of my home, and openly declaring my commitment to the Religious Life, I had already begun to move into a different world. It didn't stop me enjoying local wines and trying out Syrtaki dancing in Crete, or riding a very temperamental camel along the pyramids road in Egypt, all the while consciously relishing the wind in my hair, the sun on my bare arms and legs. It was indeed an experience to be savoured. I could hardly bear to think of the time coming so soon when my head would be covered by a veil for the rest of my life and my arms and legs by a habit.

The final weeks at home have become a blur in my memory. I remember only the weariness of turning out, sorting, burning and packing. There were endless letters to be answered and a round of farewell dinner parties. If I had my time over again, I think I would just slip away without saying anything to anyone, but that would probably have been very unkind to my friends and already they had been hurt enough. It was my hairdresser who, for my final visit, laid on the most novel farewell. To every customer that night she served a glass of wine under the hairdryer in honour of my becoming a nun.

Perhaps the most painful moment of all was the closing of my front door for the last time. A little group of neighbours gathered to wave me goodbye. I somehow managed a smile and a cheery greeting, jumped into the car and put my foot down. As soon as I was over the brow of the hill and out of sight, the flood waters burst their banks and the tears poured down uncontrollably. Somehow through that blur of tears and with a terrible ache inside I drove to friends who were giving me hospitality.

"How would you like to spend the last weekend?" they asked.

"Well, I would like to get to the sea again and be able to sit on the beach once more in ordinary clothes and swim and sunbathe," I said.

So we headed for the South Coast, deciding to take a fast train from Victoria. Still feeling that I was living through a dream I queued up for tickets, barely conscious of others in the queue. Suddenly an irate lady pushed me aside with great force, saying, "Can't you see that Sister is waiting for a ticket, let her through at once." An embarrassed nun was then pushed to the front of the queue right up to the ticket office. A wicked instinct made me want to grab the irate lady and say, "I am almost a sister, can I go next?" But then my heart sank. 'Oh God,' I thought, 'will I spend the rest of my life being singled out for special treatment? Will I be allowed to be a normal person again?'

The penultimate day arrived and I went for a final visit to see Pompey. Always adaptable, he had settled in very well and despite my own ache inside I knew the problem of letting go was mine, not his. Then came the farewell to my other faithful companion: for my job had involved a lot of travelling and I had spent literally hours of my life in my car. I watched and waved until at the end of the road the car turned left and vanished from sight in the hands of its new owner. It all seemed terribly unreal, I just went indoors, made a cup of tea, sat down and watched a test match on the television. There were no tears this time; I had almost gone beyond that point, there had been too much trauma in the last few weeks and now one by one I had said goodbye to my symbols of independence. My home for its security, my job for its satisfaction and fulfilment, my telephone for instant contact with friends, my car for easy mobility, Pompey for undemanding friendship. I wonder if we realise how much our sense of security often lies in these things. Still, I had not given up my cheque book or passport, I could cling on to those for a bit. If things didn't work out there was always the possibility of a new start either here or abroad.

I checked my suitcase for the morning. At the bottom I had packed a selection of secular clothes, and on top placed the new things I was required to take, together with the black skirts and white blouses I should be wearing for the next few months. It had said on the clothing list 'Underwear for three years'. Taking the instruction literally there were certainly enough new underclothes for three years. 'Did it mean just underclothes or toilet requisites too?' I wondered. I decided to play safe, so included a dozen toothbrushes, all of vivid colours. If my outward clothes were going to be black and white, I might as well ensure colour in other aspects of my life if only in something as simple as a toothbrush.

For my journey to Wantage I had chosen my favourite and most feminine dress. We had booked a table at a hotel overlooking the river in beautiful countryside, not too many miles from the convent. "A table by the window please," my friends had requested over the telephone. It was elegant and peaceful and yachts glided by on the water as the waiters moved smoothly and gracefully between the tables. It was a good idea in one way, but perhaps piling on the agony in another. True we had to eat our lunch somewhere, but perhaps a quick picnic would have been more appropriate. Fingering my glass of wine almost guiltily, I looked around at all the guests in the hotel. They of course were behaving quite normally and naturally. For them this lunch was no different from any other. Tomorrow they would carry on just as usual, but for me it was the end of one life and the beginning of a totally new one.

It was a relief to arrive at the convent and suddenly meet with a very calm almost casual welcome, everyone treating this as the most normal occurrence. There was no great fanfare of trumpets. The Novice Mistress came out and hugged me, looked at what I had thought to be a modest amount of luggage (after all I had packed up an entire house and office and reduced it to two trunks and a suitcase. 'Not bad' I thought), and said, "Well, it looks as though you've come to stay." The rest of my stuff vanished as though by magic from the back of the car, wafted away by willing novices, and I crossed the threshold into my new life.

2

ARRIVAL

I had never before been inside the novitiate room, for it was part of the enclosure within the convent, and the initial sight of it therefore came as a very great shock. The guest wing where I had stayed on my previous visits was simple enough, but this was austere. I looked at the bare, polished boards of the floor and the curtainless windows, the clear table and cupboard tops and plain walls unadorned save for a large crucifix, with a queer sinking feeling inside that was gathering momentum with every minute that passed.

The Senior Novice took me up to my cell in a corridor where the novices slept. I really don't know what I had expected, but I remember I was knocked sideways as she opened the door and ushered me in. It was, I think, the absence of colour that filled me with immediate dismay. There was nothing to relieve the cream walls, white chest of drawers, white chair, white washstand and white twill counterpane with a large red cross on it – except the dark stained floorboards, dark brown paintwork and curtains that had been dyed an uneven khaki. The décor was certainly not intended to please the senses. And I hadn't seen a black iron bedstead like that since I left school.

I gaped in silence, and into my mind came the picture of my bedroom at home with its restful, pastel shades and soft carpet, and all the little touches that helped to add beauty to the room, and this seemed like prison. In my initial horror I made a joke about it to the Senior Novice who was still waiting to show me the bathrooms and broom cupboard. It fell completely flat. Naturally. Anyone accustomed to monastic simplicity doesn't find it particularly amusing nor a laughing matter. She was obviously puzzled at my reaction. But laugh I did – not just at that but at practically everything, much to the annoyance of the other novices. And they can hardly be blamed.

All the nervous tension of the past weeks had left me in a state where I found everything new or strange acutely funny, and shook with helpless laughter at most inappropriate moments. It was wearisome for the others, but the only way by which I could cope. If it hadn't been laughter it would most certainly have been tears.

A large pile of letters on the novitiate table awaited my arrival, and everything in me reached out in longing for them and the contact they would give me with the friends and well-wishers who had written them. In this strange new world I was already feeling bereft of all that I had left behind – especially my friends. But every time I moved towards that pile of letters, hoping to pick them up in a nonchalant way that did not betray my eagerness, I was rushed off to get this or do that or be shown the other. Books seemed to appear from nowhere – "You'll need this for Lauds and here's another for Little Hours. Keep this one separate, we only use it at Compline . . ." and so it went on and on, gently flowing over my befuddled brain.

In the midst of it all, the novitiate door burst open and all the novices leapt to their feet. In the doorway stood the Novice Mistress cradling a large and magnificent bouquet, wrapped in cellophane with a beautiful ribbon and all.

'Well,' I thought. 'That's the nicest thing that's happened to me so far. What a super welcome. And how clever to wrap it so professionally.'

Words failed me as I tried to say an adequate thank you. "Are the flowers from the garden here?" I asked innocently, as, pink with embarrassment, she thrust the bouquet into my hands and withdrew rapidly. Then I saw the attached card from Interflora saying, 'With very best wishes

27

and love from us all – Naomi, Gail, Julian and Luke.' My ex-colleagues! Bless their hearts – what a wonderful and thoughtful gesture.

It was a very long time before I realised how absurd my gaffe had been, and how contrary to all community custom it would be to present flowers to one who had just crept in through the back door, as it were, as an aspirant. No official welcome is given, and, indeed, there is no formal admission for several weeks. There is a merciful period for adjustment whilst one gets acclimatised to a wholly new rhythm and approach to life. After that, the first tentative step forward is taken as the aspirant is received officially as a postulant.

I feasted my eyes on the gorgeous flowers. "Well, they'll make a lovely splash of colour in here," I said cheerfully as I gazed round the bare novitiate room.

"I should take them along to Sister Philippa in the sacristy, if I were you," said the Senior Novice as tactfully as she could. "She'll be delighted to have them for the chapel."

That was gaffe number two – not that we were never to have flowers in the room. On the contrary, many of us were to find real joy in arranging flowers both in the novitiate and in Sister Geraldine's office. But a bouquet. That was too special to keep to ourselves. Something of that nature would be shared with the whole community. It was clear that despite my many visits to the convent, I really had very little idea about the Religious Life and the way in which it is lived.

It was a warm September evening I recall, and I had arrived in a flimsy, summer dress. But now I was dressed in the heavyweight skirt, blouse and cardigan of an aspirant. Yet I was shivering and my teeth were chattering.

"Come and have a chat before supper," Sister Geraldine, the Novice Mistress, had said. And for half an hour I continued to shake and chatter whilst we looked for suitable spiritual reading and Sister talked about the timetable and the manual work I was to do.

"You've settled into your cell, have you?" she enquired.

28

That did it. My fear and anxiety rose to the surface and I blurted out, "I don't understand why the cells have to be so ugly. Surely that isn't honouring or pleasing to God?" In my own mind I was persuaded that I wasn't just arguing on the basis of likes and dislikes, or pandering to the senses. "It seems to me it is a matter of Biblical principle," I continued (a nice piece of rationalisation.), "God is the author of beauty. He loves beauty and he has created us in his image – also to be authors and lovers of beauty . . . so shouldn't we . . ." My voice petered out.

The large, blue eyes opposite searched mine with a pensive, almost bemused look, and after stroking her chin silently for a while, Sister Geraldine said, "I can see we are going to have some very interesting discussions." Only later did I come to appreciate her charity on that first night when I was feeling so insecure and defensive and manifesting my ignorance at every turn. She, secure in her understanding and acceptance of simplicity and poverty, was far too wise to enter into an argument with me, or defend the ways of a religious community. As I was to discover, many times over, her policy was to give people time – time to find themselves and become part of the community, time to put down roots. If the soil was right they would grow. If not, it would soon become clear to all concerned.

"I think," she said, "when you've had your supper it would be a good idea if you went to bed and had an early night. And perhaps (viewing my goose pimples), you had better have a hot water bottle."

Diving into a cupboard she produced one triumphantly, and I meekly thanked her. Obviously this was a rare concession and I hadn't got it in me to admit that I had one in my case anyway.

Then with a wealth of understanding and compassion, she swept me into her arms in an enormous hug and said laughing at me, "Are you very apprehensive?"

"Apprehensive!" I exclaimed, "I'm plain terrified."

We are all so different, and we come in different ways – some raring to go, hardly able to wait to get started; others dragging their heels fearfully and reluctantly (that was me);

29

others quite convinced that it is all nonsense and they won't stay for long, but unless they give it a try, they will never be able to look God in the face.

After supper, I finally made a grab for my letters.

"We don't read letters in our cells," said a rather tight voice.

I turned round to see a novice directing a very disapproving look at me.

"Sorry," I said, in an equally tight voice, "for this once I'm going to have to – what other chance have I had of opening them?" Inwardly I knew that I desperately needed my friends around me on that first lonely and bewildering night. And that was the measure of my detachment as I started my new life.

I didn't sleep much. People crept along the corridors and around their cells as quietly as possible, but the old wooden floorboards creaked and I was conscious of the close proximity of the other novices around me which felt very strange after years and years of living alone. I lay in bed thinking, "What have I done? Oh God, what have I done?"

There was no mistaking the rising bell; the shock of it practically propelled me out of bed towards the washstand with its bowl and jug of cold water. Life in community began in earnest when, covered in a very smart new overall, I launched into the chores assigned to me. So much of me had rebelled at the idea of coming, but now that I was here I wasn't going to do anything by half measures. I really wanted to go right in and throw myself wholeheartedly into my new life, even if the things I was asked to do were strange and unfamiliar.

Right from the outset, I was stunned by the speed at which everyone got going, almost as though the community went straight into top gear. It wasn't exactly that they tore round in a frenzied way and yet, at the same time, there was a curious feeling of being caught up in the rush hour, or in the slipstream of a large vehicle. In those early days it left me feeling perpetually breathless. Sisters moved briskly and purposefully from one thing to the next. They didn't pause to chat, nor lingered around waiting for one another.

And over everything hung a great silence – something far more than a mere absence of words and noise. It was more like a concentration of energy, a total absorption. I was reminded a bit of the ant-hills I had seen when I lived in Africa. From a distance they gave the appearance of absolute stillness. But a poke with a stick would reveal thousands of ants bent on their business in a ferment of activity . . . with no wasted energy. However, as a newcomer feeling very strange, it seemed to me that the sisters passed each other like ships in the night and I wondered if we ought not to be affirming one another more with a cheery word or with smiles. It took me quite a while to discover that the deep bonds cemented and experienced in silence and in a common purpose are far stronger than those made by eye contact or verbal greetings – and more real. Certainly there are times and occasions when sisters do linger to converse, but not as they go about their work. "It has to do with single-mindedness about what one is doing," said Sister Geraldine when I spoke to her about it. "We believe strongly that time is a gift that we receive from God, and therefore we try not to waste it, or squander it, or abuse it."

The effect of this kind of thinking is perhaps to give a feeling of non-stoppiness, to a newcomer at any rate, and yet not one of anxious rush and frenetic movement. I noticed that, at the sound of the chapel bell, everyone stopped her work and made for chapel. To me it seemed a living sign demonstrating the centrality of worship in this life, as from every direction and through every door the habited figures of sisters appeared surging silently yet purposefully towards that one focal place – chapel.

The whole of the monastic day is built upon the saying of the Divine Office. It is the first work of a Religious, sometimes called the Opus Dei, and is the public offering of praise, penance and intercession on behalf of the church and for the world to the God who is, and who is supreme. The bell summoning us to chapel is like a call from God himself and we leave everything else, since it is secondary in importance, in order to give God the praise and worship of

31

which he is worthy, and to engage the world to him through prayer.

If we had to justify our existence and our way of life . . . that's it. Not always understood by those outside the Religious Life, but that is hardly surprising, and we are not deterred.

In the Community of St Mary the Virgin, each sister is given an hour each morning for personal prayer. It is not time off from work, but is carved into the morning as a regular commitment which is as much her work as cooking, cleaning or scrubbing. After my struggle to find time for prayer in my previous working life, this was gift indeed, and I set off with great joy on that first morning towards one of the smaller chapels. Quietly opening the door, I crept in and then stood transfixed. The chapel was almost full. 'Where should I go? Which seat should I take?' I stood dithering for some while trying to spot a vacant place, hardly daring to move, for all the sisters were sitting or kneeling absolutely motionless in prayer. I badly wanted to be alone and suddenly it was very hard to cope with all these people around me. And it was a bit unnerving too, for as I stood there wavering, the absurd thought struck me that it was for all the world like walking into a room at Madame Tussaud's. Then a sister sensing my plight gave a discreet cough (that was reassuring . . . not waxworks after all) and signalled me to a seat with her eyes. I sat down and dared not move a muscle. The Bible and notebook I had brought with me remained on my lap unopened.

Next day I decided to try and find a little more solitude, and after exploring for a while came upon a little chapel that was quite empty. Thankfully, I sank to my knees. 'What a relief to be alone – no need to fear disturbing anyone or causing distractions.' It was jolly cold but that was a small price to pay for my solitude. Each day I made tracks for my bolt-hole. Each day I found it empty and rejoiced to be entirely alone. Then one day, after about three weeks, I found the door of 'my' chapel locked. 'Why?' I wondered. 'Has someone discovered my use of it, and is it, perhaps, not meant to be used?'

Later, I asked the Senior Novice about it. "Oh," she said, "Sister Perpetua's body is resting in there. Didn't you know? That's the mortuary chapel."

Shortly after my arrival, I was joined by another aspirant, Thelma. It was good to have someone else equally bewildered – we were able to help each other, imparting snippets of wisdom as we gleaned them. It was also very hard. For I, who was having great difficulty in controlling my laughter on so many occasions anyway, needed no encouragement; but Thelma gave it. We were bad for one another for we both saw the funny side of things at the same time and in the same way. There seemed to be an unspoken communication. It was very tiresome for those who were quite unable to see what was amusing in these situations and very embarrassing when we were smitten in chapel, as we frequently were. Mercifully, from our seats at the back, we could not be seen on the occasions when we doubled up and buried our faces in our handkerchiefs in an attempt to conceal our mirth.

The mornings were my Waterloo. I had been accustomed to going to bed very late. I remember how frequently I would seem to turn into the drive at home as the church clock in the valley was striking midnight, and there would still be post to deal with and Pompey to take for a last walk. Consequently, I was not good at early rising. In the Religious Life, everyone rises early to start the day's work before most of the world is awake. And correspondingly we go to bed at a time when most people are settling down to their after-dinner TV viewing. Sisters seemed to emerge from their cells so rapidly after the rising bell had rung, and would be on their way down to chapel before I had finished washing.

"How do you all do it?" I wailed at Sister Geraldine. "I simply *can't* go any faster."

"You will," she said, "and once you are clothed in the habit it will be easier. It is a very quick garment to put on – there aren't all the buttons and hooks that you have with blouses, skirts and cardigans."

Hurrying as I did, I would get to chapel feeling slightly

giddy and then sit through the first twenty minutes or so with waves of nausea sweeping over me. Always Sister Geraldine was there in her stall kneeling upright, alert . . . almost as though she was listening for something. That, of course, is precisely what she was doing.

Most of us in the novitiate were allowed to sleep in on one or even two mornings of the week and also to go to bed early on occasions. Sister never did. Morning after morning she would be there on duty just like a watchman. 'Doesn't she *ever* feel tired?' I groaned to myself inwardly one morning. 'Couldn't she oversleep just once?' But that was the cry of someone who hadn't yet found the rhythm of the life or adjusted the inner clock. It moved me deeply to see the old sisters, stalwart in their seventies and eighties, faithfully appearing each morning. How easy it would have been to argue that, 'At their age they could surely sleep on in the mornings.' But these were sisters who, all their professed lives, had risen early to be at Mass each morning and only for health reasons would they break that habit. There is no such thing as retirement for the Religious.

Since the Novice Mistress is the sister with whom the novices are most closely associated, she is a kind of model to them – though in no sense is there one blue print or one mould. Nevertheless, it is important in those formative years to see the life lived faithfully and according to the Rule. Thomas Merton once said: "The way to be a saint is to give yourself entirely to your Rule and the circumstances in which God has placed you and work out the secret which is his will."[1]

That is certainly the direction we all hope to take, but in the early stages one needs to see a living example of it. So, I sometimes looked at Sister Geraldine to see if she ever looked saggy or draggy. But no. She always had that alert look of someone who has gathered up her energies so that her whole being is pointing one way – Godwards. Did she ever feel annoyed at the things she was asked to do? Or want to refuse? I'm sure there must have been times when demands impinged on her own will and perhaps she had to say her 'Yes' through gritted teeth. But one felt that here was someone so completely given that she actually found joy in those things which presented themselves as a Cross.

One might imagine that all this discipline and recollectedness would lead to strain. But on the contrary, the sisters who struck me as being most disciplined also seemed to be the most relaxed and free ones. More and more I began to realise that my previous indiscipline had made me flabby (physically and spiritually) and dissipated in all sorts of ways. There was certainly a lot of shaping up to be done in the years ahead.

It never ceases to amaze me, when I think back, how long-suffering the sisters were at my blunders and the disruptions I caused as a newcomer. Thelma and I were assigned to washing up most evenings after supper. It was not arduous work, but it took quite a while since there were large piles of plates and dishes. Which of us started it I don't remember, but I blush to recall how we thought we would jolly things along with a little singing. We had no idea how this jarred on the other sisters working in the scullery, and what an intrusion it was into their silence. Even chores are better done when there is a total concentration on the job in hand, and we were tackling this area of work in a slap-happy, undisciplined way as though we were at a holiday camp. After they had borne it to the limits of their endurance, one of the sisters remarked very gently that it "isn't our custom to sing whilst working". This didn't mean a total lack of communication or conversation. There was often a good deal of light-hearted banter, and from time to time gales of laughter would sweep the corridors of the convent. The first time I met it, I was slightly surprised. It was so unrestrained, but so very real. And yet, why should it be surprising? Of all places, a convent should be a place of gaiety, laughter, merriment – a true and holy *hilaritas*. It would be far more surprising if the joy and fulfilment sisters find in their vocation did not find expression in laughter. I can't imagine how grim it would be living with a group of women who all took themselves too seriously.

I had been at Wantage for exactly four weeks when the

first pull from outside came – an attractive offer of a post at my old college. Momentarily I let my mind dwell on the possibilities. How I would have loved to take it up, had I not been where I was. I re-read the letter. '. . . a house provided . . . annual increments . . . car allowance . . .' It was dreamy! 'Why did it have to come now?' I thought, 'when I was so sure that God was calling me to test *this* life.' It was far too soon to know if he meant this to be a life-long vocation and I had to accept that if I turned down this offer and then later left the community, I might bitterly regret having lost this opportunity. Before I could be tempted any further, I took up pen and paper and wrote a letter declining the invitation. I knew I had got to stand firm in my conviction that I had to do what I was doing regardless of alternative proposals. There would probably be other luring voices, as indeed there were, but whatever happened I must not jump at chances but wait for God to lead me out – if he wanted so to do. The choice I had made in coming had been hard. Now I began to see that it was not enough. I should have to renew that choice again and again.

3

LIFE TOGETHER

Stranded on a desert island – how would you adapt? That's how it felt. Suddenly all the familiar things were gone, the props removed. It's true that at first, as postulants, we had access to our own money but both because we wanted to begin our new life the way it would go on, and also out of consideration for the novices (curiously, I thought they might find it hard – whereas they were thinking the same about us), we didn't spend it except on essentials like toothpaste and stamps.

It was challenging to have to make things out of nothing – as it were. We none of us know what resources of ingenuity lie hidden within us until circumstances force them to the surface. Many who spent years in prisoner-of-war camps will testify to that.

From now on, it was going to be a case of making cards rather than buying them for Christmas and anniversaries, so, within weeks of arriving, I was learning to do italic lettering, watching and copying Denise as she illuminated capitals.

"Once you are clothed, you will no longer be able to spend money on presents," Sister Geraldine said. "But often a hand-made card, that is the fruit of your own creativity, means far more to people than a shop-bought gift."

Recreation is the part of the day set aside for leisure

activities. It is as much a part of the day's timetable as Office or meals, and it is 'of obligation'. For half an hour (on most days) it is reckoned that sisters engage in some recreational activity together – as part of our 'making community'. In the history of religious communities it has tended to be fairly formal – spent together as a whole group, with the Superior of the house at the helm.

Now there is far more variety and less formality. Twice a week we had a formal recreation as a Novitiate but, even so, it wasn't stereotyped into one pattern. Often we sat and talked, doing mending or other forms of needlework and embroidery. Sometimes we listened to music. Occasionally we went out for a walk or sat in the novitiate garden. There was always a good deal of laughter and leg pulling.

Some of us were keen on table tennis and since we had a reasonably large table in the novitiate, we made ourselves some bats out of scraps of hardboard and wood. One novice knitted a net out of string, and we were raring to go. We couldn't think of any way of making the balls, however. But when a friend asked what he could give as a birthday present, he had an immediate answer. In no time a box of balls arrived, and we were away. We had a lot of fun out of our rigged up equipment.

We often seemed to be making posters or doing collage work for various special occasions. Whereas in modern educational establishments there are adequate supplies of materials in stock cupboards, and one has but to help oneself, now our supplies consisted of saved up scraps. We carefully ironed old Christmas wrappings, colourful toffee papers or silver foil from chocolates. We kept a carton for oddments of card and material and it was a constant source of surprise to find that we had within us creative resources to draw upon that we didn't know were there.

One suddenly had a new attitude to the lifespan of clothing. I watched enthralled as sisters darned and patched most beautifully, reinforced garments with an extraordinary variety of materials, and gave longer life to things which in former days I would have thrown out as beyond repair.

This side of holy poverty actually struck me as fun. It rang bells from my childhood, for I can just remember World War II and the way people got round the difficulties of food shortages and rationing by amazing resourcefulness. More than the challenge and fun in my new situation, however, my new attitude to clothes spilled over to other material things. I recognised that a new reverence was beginning to develop, a new caring in the way I used and handled things – for three reasons. First, one suddenly realises that if there are breakages, one cannot just write a cheque to replace them. That came home to me very forcibly when I had a bump in one of the community's cars. I was appalled and pleaded with Sister Geraldine to let me pay the bill.

"The money's there in the bank," I said, "if you will just let me write a cheque."

"No," she said, not unsympathetically, "you can't do that. It is one of the hardest lessons of dependence that we have to learn when we must accept that the community will pay for our mistakes."

Seeing my crestfallen face she added, kindly, "It has happened to practically all of us who are drivers, at some point or other."

Second, a new caring springs from a desire to make things last. That is indeed part of the upbringing of most of us anyway, but there are special hazards about the care of property in any form of institutional life. It is sometimes more difficult for individuals to feel the same degree of responsibility towards something shared corporately than for things owned as personal possessions.

Third, and more importantly still, was the new sense of respect for material things as 'created' – created perhaps by craftsmen in the first place, or created by machines out of natural materials and from plans drawn up by a human mind, but all reflecting and participating in the Creatorship of God. It was not just 'care' of things that mattered but 'reverence' for them, and a proper use of them for the function and purpose for which they were designed.

There were far deeper and more painful aspects of

poverty that we hadn't even glimpsed as yet, for holy poverty is far more than a material thing. When Thelma and I came to the day when we were to be admitted into the community as postulants, we were led to the sanctuary steps just before Vespers in our new grey veils and there questioned by the chaplain.

"Do you realise that what you are asking is a hard thing?"

"I do," we each replied.

Despite the two days of retreat when Sister Geraldine had prepared us for this step, one can only digest at a certain rate, and we had no idea at that stage how hard it might be, and in what ways we should find it hard.

"Are you willing . . .?"

"I am," we said. But neither of us could have guessed the full implications of that either. Any new undertaking involves a leap of faith.

Now that we were postulants, Thelma and I sat in choir for Vespers – not yet in stalls, but at prayer desks in the aisle.

Feeling horribly conspicuous I thought with panic, 'Whatever would happen if we couldn't control our mirth now? There would be no way of hiding it.' Things unexpected still tended to spark us off and reduce us to helpless laughter but, on the whole, the intensity of the first weeks was easing off.

Now that we were in choir and taking a more active part in the singing, it was decided that we should begin singing lessons. Sister Rachel was appointed to take us through our paces. Thus we were launched into the mysteries of plainchant. Each week we attended our class. Each week I wrote down notes of all that we were taught most conscientiously, listened with great attention, tried to follow all the intricacies – and always came away completely baffled. Thelma romped along seeming to find it quite easy. I was puzzled. Was it due to some kind of built-in resistance? What was wrong with me?

'I read ordinary staff notation with reasonable facility,' I thought, 'so why is this so incredibly difficult?'

It was a little like learning a foreign language; but I had had to do that in the past, and had enjoyed it.

The inability to grasp the fundamentals of this music made me miserable, for singing plays a very large part in our worship and I was beginning to lag further and further behind.

What with this and the very different atmosphere I was experiencing in the community's daily worship from anything I had known previously, I felt the need of some kind of theological and liturgical decompression chamber.

Three days after becoming a postulant, I was in the pantry helping Sister Olwen when the chapel bell began to toll. Sister Olwen stood still, crossed herself and murmured, "How lovely!" Seeing my puzzled expression she whispered, "It's Sister Eva, that's the passing bell." The bell tolled very slowly for one minute telling the sisters, wherever they were in the convent or the grounds, that Sister Eva had just died. It also informed the whole of Wantage, for being situated on rising ground on the edge of the town, when the wind is in the right direction the chapel bell can be heard quite clearly in our other house about a mile away. I had not met Sister Eva. She was old and had been nursed in the infirmary wing for some months. Throughout the convent there was an atmosphere of joy and thanksgiving that, for her, the earthly part of her pilgrimage was over.

After death has been certified, a sister is washed and fully dressed in her habit and veil, and her crucifix is placed in her hands. Two candles are left burning within the room where she is lying and sisters may go in to pray and give thanks for her life and all that she has been.

Sister Olwen stopped me in the corridor later that day.

"As you never had the chance to meet Sister Eva," she said, "I wondered if you would like to see her before the funeral?"

I said I would, and so she kindly took me along to point out the room.

Since that day I have been with sisters when they have died, and have seen many after death, and I am always

41

struck, as I was on that first occasion, by the amazing serenity and peace on their faces.

Fully dressed in the habit, they often look as though they have just stretched out on the bed for a short rest and are deeply asleep.

I wondered why Sister Eva was not wearing her community cross. When I enquired of the infirmarian, I discovered that the cross is not buried but is handed down from one sister to another, so that, at profession when a sister is first given her community cross, it comes to her with a history.

The Requiem Mass was to be sung on the following Tuesday. On Monday evening we gathered in chapel for the Office of Placebo, a very gentle and moving Office which begins with the coffin being borne in on a bier by four sisters and placed in a central position in choir. Four amber-coloured candles stand at the corners of the bier which is covered by a pall bearing a large red cross.

'Just like our bedspreads,' I thought.

The music of the Requiem is very lovely. For Sister Eva's service, a single vase of flowers had been placed on the westward side of the coffin. There were no visitors or members of the family, for Sister Eva, being of a ripe old age, had outlived her natural sisters. So it was just her community family who gave her the final send-off. And how moving and symbolic the burial was, there in the Garth with its lovely trees and huge rood.

Sister Eva was lowered into her unmarked grave and the community filed past dropping sprigs of box on to the coffin. It was a custom I had not met before. What really came as a most unexpected delight was the sight of the grave itself as I approached. The gardening sisters had lovingly decorated it, and the four sides were studded with colourful autumn leaves and flowers.

Then the procession moved off, back through the Garth and the east wing garden, to enter the convent by the cloister door and return to chapel. The final hymn had started by the time we postulants, bringing up the rear of the procession, had reached chapel.

> Love's redeeming work is done;
> Fought the fight, the battle won:

the choir was singing, and I looked round in amazement. I don't think, up to that point, I had ever seen so many smiling faces in chapel. And my word, how the sisters sang! No quiet restraint now. It was a case of full organ and full voice triumphantly celebrating the resurrection life,

> Thee we greet triumphant now;
> Hail the Resurrection thou![1]

rang out the choir as joy and the volume of sound increased together. The procession filing out, to more triumphant organ music, had more of the flavour of a Wedding March than a funeral, but as we joined the community for a festival elevenses, it struck me that, of course, we were celebrating Part II of a wedding that, for Sister Eva, had begun at her profession service.

Now that we were postulants, Thelma and I had really begun our community life in earnest. Our first month as aspirants had been a gentle breaking in and we had still been partly treated as visitors. Now the training was for real. Sisters became slightly less tolerant of our mistakes. There began a period when I felt I could do nothing right. I blundered and floundered all over the place, and suddenly cricitisms about me seemed to pour in daily to Sister Geraldine. Even though she used discretion about how and when to pass them on, I reeled under some of them. Often the faults had been committed in ignorance; I was trying desperately hard, but since I was so new to the life and doing unfamiliar things, I was bound to make mistakes. And, of course, I was bound to be corrected . . . and not necessarily with a kid-glove treatment. Perhaps it is part of simplicity not to wrap rebukes in layer upon layer of soft tissue so that the impact is cotton-woolly. There are times when it is right to be bracing. Certainly I had to learn that it is part of simplicity to accept one's mistakes and the corrections that follow without getting hurt and downcast.

This didn't come at all easily and I frequently escaped into my memory and thought of my former professional life where I had felt secure and knew how to get things right. It was hard always to remember that if I had made mistakes before and annoyed my colleagues, come the end of the day we went our separate ways and by the morning it was a new day and the heat of any previous friction would have dissipated considerably overnight. But in community, you go on living with your mistakes, and with your sisters day in, day out, cheek by jowl.

I remember thinking, 'If I stay, I must try and remember these early days and, for the sake of others who will find it equally hard, not just forget how it felt to be a new postulant'.

We are human and there is always the possibility that we shall get exasperated when someone upsets the smooth routine of life, or leaves jobs half finished, or simply doesn't turn up to work. Such mistakes are by no means limited to postulants or novices, and it has been a growing joy to discover the charity and forgiveness one receives from one's sisters, but as Postulant Kirsty I had yet to come to that discovery. In my over-sensitivity there seemed to be a lot of hard hitting, not backed up by much affirmation, and it was all a bit unnerving. This kind of sensitivity often goes with what might be loosely termed a creative, artistic temperament, but it can also be the direct fruit of pride, or it can be a sign of insecurity. It was a bit of all three for me, but it was going to take the next few years to unravel the strands and determine their respective strengths. In the meantime I crumpled under my unexpected failures – or so they seemed to me.

Sister Zoe was always there in the background, but now that I came under the pastoral care of the Novice Mistress, we actually saw less of each other than when we had lived eighty miles apart. That may seem surprising but, in a large group of people, it is perfectly possible to go for a week or more without seeing a particular sister. Naturally people saw quite a bit of the sisters in their departments of work, and for us, we met fellow postulants and novices every day.

It was painful to be so near Sister Zoe and yet in many ways so cut off. We were still at that point in the community's life when it was practice for the novitiate to be fairly enclosed. We were only just beginning to mix more freely with the professed sisters and still had a long way to go before reaching the present measure of integration. Sometimes Sister Zoe and I would meet in passing in the corridor and she would whisper, "I'm longing for the day when you'll be professed. It will all be quite different then. Perhaps we'll be able to have holidays together."

Profession seemed so many light years away from where I stood at that point, but sometimes I would take a fantasy trip and she and I would roam over hills and beautiful country talking at length as we had done when I was an oblate. Just having her around at the convent praying and loving helped me greatly, even though there was little verbal communication.

One retreat day I was feeling particularly low. The merciful anaesthetic that God seemed to give in the period when I was preparing to come to Wantage had been wearing off bit by bit, and pain that had been deadened began to hurt. On this particular day I was hurting rather more than usual for the job I had left, thinking wistfully of the work where I had felt safe and wanted. I went to Saint Mary Magdalen's chapel to pray. Only one small reading lamp was on at the back, otherwise it was dark. I sat halfway down the chapel where I could just pick out, in a niche in the wall, the line of the carved figure of our Lord in his third fall (the well-known carvings of the Way of the Cross, by our late Mother Maribel, are in fifteen niches around this chapel). I was glad that he knew what it felt like to fall, not once but again and again. I thought I was alone in the chapel and couldn't check the tears that flowed and kept on flowing. Maybe it was the general slump of my body, or the rather frequent nose blowings that gave the game away. All out of the dark there was Sister Zoe beside me. She said no words. She needed none. There was complete understanding and, not being afraid of tears (or anything else as far as I could make out), she enveloped me completely in her love. Strangely she had arrived by my side at the very moment when I had been thinking, 'Give me enough of thyself, O God, and I am rich indeed . . . but, oh I would so love a bit of human comfort too!' and then, there she was, like a swift answer to prayer. We never referred to the incident again but I know that as I sobbed out my pain, I let go something of my professional life to which I had been clinging.

We don't cut all our losses absolutely cleanly. Some are severed only gradually over a period of time, for entry into the novitiate of a community is both re-birth but also a dying, and the dying must have its rightful period of grieving and bereavement. The letting go of props and false securities may take years, if not the rest of one's life, to complete. It seems to me that it demonstrates the remarkable courtesy of the Holy Spirit in his dealings with us. He never attempts to wrest from us prematurely those things which we are not yet ready to surrender freely. Some of us come like small children clutching our trinkets but unable to let go. The Holy Spirit is not going to prise open our sticky, reluctant little fingers to get at the gift. He is prepared to bide his time.

We were a most heterogeneous group in the novitiate. Different in our backgrounds, age, temperament, experience, outlook on life, theology, churchmanship, tastes, shapes, sizes and health. We had been joined by two more postulants, Virginia and Miriam, and there were eight novices at home, making twelve of us in all. The other novices were scattered in other branch houses. We only saw them occasionally.

I often used to ponder the mystery of how God had singled us out from such very different walks of life, laid his hand upon each of us and called us with the same call. Some had been Christians almost from the cradle, others had been recent converts. Some knew their Bibles, others didn't. Some had wandered over the face of the earth, lived hippy style, seen the abject poverty of the Third World, others had been tied to home and ageing parents. It didn't matter. The novitiate is a great leveller.

Sometimes I used to gaze around the group and think, 'We are a strangely mixed bunch. We none of us have chosen one another as companions. Maybe in the world our styles and walks of life would have been so different, we would never even have met. Yet God has brought this particular group of people together at this particular time, and asks us to live together and love each other, even though we are so different.'

By and large, we got on extremely well together, but even so, there were the inevitable times of tension and confrontation unavoidable in any corporate life. We only survived as such a closeknit group by trying to work honestly and sometimes painfully towards a love that was real and founded on truth. Once, when she was leading our intercessions, Virginia gave thanks for the uncomfortable gift of community – and we all knew what she meant.

Every time I was tempted to think, 'We are an odd lot. What have we got in common?' I was immediately reproached in myself. To begin with, we had one very big thing in common – our vocations. True we were still at the stage of testing them, but we were all there in the novitiate because in one way or another, God had got hold of us by the roots of our hair and guided or dragged us there as the case might be. Different we might be, but our differences didn't divide us – they just made for greater variety. One other essential thing we also had in common. We all basically enjoyed life. We had all been successful, happy people – not jilted lovers running away from life.

We were women – healthy, normal women at that. We all had the creative gifts and urges of our sex. For us, in the Religious Life, our creativity is not channelled into home-making for a nuclear family. Nevertheless the energies are there, and will out – so they are used to benefit and upbuild the bigger family of the community. If our creativity did not find outlets – oh dear! It would probably be repressed and then manifest itself in all sorts of ugly ways such as moods, quarrelling, depression.

Inevitably, in a group of youngish (the average age was about thirty-five) healthy women, there was a great deal of laughter, teasing, mimicry and sheer exuberance. Yet despite all that, every single one of us valued stillness, solitude and silence, and part of our growing together as a group was a learning process in sensitivity towards one another . . . knowing how to touch down with the delicacy of a butterfly when someone was in pain, rather than bursting into their privacy with tactless questions, crashing all the barriers like a herd of elephants trampling down a plantation. We were all undergoing massive, interior changes and sensitive awareness was desperately important. Just to come in to a religious community is a gigantic cultural shock. There was far more to it even than adapting to new routines, new forms of worship, new faces, new work, new disciplines and traditions . . . though there was all of that. There was an inner work to be done. Plunge a group of people into silence and leave them there before God, and things begin to happen. Each one of us began to get deeper insights about ourselves – who we were, what we were really like, how we looked to God and, worse still, to others. Cut off from some of the things which previously had given us affirmation we began to get in touch with the more deeply buried areas of our emotions, our fears, our sexuality. Always within this voyage of self-discovery there was the promise of joy, but, to begin with, we didn't always emerge from the various stages of the journey particularly jubilant. Yet, the road to greater inner reality was also the road to the reality which is God himself, and so we felt compelled to continue our pilgrimage along it.

If previously we had, in any way, gathered to ourselves crumbs of importance and worth because of our professional status, they had to go.

If we felt we were lovable because we had a lot of friends, a loving family, and were much sought after . . . that had to go.

If we felt we were acceptable in the eyes of our colleagues, and the world in general, because of what we could do . . . our successes . . . that had to go.

If in the course of a successful career we had made a name for ourselves . . . that had to go.

If security had been based upon possessions – money, homes, cars, books etc; that had to go.

If we felt we were strong, bouncing and capable . . . even that had to go, for there were to be times for all of us when we would know physical weakness.

If we had (albeit unconsciously) learned techniques for hiding, even burying, our wounds . . . they had to go. Certainly we had to learn not to allow those buried wounds to come bursting out all over the place in an inappropriate and undisciplined way. But in a closely-knit group one cannot conceal pain very successfully, nor hope to clown one's way through with an aching heart. All around are people whose sensitivity is acutely tuned in, and any such unreality is soon picked up. One can sit in choir with what one imagines is perfect outward composure, a poise that could well be thought to come from passivity and inner serenity. But one's neighbour won't be fooled. In all probability she will be picking up the negative vibes lying just below the surface. Another may feel the full force of the waves of fear given off by someone nearby.

Just as animals know who are those who are afraid of them – because apparently we smell of fear – so those who spend much of their lives in silence, are able to hear, perceive, pick up and interpret. It is sometimes uncanny and often uncomfortable.

Yet it is also a joy. For it means that the community (my sisters around me) are given by God for comfort, as with Sister Zoe, but also to help me move away from the sham and pretence that have often characterised my life in the past.

Sometimes in the early days, when I longed to get away from people – just from the sheer number of actual bodies one encountered day after day – and to find space and solitude, and a curious but persistent hankering after my private bathroom dogged me, I would remind myself what a gift God gives us in our sisters. I had always wanted one when I was younger. Now I had nearly two hundred of them. Also, I learned to recognise that the ones who irritated me most, and sometimes drove me to near scream-

49

ing point, did so because they were my mirrors. Their faults were mine, and I couldn't bear having them reflected back at me so blatantly.

Practically every one of us had found it terribly hard to break the news of our intention to enter a convent to our families. Indeed, some had faced fierce opposition, even complete separation. One sister told me how her father had shown her the door and told her never to come back. And she didn't. Another had been told she might visit her family but only on the understanding that she removed her habit. She refused, and her family finally relented. Others have been immediately cut out of wills. Even for parents who are basically sympathetic, it is still often hard though mostly they continue to be very loving and supportive. Some break their hearts at apparently losing their daughter. For others the greatest distress is the thought that she won't marry and have a family of her own. Others are angry that a gifted child is throwing away a career with good prospects. These are very understandable reactions. Why any child of theirs should want to do such a strange and unnatural thing is often totally beyond their comprehension. If they, themselves, are not practising Christians it is all the harder – it just seems like a crazy, senseless waste.

It is a bit like the parable of the hen who hatched out goose eggs,

> and when she saw her children swimming about on the surface of the water, she ran up and down in consternation seeking help for the unfortunate ones, and did not understand that this was their whole life to them: to roam there on the surface of the water.[2]

Not only does it tear one apart to see one's family distressed, but also it brings untold pain not to be able to provide explanations other than something pitifully inadequate. For there is no way of explaining the inner compulsion. No way can one reason it out.

In his book *Till We Have Faces*, C. S. Lewis retells the myth of Cupid and Psyche. In Lewis, the elder sister,

Orual, Queen of Glome tells the story herself. She is a study in self-centredness and possessiveness. Her guide and philosopher is an old Greek sage who preaches reason, calm, and discipline, and has no time for gods. After a long search, Orual finds Psyche, whom she feared dead after having been offered as a ritual sacrifice. But Orual lacks the spiritual vision to recognise Psyche's new happiness (Lewis has made Cupid's palace invisible to the unregenerate), and the moral virtue to let her go. She is out for Psyche's 'good', and drives her to disobedience by the blackmail of selfish 'love'. The breaking of faith with the divine lover by the human beloved is a high moment in a rich story. But it is long before Orual comes to know what she has done. She is on the point of destroying herself in the wrong way before she learns to destroy herself in the right way. "Die before you die," the god tells her. "There is no chance after."[3]

When someone feels the pull towards the Religious Life it is because, under the pressure of the Holy Spirit, she is gravitating towards *her* natural environment, just as when the geese hatched out they made for water. Why some mothers hatch budding nuns is a mystery, and not surprisingly they flap up and down on the water's edge convinced that their child has landed up in the wrong environment – unless that child happens to be a Thérèse Martin with two older sisters already in a Carmel at Lisieux.

Just as Psyche found it impossible to persuade her sister, Orual, that she was happier than she had ever been before, and had no desire to return to her old life, so it is with those in the Religious Life. Like Psyche, we too know it to be an inexplicable love affair. Viewed in that way, the conditions are not arduous restrictions but a means to a goal – none less than the Beloved himself.

Those things which to an outsider may appear ridiculous and unnecessary, take on a very different colour from the other side when their purpose is seen more clearly.

Maybe there is a particular sense in which we have to be prepared to be 'fools for Christ's sake'.[4] For love can express itself in ways that are extravagant, often foolish and quite inexplicable. The ardour and burning zeal of the early saints sometimes led to what was described as 'holy madness'. There are numerous and delightful stories illustrating their *sancta simplicitas* which sprang from such an intensity of desire for God that the world wrote these 'holy simpletons' off as crazy with love.

> Wisdom 'tis and courtesy
> crazed for Jesus Christ to be.[5]

They themselves often regarded discretion as the 'enemy of true devotion'.[5] Nowadays we tend towards greater moderation, and yet, did not their life have a tang, a salt-sting, which our lacks? They succeeded where a broader, saner way of life often fails.[6]

No half-measures, no half-heartedness, no cowardice or compromise – that was their way. Theirs was a wholeness of purpose and singleness of heart to which deep down we, too, would aspire even if the common life precludes some of the extraordinary outward excesses of the individual zealot.

Our prayer would be that of Richard Rolle:

Lord Jesus, I ask Thee, give unto me movement in Thy love withouten measure, desire withouten limit, longing withouten order; burning withouten discretion. Truly the better the love of Thee is, the greedier it is; for neither by reason is it restrained, nor by dread thronged, nor by doom tempted. No man shall ever be more blest than he that for greatness of love can die. No creature can truly love too mickle.[7]

4

ADJUSTMENTS

Whoever you are, and no matter what your previous pattern of life has been, there are colossal adjustments to be made when you enter upon the Religious Life. As with all changes, you can only partially foresee what is going to be involved, and there are always surprises, even shocks, in any new way of life. And ours has its fair share.

The adjustments have to take place at every level, but I remember the physical ones being amongst my most traumatic in those early days.

The early rising was a rude shock to my system and led to a daily battle with sleepiness during the first half of the early morning period in chapel and hunger during the second. At home breakfast had been the first thing on the agenda after getting up. Now it was nearly two hours after rising.

Sometimes I thought back longingly to the days when I had been free to come home from work, relax into a comfortable chair with a large pot of tea by my side and Pompey purring contentedly on my lap, and do absolutely nothing. Often I put on a record – organ music was always my first choice – or sometimes the radio. But, other times I just sat. I don't suggest that there was anything essentially wrong in that, but, viewed now, I could see that it often lacked discipline when I set myself no time limit and sat on far longer than was appropriate. There were times when as a result household chores were neglected or preparation for the next day's work was skimped. I'd go round to friends for coffee and stay far too late engrossed in some absorbing topic – keeping us all from our beds.

The demands of my job and church work had reined me in to some extent and saved me from becoming totally undisciplined. And it was true that I was constantly reproached by family and friends for taking on too much. Certainly my diary was always crammed with engagements and I was bad about leaving realistic spaces between them. Even so, compared with convent life I had been soft with myself all too often in those years alone when I had chiefly done things as and how it suited me. Excesses both of work and of relaxation. Now there had to be a greater balance in life, and if the training seemed rigorous it was because St Paul's words about becoming spiritual athletes were taken both seriously and literally. If we were to be capable of going flat out after God, then much of the 'slack' of our previous patterns of life had to be taken in.

Now I had to adjust to a fairly strict timetable. There were of course spaces – times when I would not be expected in the kitchen, or at classes, but it was amazing how the spaces seemed to evaporate, as one tried to fit in all the other commitments of the day. The morning hour of prayer and the five Offices are provided for in the daily programme, but each sister finds more time in the day for personal prayer and spiritual reading. These are arranged according to the nature of her departmental work. It was all too easy, I found, to fritter away precious moments and find at the end of the day that the time ear-marked for priorities had been badly eroded. I was surrounded by sisters who were clearly very businesslike about every aspect of their day's work and yet without strain. They were relaxed and unhurried in their movements, had time to be gracious and probably had easy consciences about their use of time. Whereas I so often came to the end of the day having to say sorry to God for having robbed him yet again of time that was his.

So appalled was I by this mismanagement of time, and so aware that one doesn't conquer bad habits overnight, that I admitted my failure to Sister Geraldine and asked how I could become more disciplined.

"Keep a time-book," she advised. "We always did when we were novices, and though it can lead to a rather fastidious form of clock-watching, it can also help to form good habits that will be the means to generosity."

So she provided me with a small notebook in which, each day, I wrote down the amount of time given to prayer, reading, manual work, classes, study, leisure etc. By the end of each day, I could more or less account for the hours and how they had been spent. It was a bit of a labour, but worthwhile as a temporary aid for me, though it was by no means the kind of assistance that other novices would necessarily have found valuable. On the one hand I was anxious not to be half-hearted, and yet on the other, didn't want to become legalistic. But, I hadn't left behind that happy, fulfilling secular life just to settle into mediocrity. Gradually I began to develop a new respect for the odd five or ten minutes that I had previously despised, and therefore wasted, since it hadn't been 'time enough to do anything worthwhile'. Like Parkinson's Law, if one has only ten minutes, it is amazing how much can be achieved, how quickly one can polish off an urgent letter, get one's washing in to soak or do some other necessary chore.

In this matter of the use of time, my will was facing in the right direction and there was a growing desire to reverence this gift of God, but sadly my limbs and muscles couldn't keep up. By supper time I often ached from head to toe with the unaccustomed physical labour. My body seemed to be in revolt. Every Friday evening, my inner clock told me that I could slow down a bit – the weekend was beginning and there would be a break in the daily routine. Not so, however. It was business as usual on Saturdays and Sundays. I was working in the kitchen, and, like any family, the community still had to eat. Nor did we give up praying because it was the weekend. On the contrary, Sundays always being great festivals, we celebrated with a Sung Mass. It is the one service in the week when we have a sermon. Often we had to double our efforts when we returned to the kitchen after Mass, because we would have been in chapel considerably longer than on a weekday.

Having worked according to the academic year all my life, I was used to three hefty bursts of energy during the three terms and three long spaces to recover – with half-term breaks thrown in. That rhythm now had to change completely. There had to be a steady, daily output of energy without the prospect of weekends off, half-term breaks or a long holiday as a kind of recuperative sandwich filling. Like so many other people, I would now have only three weeks holiday a year.

There was the kitchen work to do in the mornings and evenings and often classes or study in the afternoons – though sometimes we were free to go for walks, write letters, do some gardening or enjoy another creative activity. Even though some sisters reminded us from time to time that life was far less pressured for us than it had been for them, there were no more evenings off to go to the theatre or sit and watch the TV.

All this I had known and accepted in advance, of course, but the reality of living it out in those early stages was very hard. We knew in theory that once the rhythm of the life had taken hold of us it would greatly reduce stress and enable us to take the 'going on going on' in our stride in the same way that people who work rhythmically can sustain their efforts longer than those who work erratically in fits and starts.

In actual fact, I was getting far more regular hours in bed – not always asleep – than I had had for the whole of my adult life. And yet I began to crave for sleep with an unholy craving. 'If only I could just be left to sleep on until I woke naturally,' I used to think. 'Even just occasionally – I would then feel really refreshed.' Even though we were free to rest till breakfast on two mornings a week, it was still early by previous standards and I felt constantly tired.

I was terrified that I'd drop off in Vespers and that the large, heavy volume of the Order of Vespers would slip out of my hands and crash into the middle of the aisle announcing to the entire choir that I was very far from saying the

Office with attention and devotion, which is our intention at the beginning of the Office each day. It was a perpetual battle to keep awake at that time for it coincided with my personal zero-hour, the low ebb period, the time of day when previously I would have been dozing with Pompey sprawled on my lap if I had been home at that point.

Suddenly feeling quite desperate about the weariness I decided what to do. It was pretty obvious, to me, that I needed a break just to catch up on sleep and to view life from a distance so that I could get things into perspective. It was all beginning to get rather on top of me.

Confident in the good sense of this decision, I went to tell Sister Geraldine and to ask if I could spend a weekend with Naomi.

"I know she'll have me," I said.

Sister Geraldine's reaction took me wholly by surprise. "Oh no! We don't just take weekends off like that," she said. "In fact, it is not usual for a postulant to have any holiday at this stage."

I groaned to myself. "We don't," she had said. I would, given half the chance. It seemed to have slipped my memory completely that I was no longer in a position to take decisions of this sort and to organise my own affairs so freely.

"You needn't be afraid that I wouldn't come back," I parried. "It's just to enable me to carry on."

"But, I'm afraid you'll have to learn to carry on without weekends off," she replied kindly but firmly.

Much later on I came to see that one of the tests for me had to be whether or not I could sustain the life without hunting around for escapes. Maybe it had been difficult for Sister Geraldine to be so seemingly hard, but it was necessary.

Brother Ass continued to be unco-operative, or was I just paying the price of having sadly neglected him for too long? At any rate, I was convinced that I would be able to cope if only it weren't for my wretched body. But it was no good having one's heart and mind in one place and the body lagging behind.

57

Once more I watched some of the professed sisters – particularly the ones who had heavy responsibilities. They didn't seem perpetually tired. They walked buoyantly enough, looked as though they were thoroughly enjoying life and living it with zest and enthusiasm. Mother Candida had a fearful load to carry, but she didn't move round the convent as though weighed down by it. Sister Harriet Ruth, her assistant, had alert, striking eyes that gave her a look of being fully awake, joyful and ready for anything. Sister Madeleine, the Convent Superior, appeared to do five people's work without ever looking het-up or hustled. And then there was Sister Geraldine, practically being devoured by other people's needs, yet receiving each day as a gift and living it with energy and joy. None of them ever gave the impression of being bowed down by the burdens placed upon them by the community, yet they obviously knew great physical tiredness at times.

It was too early for me to have discovered that the secret to this particular adjustment lies in the depth of one's dedication. One's inner clock can be altered, but not just by conforming to community customs and promptly leaping into action at the sound of a bell. For me it was going to mean a radical transformation of my former rhythm and pace of life, a transformation that could only come from a desire to be wholly given in a life which is itself rhythmic, with its balance of work and rest, and its punctuation by prayer at regular intervals throughout the day. Such a rhythm is not initially achieved without effort and is only maintained by vigilance, but it is because it is valuable both in terms of witness and as a gift to be shared that it is worth striving for it. There is nothing particularly romantic about it, for dedication in our life is 'not a matter of romance but of routine'.[1]

Some rivers in areas of sandstone or soft rock have beds that are U-shaped. They are wide and meander about spreading themselves in an indirect path, taking in a great deal en route. They tend to be slow moving and sluggish as a result, and are usually shallow. In complete contrast there are river beds in granite or other hard rock chiselled out by glaciers during the Ice Age. They are narrow, V-shaped, deep and fast flowing. And they are very direct – no meanderings or eclectic wanderings. This latter type of river seemed to be a parable of the new, purposeful rhythm of life into which I had come. Its narrowness made for depth and directness, and I couldn't have known, at that stage, how once one has adapted to it, it is possible to find great resources of creative energy bursting forth.

'How was I to fill in the column in my little time-book if I had dropped off to sleep in the middle of the morning hour of prayer', I wondered? 'Should I count the sleep as prayer?'

"Sometimes we are so tired," said Sister Geraldine, "that our prayer is simply to 'be' in our stall. That is our offering – just planting ourselves there and staying there despite one's weariness."

She told me to read what the late Mother Maribel had once written to the community when she was in office.

> Dog-tiredness is such a lovely prayer really, if only we could recognise it as such. Sometimes I hear, "I'm so dog-tired when I get to chapel, I can't pray." But what does it matter? We don't matter. Our Lord can pray just as well through a dog-tired body and mind as through a well rested one, better perhaps . . . So just when our backs and heads are aching and it is a battle to keep awake, then is the time when to say our Office becomes a worthwhile offering.[2]

None of us sets out, of course, with the intention of falling asleep during our prayer time, but it was a comfort to have this reassurance that if we do God can go on using our fidelity and achieving his purposes through us. For often there is more affinity between prayer and sleep than we are prepared to recognise. After all, both are a letting go, an abandonment into the hands of God.

Great store is set by punctuality in the Religious Life. Here was another battlefield for me. With shame I looked back on the numerous times in the past when I had been full of apologies and excuses for being late. It was always the traffic, or a last minute phone call, or some inescapable pressure that had delayed me. Now I was able to see that it was chiefly due to lack of organisation, not allowing sufficient time to get from one engagement to another without breaking the speed limit, lingering too long over an interesting book or an enjoyable discussion. Much nervous wear and tear could have been avoided if I had been more disciplined in the matter of punctuality.

Well, that most certainly had to be dealt with now. Punctuality at chapel, meals, work, classes, appointments (not just with Sister Geraldine and senior sisters, but with anyone including one's fellow novices) was of prime importance. Not to arrive on time is a form of breaking a promise, and very discourteous. Arriving at 'approximately' a given time had become one of my worst failings and was soon in evidence. It was slovenly, and I quickly discovered that slovenliness would not go unchecked – and rightly so.

"If you are meant to start work at 6.15 am," said Sister Geraldine one day, "it means being in the kitchen by that time with your overall on, ready to begin." She paused, and then added, "And that will mean leaving the novitiate five minutes earlier." She was enormously loving and tender-hearted, but there was a really tough side to Sister Geraldine too, and she was not above administering sharp rebukes when they were needed. If she hadn't had that side to her, she wouldn't have been able to train novices, of course. Doubtless this particular rap over the knuckles had been prompted by the bitter complaints of an irate kitchen sister at my lassitude and casual arrivals.

It made sense of course – this premium put on punctuality – and if at times I felt uptight about what appeared as rigidity when no allowances were made for a little leeway, I also knew deep down that it was a matter of honesty, and respect to other people.

"Not only is it an outward sign of readiness . . . of being inwardly together . . . if one is punctual," said Sister

Geraldine, "it also aids and demonstrates the overall recollectedness of a sister."

By recollectedness we mean having one's energies all gathered up and harnessed for a particular purpose, not scattered all over the place and thereby weakened. It means constant mindfulness, to use a Buddhist term. 'Gather up the fragments that remain, that nothing be lost'[3] could apply to one's energies as much as to the original crumbs. Punctuality is a form of obedience, and obedience is at the very heart of our life.

Then there was the question of orderliness. It had always struck me on my early visits to the convent how neat and tidy everything was. The kitchen was always left in spotless order when the sisters went off duty. So too the pantry, broom cupboards and various parts of the convent visible to visitors as they walked through the corridors to the refectory or chapel. Everything seemed to have its right place and one rarely came across anything that had been left lying around.

Most of us enter the novitiate having had a fair amount of space to ourselves and freedom to use that space as we chose. From having had a home to ourselves and perhaps an office too, we now had one shelf in the novitiate room. Some novices kept their belongings in scrupulous order, always putting things away neatly after using them. I, in my usual hurry and habit of cutting things fine, seemed always to be in trouble. I had prided myself that, by some people's standards, I was a reasonably tidy person. By the requirements of the Religious Life I was highly disordered. I left papers and books lying around – always expecting of course to come back to them and finish off some piece of work I was doing. I had too many papers. That was the crux of the problem. There was still a lot of paring down to be done on possessions and a big adjustment to be made now that I was sharing one room with eleven other people rather than having the run of a house to myself. Again it was a matter of respect, consideration and courtesy towards others – necessities for communal life. Just imagine the general chaos that would have resulted if my disorderliness

61

had been multiplied eighty or ninety times by the sisters living in the convent at the time.

One Sunday, Sister Harriet Ruth preached the sermon at Mass. She spoke of the way in which order can bring glory to God. I never again looked on what had seemed like ultra-tidiness as the fad of a lot of over-fussy women. Whether it was in the cloakroom, our cells, departments of work or novitiate rooms, order could bring glory to God. For the first time, I began to esteem the value of the ordered books in choir, the orderly arrangement of cutlery and chairs in the refectory, the order of equipment in the laundry, kitchen, pantry and library, not just as religious duties but as part of our response of love to God and to give him glory. It is pretty obvious, I suppose. We do, after all, reckon to keep cars, typewriters, watches and so on in good working order so that we can get the best use out of them. Order speaks of reliability and trustworthiness. If then we are to offer our best to God, our lives need to be in order. Perhaps the practical outworking comes more naturally to some than others but in general, orderliness, or lack of it, is saying something about our inward state. All of us would want to say a fervent Amen to the prayer:

> Take from our souls the strain and stress,
> And let our ordered lives confess
> The beauty of thy peace.[4]

David Livingstone once said that he had never made a sacrifice in his life – he who had renounced all the might have beens as a doctor in his homeland to become an explorer-missionary in an unknown part of Africa, living among and serving its people in great isolation. But we know what he meant. We think we make all sorts of sacrifices for God only to find that he will never be outdone in generosity. We give up this or that only to find it is all given back, so often with the 'hundredfold',[5] as our Lord promised.

In all sorts of ways I found this to be true. No longer was I free to come home from work and put on an organ record, but we had organ accompaniment at Vespers every day and at all Sunday Masses. Even if the playing was not quite that of Fernando Germani it was often very consoling in those first months. In some ways it was like being in a rehabilitation centre. We had to learn to live without things which had been almost as much an extension of ourselves as limbs. Certainly this was true of my car. But losing it made me rediscover my legs. Before I had a car, I used to enjoy walking, loved to be out in the fresh air, loved the wind, and the rain too if I were suitably dressed. In fact, a good tramp in the country or by the sea on a wild, elemental day would be wonderfully exhilarating. Now there was a chance to rediscover all that, and it was good – not simply because of the physical exercise though that was important. Far more significant, however, was the fact that I began to notice things which from a car I had missed – just small, simple things like finding the first violet of the season and spotting a perfect leaf skeleton on a compost heap, picking up the incredibly soft, downy feather of a duckling along the riverside and smelling the sweet breath of the cows on the convent farm. Maybe that sounds foolish and sentimental, but people write poetry about such experiences. They are awakenings to beauty that lead to wonder, and wonder is part of contemplation. Travelling everywhere by car, and at speed, had prevented me from the awareness that comes from really seeing and hearing. Terrible as the confession may be, I began to listen to bird song, really listen that is, as though I had never heard it before. I became much more sensitive to sights and sounds, to the sudden movements of a water rat or a hedgehog and to all forms of bird and insect life around us in the garden. I began to see flowers in a wholly new way and while the blending of colours, the shapes, and the smells all gave a kind of sensuous pleasure, there was far more to it than that. It took me back to my roots – to that part of my childhood that had been spent in the country and which clearly had been formative without my realising it. More even than that however, I believe such awareness takes us to yet deeper roots, our roots in God whose life and quickening power it is that breathes through all his creation.

> Out of all the earth God's eye looks into the eye of him who seeks, and every being is the fruit in which he offers himself to the yearning soul. Being is unveiled in the hand of the holy man.[6]

The colour which had meant so much to me in my home and in my clothes, and which I thought had been renounced, was all given back in a different form. I remember one day as I was making my way to chapel along the novitiate cloister, the sun burst through the clouds and, shining through one of the coloured panes of glass in the windows, threw an absolute kaleidoscope of fragmented colour on to the red tiles right at my feet. There were such rich reds, purples and greens – I stood transfixed just soaking up the beauty of it. On impulse I sat down cross-legged on the cloister floor and decided to enjoy the colours splashed around me as long as the sun shone through. 'I only hope no one comes bursting in on this,' I thought. It could perhaps have been viewed as unsuitably eccentric behaviour for a postulant, whereas in truth it was as genuine a prayer of thanksgiving as any I have prayed.

There were many ways in which our life was enriched by colour. There was, of course, the garden – lovely at all seasons – and then, the changing colours of the downs, the marvellous floral arrangements in chapel that were Sister Philippa's special gift, the liturgical colours of the vestments and altar frontals, the art work done by numerous sisters in painting, embroidery, collage work, rug-making and intricate forms of stitchcraft. Colour abounded when one had eyes to see.

The great feasts of the Church's liturgical year were times of enormous adjustment for me but also of joyful discovery. I suddenly found myself plunged into a whole new world of symbolism, ritual, colour, music, movement, language and ceremony that seemed to involve every part of my being – cerebral, emotional, aesthetic, as well as spiritual. The tradition from which I had come had been non-liturgical, strongly Biblical and evangelical. I shall be eternally grateful for that background and all that it gave me and still gives me, but God was now, as it were, giving 'full measure, pressed down and running over', for here were new riches, new forms of expression, new insights coming in and through symbolic and sacramental channels.

I was no stranger to festivals such as Christmas and Easter, of course, but even these took on very new dimensions.

"Christmas is beautiful in community," Novice Helen told me one day.

"In what way?" I asked.

"You'll see," she said. "I'd spoil it if I tried to describe it in advance."

It was going to be very strange not being with my family, not having a great pre-Christmas shopping spree, not engaging in the special rituals that every family evolves.

I was involved in the domestic arrangements for Christmas at the convent, of course, because of working in the kitchen.

"Would you like to ice some of the Christmas cakes?" said Sister Frances, the housekeeper.

I had never iced a cake in my life but said I'd like to try. We had made the cakes as a team and now we each took two of them and went to work. Following very carefully the instructions Sister Frances had given, I put some colouring into the mixture to make the icing a brilliant white, but horrors! It turned out a vivid, Saxe blue. I had put in far too much.

"Well it does look a bit hectic," said Sister Frances trying not to be discouraging. "But perhaps you can think of a way of decorating it that will draw the eye away from the colour?" No way. I turned it into a skiing scene, hoping people would be able to imagine that the sun had just set behind the skiers as they descended the slopes. I tied a wide, dark blue ribbon round the cake. It looked pretty presentable, I thought. We put it out for one of the special tea parties for visitors on Christmas Day, but it came back untouched. It's funny how, on the whole, people don't like eating blue food – even if it is perfectly wholesome. (Eventually it was eaten by the sisters.)

In the novitiate we were busy at work on our own cards and home-made decorations. I found myself drawing, painting, lettering and illuminating in a way I couldn't have imagined possible three months earlier. Already creative forms of expression were emerging that I hadn't known were there inside me. All the fun of preparing and giving was there, yet we didn't go near a shop.

It was however, the last Christmas when I would have access to a cheque book and I asked Sister Geraldine if it would be all right to send small gifts to my family and one or two close friends. She agreed, and I sent a short list to a friend in Manchester who had volunteered to do the shopping for me and posting of the parcels. They were just token gifts and one couple receiving a package from Manchester addressed in an unknown handwriting, promptly rang the police. (There had at the time been a flood of letter bombs all bearing Manchester postmarks.)

"Don't attempt to open it," they said. "We'll be right round." Within minutes the police arrived and took the packet. Setting off in one car, followed by my friends and their visitors in another, they drove out to some waste land. There, very gingerly, the police opened the package.

After minutes of suspense, one of them called back to the watching group, "Do any of you know someone at a St Mary's Convent, Wantage?"

"Kirsty," they choroused, and burst out laughing.

I'm glad my last bought Christmas present was given such a spectacular reception.

The chiefest preparation for the season was in our worship. Sister Geraldine took us through the Office and we looked up the many Biblical references and tried to look ahead to the riches in store. For the first time I encountered those marvellous and ancient antiphons, the Great Os. Throughout Advent, expectation had been mounting and now in the final week before Christmas Day one felt fairly bursting with excitement.

"Stand ye still: and ye shall see the salvation of the Lord", we sang again and again.

"It will be a busy time for many of you," Sister Geraldine said. "You will probably be tired at times. So it is important to 'Stand still . . .' to ponder the mysteries of the Incarnation, to enter into the silence of that first holy night, and not to get caught up in a complete whirl of activity."

Then on Christmas Eve the great versicle and response pealed out,

Ye shall know this day that the Lord will come:
And in the morning, ye shall see his glory.

and we knew we were nearly there.

The Christmas Office grows richer and richer each year, but there was an unforgettable freshness about it that first year. I can still recall its impact.

As we came down to chapel for Midnight Mass, all was immensely still. Supper and Compline had been early so that we could rest a little beforehand. Dreading the thought of oversleeping I set my alarm clock and left a large note by it to remind myself to go and light the gas under the double boiler of cocoa before going to Mass.

In chapel, the tree and crib were illuminated but otherwise there were no lights. The stillness was intense. As the time for Mass approached, visitors began to creep in and fill up the ante-chapel. Then without warning, the organ gave a few soft introductory bars, a few lights went on and very quietly we began to sing our first carols of Christmas. We had been saving up for that moment – no pre-Christmas carol services – and the sweetness and devotion of the singing were deeply moving in the semi-dark, with all the stillness and expectation.

Lauds followed straight after Mass so that, all in all, we were in chapel for quite a long stretch in the middle of the night. Yet it flashed by, such was the joy and the sense of being caught up in a wonderful mystery. Nevertheless, the cocoa was very welcome as the tired but happy procession made its way from the chapel to the refectory.

Anyone involved with food at Christmas has a fairly busy time, but careful planning by Sister Frances meant that we weren't slaving in the kitchen the whole time. Indeed, so anxious had she been that the dinner arrangements should go smoothly and with clockwork precision, she had drilled the team as though we were preparing for a commando operation. We were grateful to her for her forethought in the menu-planning, however. It meant that though the food was festive, the emphasis was on simplicity, so that our main energies could go into the worship and celebration in chapel. At dinner we broke our customary silence and greatly enjoyed the rare treat of some wine to go with the meal – the gift of a kind friend of the community. Celebration indeed.

Suddenly, by the afternoon, on that first Christmas in the convent, I felt a little bleak. Everyone seemed to have disappeared from the novitiate and I sat for a long while entirely alone. It was quite good to have some silence but, inevitably, my thoughts turned to my family. 'By now we would be on our customary Christmas afternoon walk in the forest,' I thought. Sister Geraldine had given Thelma and me permission to make phone calls home as we were still postulants. This, then, seemed the right moment to ring, for later on we should all be gathering in Sister Geraldine's room for a novitiate tea party.

Despite the momentary nostalgia, the festival was a time of tremendous joy because of its sheer simplicity. There was time and silence to savour the inner meaning of it all without getting bogged down in the externals – beautiful as they may be.

An overwhelming gratitude welled up inside that I was where I was. Pain there might have been in the months since my arrival, but here was some of the pure joy of this life. Everyone seemed relaxed and happy. Peace and goodwill abounded, and I could only agree with Novice Helen's prediction, "Christmas in community is beautiful."

If Christmas is beautiful, Easter is an even greater highlight to my way of thinking. After the many previous Easters that I had spent in action-packed conferences, the intensity of that first Holy Week at the convent is an experience I shall never forget, even though it continues to make a deep impact with each succeeding year. Perhaps it had something to do with the seriousness of our preparation, both corporate and personal, throughout Lent. Certainly there was an increasing sense of being caught up in the drama of the first Holy Week and the Passion itself through the ceremonial re-enactments and the visual aids of the Maundy Thursday 'stripping of the sanctuary', the night vigil and the Good Friday 'Stations of the Cross'.

Sister Geraldine had taken us through the week step by step in class, preparing us for the special liturgies of Maundy Thursday, Good Friday and Holy Saturday. We couldn't have had a more thorough grounding. Yet, even so, when the impact came it practically pole-axed me.

All through the week a curious tension had been building up – like a general purging and there was a strange mixture of heaviness and expectation.

Never could one forget the haunting cry of the Lamentations echoing round chapel on the three nights of Tenebrae, the total darkness at the end and out of the darkness the triple Kyrie Eleison sung by two novices. Then the community's response of "Christ the Lord became obedient unto death", with the final high notes of a lone voice piercing the darkness with the words, "Even the death of the Cross". And, after complete silence, the low murmuring of Psalm 51 . . . and the final three raps from Mother breaking rather eerily into the silence and dispelling the darkness as it was the signal for one large candle to be carried in slowly and placed on the sanctuary steps. An incredibly moving service.

Symbols are, of course, very much more than mere visual aids. They are powerful vehicles of truth, and in this week truth was making its impact from all sides and at every level via the wealth and variety of symbol.

Before the Maundy evening Mass, we gathered in Sister Geraldine's room for a fellowship meal and then, after greeting each other very lovingly, we entered the deepest and strictest silence of the year. There was little work to do in the kitchen until the following evening for the community fasts on Good Friday. The deep hush, the Way of the Cross, the Good Friday liturgy, the low note of the Office all conspired to lead one into a creative sorrow that perhaps finds its most poignant expression in one of the responds at the Good Friday Tenebrae. It seemed practically wrung out of the community that night when I first heard it.

"Eloi, Eloi, lama sabachthani."

There is a curious stillness about Holy Saturday, rather like the day after some crisis in an illness or after an operation . . . there's a need just to lie back and regain strength. Yet, despite the hush and the 'recovery', there was considerable activity in the convent.

The Easter Garden was being prepared. Flowers were being brought in and arranged around the house and chapel. The tabernacle stood empty on the altar, the sanctuary lamp was extinguished. Everything and everyone was waiting expectantly for the great explosion of the Paschal liturgy on the Saturday night with its lighting of the new fire and renewal of baptismal vows.

This is the night when first you saved our fathers:
you freed the people of Israel from their slavery
and led them dry shod through the sea.

This is the night when the pillar of fire
destroyed the darkness of sin.

This is the night when Christians everywhere, washed
clean of sin and freed from all defilement, are
restored to grace and grow together in holiness.

sang the chaplain in the Exultet as the candles flickered all round chapel.

We had 'buried' our alleluias at the beginning of Lent. We had sung our last Gloria at the Maundy Thursday Mass.

Now it returned with a great outburst of bell ringing and organ accompaniment. It was a thrilling, nerve-tingling moment. Every available handbell from the convent had been pressed into service for the occasion, and between them they voiced the resurrection joy we were all feeling.

What a rich liturgical diet.

Mother began the Litany of Saints. It was almost like a roll call of the Company of Heaven and one could imagine them appearing in the sanctuary in response to their names and gradually filling it with their swelling numbers.

"This is the night . . ." had sung the chaplain, as we recalled the great redemptive acts of God towards his people in the past.

'This is the night', I thought, 'above all others, when the veil between the seen and unseen is split in half, when heaven touches earth with an electrifying shock and resurrection life bursts out of so much that is seemingly dead. This is the night when renewed in our baptismal freshness we cast off the heaviness we may have carried through Lent and Holy Week, and leap and dance for joy in our hearts.'

Paeans of praise rose up, of course, throughout Easter Day and for the rest of the week. Everywhere there was a light-heartedness, a release of new vigour.

There was so much in this new way of life that was sheer gift and sometimes it was almost as hard to adjust to the exciting, enjoyable things as to the hard and difficult ones.

One's belief that there is no essential dividing line between sacred and secular, work and worship, is expressed fairly strikingly when one is literally scrubbing out a saucepan in the sink or rolling pastry one minute and five minutes later kneeling in chapel waiting for an Office or Mass to begin; when one doesn't change into special clothes for worship. If it is not always easy to 'wipe one's feet on the threshold'[7] of chapel and drop all distracting thoughts; if one finds oneself in the middle of the sermon worrying about the prunes boiling dry, it has the reverse effect too, and worship flows out easily and naturally into the kitchen, into the pastry-rolling and dishing up of prunes. The new cohesion I was finding in the unity that came from the structure and rhythm of the day was a joy, despite the fact that there were times when it was still hard to adapt to it.

Anyone arriving in the convent kitchen to work had to adjust to one very major thing – the oven. I should perhaps say, the 'late' oven, for this remarkable museum piece has now been replaced by a modern counterpart. Our oven, however, was one of the convent's show pieces to fascinated visitors. It stood about eight feet high and had two long drawers (a top and a bottom) that pulled out for about six feet.

"They look just like mortuary drawers, don't they?" I said to Thelma when we were first introduced to it. "You could easily get two bodies side by side on each drawer – two up, two down."

It remained switched on all the time since it took several hours to heat up. In the winter it provided one of the warmest places in the house. In summer it sometimes made the kitchen unbearably hot. But it had great advantages. It could cook the whole of a two course meal for eighty or more people at once. It had some peculiar quirks but most of us had a healthy respect for it.

My first experience of using it was in biscuit-making. Since I had never cooked for large numbers before, this seemed a gentle breaking in.

"With a sale of work coming soon," said Sister Frances, "you can't make enough. They will always sell."

So each day I mixed and baked biscuits, experimenting with all the recipes I could find.

"There's one thing about it," I said to Thelma, "if I have to leave the convent, I could always get a job with Huntley and Palmer now."

"Gingerbread-men are extremely popular," Sister Frances volunteered one day.

So, gingerbread-men it became – day after day.

'What in the world would Naomi, Gail, Julian and Luke say if they could see me now?' I thought. 'Chief manufacturer of gingerbread-men.'

Gradually I was promoted to cooking meals, or part of them. At first it was the puddings. Unused as I was to this kind of domestic activity, I enjoyed the creativity of it. It was all a far cry from my solitary lamb chop and packet of frozen peas at home, but there was something very satisfying about producing a meal and knowing people were enjoying it. It was also very humbling when one's efforts were a disaster and the sisters ate the food just the same without batting an eyelid. There was a certain amount of beginner's luck, but there were also some very bad moments such as the time a banana recipe did not warn me that the pudding would turn a delicate lilac if left overnight in the cold storage room. I was terrified and fervent were my prayers that the Lord's hand would be upon the community's stomach that day.

There were other times such as the morning when I woke with a jolt at 2.0 am sure that something terrible was about to happen. Suddenly I knew. The apples! I had put them into the bottom oven at 7 o'clock the previous evening to stew slowly, and had clean forgotten them. Throwing on some clothes I flew down to the kitchen, opened the oven and was nearly knocked backwards by the smell. The huge pan was ruined, of course, and we had to switch the oven off and let it cool down before we could scrape the mess off the drawer.

The more experienced sisters in the kitchen bore with these lapses of memory and their consquences with great fortitude, and they always came to the rescue when our mistakes led to a crisis. That sounds a fairly mild statement to make, but behind those rather ordinary words lies, I can assure you, a most extraordinary quality of charity, patience and good humour.

When Carlo Caretto entered the Sahara desert to join the Little Brothers of Jesus, he took a thick notebook containing thousands of addresses of friends and burned it behind a dune. I marvelled when I read of this act.[8] What courage! "*Il faut faire une coupure*," his Novice Master had said to him.

If I had been able to do that, it would certainly have spared me one of the most painful aspects of my novitiate, but I am certain that it would not have been right. As postulants we were free to buy our own stamps and, in theory, we were not restricted in our letter-writing. In practice, of course, we were – simply by virtue of the time factor. Our days were full. Trying to keep abreast of correspondence became a losing battle, and frequently it led me into a wrong choice about the use of my time. After 'Clothing,' I knew that I should be able to write only two letters a week. The restriction is part of our poverty, not just in terms of economy on stamps, though that is certainly a consideration, but at a far deeper level it touches on our poverty of time. We offer ourselves to God in a life that, by its very commitments of prayer and of enclosure, precludes a vast correspondence. Sometimes it is hard to write one letter a week, let alone two.

For some sisters this is not a problematic area. Either they had more clue about the life they were going to lead and gave their friends no false hopes about letters, or in some cases, they just don't like writing letters.

For me it became increasingly difficult.

"Will you be allowed to receive letters?" many had asked when I told them of my intention to enter a convent.

"Oh yes," I had replied with alacrity. So anxious had I been to allay their fears about this extraordinary venture, and assure them that it would not be a heavy, repressive regime, that I had not anticipated the complications my cheerful assurances would bring.

At first there were a lot of letters. Friends were very loving and, I think, badly wanted me to know that even if I had chosen to go behind walls, they weren't going to forget me. I blessed them for that and it was heart-warming. It became very hard, however, when after a while practically every letter that I opened began, 'We haven't heard from you for so long.' 'Did you get our last letter? We haven't had a reply'.

Increasingly I felt reproached, guilty and miserable. It seemed a hopeless situation. It was not that I now needed the letters, as I had done at first, to act as pain-killers, much as I loved receiving them. The problem was that I hated the thought of hurting these loving, generous people. I was tremendously grateful to Sister Geraldine who, when I asked her if I could send out a circular at Christmas said, "Yes, that's a very good idea – if you can get someone to duplicate it for you."

Inevitably, the number of letters decreased as time went on but some people have written faithfully over the years knowing that replies will be infrequent. That kind of loving almost hurts.

The adjustment in this whole matter was as much one for my friends as for me but, as was impressed upon us on a number of occasions in the novitiate, one never really loses a true friend because one cannot correspond frequently. The bonds are too deep. The 'coupure' in this area of our life is not a cutting of those bonds. If anything, it makes for greater availability and closeness through prayer. As Carlo Caretto said,

> Burning an address is not the same thing as destroying a friendship, for that I never intended to do; on the contrary, I have never loved nor prayed so much for my old friends as in the solitude of the desert. I saw their faces, I felt their problems, their sufferings, sharpened by the distance between us. I am completely convinced that one never wastes one's time by praying; there is no more helpful way of helping those we love.
>
> The address-book is mine no longer, but this is of no importance because there are other ways of reaching one's friends.[9]

5

BE CLOTHED WITH HUMILITY

"So you feel you are ready for clothing, do you?"

The question came right out of the blue, and I could scarcely believe my ears. Gasping in unbelief, I stammered, "Could . . . could you repeat that please, Sister?"

"So you feel ready for clothing, do you?" said Sister Geraldine, laughing at my wide-eyed astonishment.

"But – I'm so awful. I can never do anything right. You can't really mean it!" I blurted out.

We were sitting in the garden. It was a lovely spring evening and suddenly the sky looked bluer, and the budding trees looked even greener, and our tame robin flew down and perched on the arm of the garden seat to share in the excitement. We had only been talking for about ten minutes when Sister Geraldine popped this question. It seemed she hadn't actually planned to ask me on that particular evening, but somehow the conversation must have taken the kind of turn that made it the right moment . . . and suddenly, out it came. My joy knew no bounds. For once I was without any words and could only sit there grinning like a cat after a saucer of cream.

It was strange really. So much of my life at St Mary's up to this point had been desperately painful. If Sister Geraldine had said, very kindly, "This honestly isn't the life for you, is it? Surely you must feel that for yourself?" it would have been a very respectable way of leaving it all, getting out and going back to the life I had loved. After all, I could be quite satisfied that I'd given it an honourable try. Not one of my friends would have been surprised and certainly none would have blamed me. Indeed, I know they were rather hoping for it. "Give it six months," some of them had said, "and then she'll have got it out of her system."

Why then did it matter so much – this going forward to the next step of the Religious Life? Why did the mention of clothing bring such joy? And you will note that it was put to me in the form of a question. All the way along, the choice had to be my own. No one is coerced or directed against her better judgement or understanding of God's will for her.

It mattered desperately because I had caught a glimpse of something that absolutely captivated me. It would be impossible to put it into words, though the New Testament calls it 'the pearl of great price', and I felt sure that, for me, the pathway to that pearl lay in the Religious Life. The moments of vision and certainty had only been fleeting and rather like a light at the end of a long dark tunnel . . . but enough to hold me to my course. Somehow I couldn't turn back (though there were to be some temptations to do so later), even though the light was a mere pinpoint and the tunnel exceedingly long. The imagery has many overtones of birth and there were all the ingredients of that kind of trauma ahead. It was indeed going to be a long, tough journey. And I knew it.

'Clothing' in a religious community is that ceremony in which a postulant receives the habit of the community and becomes a novice. Up to that time, the postulant has been knocking and asking (Latin: postulare = to ask), "Is this the call of God to me, or not?" It may not be, and, in that case, the postulant leaves and there is no disgrace in that and, hopefully, no bad feeling. If someone has a pull to the Religious Life, the only way to find out if it is a genuine call of God is to try it – to test the vocation. The testing necessarily has to be a two-way thing, for the individual must know if it is right or not, but so must the community.

No one can leave a community without there being a

sense of loss and sadness even at the early stage of postu-
lancy. But it isn't an occasion of major upheaval for it is
inevitable that some will go and some will stay. One day,
Moira didn't appear at meals or chapel. I suppose we
assumed that she wasn't too well and had been told to stay
in bed for the day. But later, Sister Geraldine stopped on
her way through the novitiate, and told us in a very low-key
way that Moira felt she had come to the end of the road as
far as her life in the community went and had asked to
leave. Sister Geraldine had felt she was right in her decision
to go, and so Moira had slipped away quietly. She hated
farewell scenes and therefore had just left messages of love
and returned to her home on a farm in North Wales.
Naturally, we all missed her but after a while she was able to
come back and visit us and she was so obviously happy in
her new life and work that we were happy for her and with
her. If someone leaves – it isn't failure and it isn't rejection, though it needs careful pastoral handling to ensure
that no painful feelings of either are lurking around. It is the
sign of a healthy novitiate if there are comings – and
goings – for it shows that it is a true testing and that there is
real open-ness to the Holy Spirit.

'Is this for me?'

For some the answer is 'Yes', and for others 'No', and for
yet others, 'For a while only'.

Sometimes it is obvious that a person has got a vocation
to the Religious Life in some form or other, but perhaps not
'to *this* community'. It is usual then for arrangements to be
made for the postulant or novice to spend some time in
several other kinds of community so that he or she is given
as much help as possible in finding the right one. Religious
orders form one big monastic family, and there is far more
interchange than is generally realised. The thing that everyone is wanting is God's will, for the individual as well as for
the community, and I remember being very impressed at
the enormous integrity shown when an acquaintance of
mine who was personable, experienced, who had many
desirable qualities and numerous good qualifications including a double First from Oxford, was advised to try

another Community nearby since Sister Geraldine felt sure "they would be right for her and she for them."

For those for whom it is right to continue the period of testing, clothing is the occasion when the habit is blessed, given, received and put on for the first time in a ceremonial act. It is a great moment, for this is no mere dressing up – in a theatrical sense. It is far more than putting on a uniform, though certainly it does identify the sister as belonging to a particular group. But the habit also speaks of the sister's new relationship to Christ, to the Community, to the world and to herself. It symbolises an unchanging covenant – and so she wears it all the time. To receive and wear the habit is a putting on of the Lord Jesus Christ. Of course we have already done that at our baptism but clothing is a public renewal of that baptismal vow and a declaration of our intention to live out those vows in this particular way within the context of this particular life.

"Will you be able to take your habit off when you are on holiday?" people asked me. "Or when you want to go riding or sailing?"

"No, I won't," I answered.

'Wear your habit at all times . . .' says our Rule and since it symbolises a commitment and a relationship and a consecration of the whole life, we no more think of hopping in and out of it to suit our own convenience than the majority of married people would dream of removing their wedding rings if they seem likely to get in the way of a particular activity. And for the same reason.

For the novice, the habit does not yet speak of vows, but it indicates that promises have been taken to follow a particular path as far as God leads. He may lead right on through to final commitment and life vows, or he may eventually lead the novice sister back into her secular life in order to share more widely the insights and fruit of her time of withdrawal and training. Either way, at her clothing, the new novice promises fidelity and a willingness to be guided by the community in all matters regarding her vocation.

In other words, she is free to leave at any time *if it seems to be the will of God*, and both she and the community agree on this. She is not free by her promises to walk out or run away because life has suddenly become pretty intolerable, or because a sister has spoken a hasty or unkind word to her, or because she has been given an unpalatable job to do. The same promises bind her when she feels tempted to pack her bags and go because she is bored or frustrated.

All Novice Mistresses are probably familiar with the kind of angry outburst in which a novice fumes and declares that she "can't stick it a minute longer and will have to leave." And they are usually armed with the kind of deflating reply given by one of our Novice Mistresses on such an occasion. "Yes dear. What time is the next train?"

The habit, then, is the outward sign of a binding, of a contract, of a consecration. Even to the uninitiated, who may not understand its full implications, the nun announces by her clothing that she is a Christian, that God matters more than anything else, that he is supreme and has total claim on her, that she desires to give herself to him wholly through a life of prayer and service. Often times she is treated with kindness and even respect – because she is in a habit. And other times, she is the target of taunts, abuse and even obscenities.

"Won't you find it hard always to wear black and white?" a friend had asked me. I still couldn't be sure about this, for colour had played such a very large part in my previous life. It might indeed be hard – some women certainly find it much harder than others, but already I had been discovering in the matter of colour, and in other things too, that what he takes away in one form, God so often gives back even more richly in another.

"Won't you feel that you have lost your identity?" asked someone else. "All dressed alike, you'll feel . . . so . . . anonymous."

None of these things bothered me as Sister Geraldine and I sat discussing my clothing in the garden that evening. I only knew that I wanted to go on, that it felt entirely right to go on – though indeed it was 'against all reason' – and that therefore, the sooner I got on with the next step, the better.

However, there were a few weeks of preparation ahead and they were going to be busy weeks. With a twinkle in her eye, Sister Geraldine said "Would you still like a long weekend with Naomi?"

"Oh yes . . . I would," I said with great enthusiasm, "but not for the same reasons as before!" And we both laughed.

"Make it a week," she said. "You need some rest before the clothing."

There were invitations to be sent to my family and a few close friends. There were preparation classes and frequent visits to the habit room to be measured and fitted for my new clothes. How strange they felt . . . and surprisingly comfortable. They are not designed primarily for comfort, of course, but in fact loose-flowing garments do give freedom of movement and very conveniently trap cool air in the summer and warm air in the winter so that they practically provide their own built-in thermostat. There are times for all of us when it is necessary to wear clothes suitable to a particular lifestyle or activity. One puts on gardening togs for the garden and overalls to service the car. So with us, our clothes are designed to aid and to express the simplicity of life that we all desire.

Despite all my packing up, sorting out and destroying of superfluous belongings before coming to Wantage, I still seemed to have collected a great deal of clutter in my months as a postulant. Before clothing, I was to be stripped of all possessions other than essential things. So, I set about doing my own preparatory sorting and sifting. And, once more, I discovered how very hard it is really to be detached from things. Disposing of a home, a car, books, clothes, boats, animals and other belongings is only stage one. As one of the early fathers said, a monk can become as attached to a particular pen or needle as a rich man to his castle. The degree of attachment and possessiveness can be just as great over small things as large. In accepting a vow of poverty (in the monastic sense of that word), we hope that perhaps we will help in some way, albeit a small one, to counteract the acquisitive spirit of society today which takes the attitude, 'I want, therefore I must have.' But lest our protest betray in any way a holier than thou attitude, let us come clean and admit that even though we are trying to take a stand against that attitude, we quickly discover that hidden deep down in most of us is the spirit which says, 'I have, therefore I must keep.' In this whole area of attachment there is need for continual vigilance.

For me, when it came to this further attempt to get rid of unnecessary clutter, it wasn't only or even chiefly the spirit of attachment that I had to fight. It was a battle with fear. I have always found it hard to let go of things for fear that the minute they are destroyed or given away, I shall need them again. So, throughout my life before community, I had hoarded files of lecture notes, addresses, sermons given, articles written, sketches made. And to divest myself of them was a real wrench – a form of loss and separation. But as I fed the fruits of my creativity into the incinerator, I tried to convince myself that the God who had been sufficient in the past, would be equally sufficient for the future.

It isn't that things in themselves are wrong, or that those who have great possessions are in grave error. But each way of life has its own disciplines and renunciations. The ballerina has to eat a disciplined diet and watch her weight. The concert pianist may have to put strict limits on his social life to safeguard the necessary hours of practice. The mountaineer must learn to travel light and carry all his survival kit in one pack. These are disciplines which lead to excellence and freedom . . . Oh, to be able to dance like that! Or play like that! Or climb to a mountain peak and get that breathtaking, panoramic view. Sometimes we forget the sacrifices that lie behind that seeming ease and mastery.

So with us. We are offered certain goals and freedoms, but to reach them, we too have to travel light. One would-be follower in the Gospels was told by Jesus, "You have all the necessary qualifications except one. Go and sell all your possessions and give the money away. When you have nothing, then come and follow me." But the young man baulked at that. We are told that he had many possessions and, at that stage, the demand was too much for him, so he turned away sadly. He has had many successors.

I was to have a week's retreat before my clothing and the 'stripping' was to take place immediately beforehand. Even after all the pruning, it still looked such a lot when I came to set out my remaining possessions. I can't remember now exactly what there was that covered the full length of the long table, but I know I waited fearfully and with deep embarrassment for Sister Geraldine to arrive. At the appointed moment, she came into the room, smiling encouragingly, and, though she was tender and sensitive to my tremblings, it was obviously an occasion of great joy for her. The fact that someone wanted to divest herself of unnecessary burdens in order to move more freely on her path to God was not a matter for sighing and sorrowing. Things which would be useful to us all, and that could be shared, were ear-marked for the common stock, so that file-paper, records, pens, paints, embroidery silks and those kind of things became 'ours' instead of 'mine'. Other articles which would have been an extravagance for us were stored away for Christmas when they could be given as presents to some of our helpers.

My heart gave a lurch as we approached the beautiful new leather writing case given me by my Youth Club when I gave up the leadership. But mercifully, that was deemed something that I should need, to keep my letter-writing equipment in an orderly fashion. "You won't need both of these toilet bags will you?" she said, picking up the prettier of the two. Although she was gentle in one way, Sister Geraldine was also very matter-of-fact, unsentimental and business-like about it all. She had naturally assumed that I welcomed help in ridding myself of my possessions and so was only too prepared to give it generously, and in as unfussy a way as possible. Of course I wanted it, and longed to be the kind of cheerful giver that God loves, but . . . oh dear! How the head and heart can pull in opposite directions at such times. I suddenly realised that one has got to be very free and secure in oneself to let go and in joyful abandonment 'naked follow the naked Christ', as Thomas à Kempis puts it.

Soon the stripping was over and, beaming at me, with joy popping out of her eyes, Sister Geraldine strode off down the corridor, laden with an assortment of things and scattering my prudent stock of psychedelic toothbrushes in all directions. She had my cheque book, passport and other personal documents firmly tucked under her arm ready to go into a personal folder in her filing cabinet, to be locked away as 'frozen assets'. They would not have to be dealt with until profession . . . or my leaving.

Then with farewells all round in the novitiate, I went off to the distant part of the convent where a room had been assigned me for my retreat. A whole week! I'd never had as long a retreat as that before, and I was looking forward to it immensely. I was longing for space to get away from the many practical details of the clothing preparation, to dwell more on the inner meaning of it all.

I had a little weep when I arrived in my retreat room. The Novitiate had been there before me. On the table was a most beautiful arrangement of flowers, and on the mantelpiece a card, exquisitely lettered and illuminated, bearing the text chosen by Sister Geraldine as the theme of my retreat. The ways by which we discover we are loved in community sometimes knock us sideways taking us right off guard – they are so sudden and unexpected. This was one such occasion and I felt quite overwhelmed.

Sister Geraldine was to give me one address a day, but for the rest of the time I was free – to pray, read, relax and get out into the fresh air. I had even been loaned a bicycle so that I could cycle out to the downs and enjoy the wonderful views of the Vale of the White Horse.

"Now you are not to worry about the clothing at all," said the Senior Novice as I began. "From now on, the community will carry you and take care of all the details."

"We'll have a rehearsal on the day before the clothing," said Sister Geraldine. "In the meantime just rest as much as possible and be open to God and to the way he wants to lead you."

So I did. I dropped all concerns about practical details. No one could reach me for this week and I could be entirely alone with God. My meals were to be sent to me in my hideaway, so that I wasn't expected to rub shoulders even with the community. The only time I saw my sisters, and they me, was in choir.

Silence and Solitude. They were like great waves that closed over me and left me with that profound sense of alone-ness that one feels when swimming under water. I was deeply happy – but not in any schizoid way. For just as sounds carry further or more clearly under water, so in retreat the inner ear becomes far more sensitive, and not just to the voice of God. 'We withdraw only to listen more intently to the cries of the world,' as Thomas Merton puts it.

I was absolutely at peace about the rightness of the step I was about to take. Often, in the days after, I looked back with great thankfulness to that retreat and its certainties, for there was indeed much pain to come. But the reality and God-given insights of that time were to follow me like goodness and mercy all the days of my novitiate life.

On the eve of the clothing I began to get decidedly nervous. I was convinced after the rehearsal that I wouldn't be able to remember a thing – that I'd kneel when I should stand, or trip on the steps in the unaccustomed long clothes. As I took in all the preparations that were being made and smelt the polish and heard the singers practising the anthem in the song room, it suddenly struck me, 'They are glad. They are all rejoicing with me and for me at God's strange, mysterious call'. Looking around the chapel and musing, my eyes suddenly fell upon the floral arrangement in the sanctuary, and I gasped out loud. It was stunning. My beloved Sister Philippa, knowing my love of colour, had done a massive arrangement of deep blue delphiniums and small pink roses. Inevitably and typically, the beauty of it all and the love that had gone into it brought tears to my eyes. Suddenly I had the feeling of being swept up into the community's love. I crept up to the sanctuary, perched myself on one of the steps and feasted my eyes on the marvellous display for a long time. There wouldn't be time to gaze at it protractedly in the service tomorrow, so I attempted to memorise all the details so that I could enjoy them later at my leisure.

My new habit, veil and cross lay upon the altar all that night by the Blessed Sacrament. As I left the chapel after Compline to retire to bed for the last time as a postulant and for the last time in ordinary clothes it was somehow comforting to know that the new garb which would symbolise a new stage in my spiritual life would remain in company with, and close to, that Divine Presence while we slept.

While we slept . . . but, I didn't. I was far too excited and nervous.

"Don't come down early in the morning," Sister Geraldine had instructed. "It will be a long tiring day and you should get a good, long night first. Your breakfast will be brought up to you."

What a luxury, and how galling not to be able to make the most of the opportunity to sleep on. Eventually the Senior Novice arrived with a breakfast tray that included toast – a special treat – and a diminutive posy in a cut-glass vase. After a quick and cheerful greeting, she left me to it. It was then that I noticed the envelope. I opened it wonderingly and pulled out an absolutely beautiful card. The words had been chosen by Sister Geraldine and the card designed, lettered and illuminated by Novice Denise. It was so lovely, it completely took my breath away and it was quite some time before I could put it on my bedside locker and turn my attention to the coffee and toast.

There is always great precision of timing in a convent, and on special occasions such as this even more so. The whole programme is timed to the last minute. At the ringing of the first chapel bell, the sisters file in. At the ringing of the second, the novices process in. Precisely five minutes before the service was due to start, the Novice Mistress would come to collect me and escort me into choir. After that the clergy would enter and the service would have begun.

It's surprising what absurd and irrelevant thoughts assail the mind at really important moments in one's life – just when one wants to be most recollected. With my heart pounding wildly and stomach somersaulting, my attention at this auspicious moment was wholly absorbed in wondering how it must feel to be in the condemned cell waiting for the arrival of the prison warden to lead you to the gallows.

The clothing ceremony is very beautiful and moving . . . dramatic too. The postulant begins the service in her ordinary clothes. After the Scrutiny, in which she is questioned by the Warden of the community, and an address, the novice-to-be makes her promises and receives the habit which the Warden has blessed. As the Warden gave me mine, he said in a booming voice, "Novice Kirsty . . ."

(There it was! The first public announcement of my name in religion. Just as in the Bible a change of name often indicated a change of role, or a new spiritual relationship; so with us the taking of a name marks an important first step into a whole new way of life. In itself Kirsty means 'Christian', but now it took on further significance, for it spoke of an even deeper commitment.)

". . . Receive the habit of this Community of St Mary the Virgin, the sign of the putting on of the Lord Jesus Christ — and be clothed with humility."

"The putting on of the Lord Jesus Christ." There in a nutshell is what this ceremony is all about, and a definition of our lifetime's work.

The novice is then led out of choir to a separate room, where each part of the religious dress is put on with special prayers. Finally, dressed in her new habit, a white veil, and wearing a novice's cross, she is led back in procession into the chapel where the choir is singing, and community, relatives and friends all get their first glimpse of her. In C.S.M.V. we have never worn wedding dresses or been given away by our fathers as was customary at one time in some orders, but the change from secular clothes into the habit is still a very dramatic and joyful moment.

I remember every detail of the first part of the service but from the moment I left to put on the habit I can remember practically nothing except the overwhelming feeling of joy. I seemed to be in a kind of holy daze but kind hands guided me here and shepherded me there and it was all quite peaceful and straightforward.

Everything was beautiful. That I do remember. "We do do these things rather well," Mother said laughingly to my parents afterwards over a cup of coffee. And it was true. The singing was superb. The organ, which can be quite temperamental, was on its best behaviour and pealed out wonderfully to the greater glory of God. And, to crown it all, the sun streamed in through the east window scattering fragments of coloured light all over the sanctuary steps and carpet.

When it was all over, there was a joyful reunion with friends. But on such occasions it is also frustrating that, after they have made long journeys to be there for the service, one can only greet friends briefly. Naomi, Gail, Julian and Luke were there smiling and laughing – and I was dying to hear all the news of my ex-colleagues. I wanted to introduce all my friends and family to Mother and Sister Geraldine and make sure that no one was left out. Yet I also wanted to give the lion's portion of my time and attention to my family. For families, there are inevitably very mixed feelings on these occasions. The son or daughter is moving into a way of life that cannot be fully understood from the outside and would seem to mean a severing of family bonds. From now on the community is family and the convent home – and that can be pretty hard for a mother and father to accept. It takes time for them to come to experience the new, but equally deep relationship which grows in place of the old, and to find themselves included in the community's love and concern.

It was wonderful, it was joyful, but it was also incredibly tiring. All that talking – and after seven days of total silence – left me with a dry throat and aching head. There were still all the sisters on the infirmary wing to greet, and a special tea party later on.

I went to thank Sister Philippa for her wonderful flower arrangement. She greeted me rapturously and said, "Kirsty, you look absolutely right in the habit. I can always tell." I so hoped she was right . . . yet vaguely wondered why. After all, the important thing is simply to be where God wants us to be, and if, later on, he led me out of community, surely that would ultimately be for joy?

At last I could slip away thankfully to bed. I would go back into retreat the next day, and how grateful I was at the thought of that. It needed a bit of time and space to recover from the emotional intensity and physical exhaustion of the 'clothing day', and reflect on the wonder of it all. But alas, sleep did not come . . . not for many hours. The immensity of what I had done, or rather what had been done to me, left my mind wide-awake but my spirit peacefully happy. I lay there rejoicing, musing . . . and wondering if I would finally drop off, and start my new life as a novice by oversleeping.

Thankfully I didn't. It was a beautiful summer day and I packed a picnic lunch, picked up a book and the pile of cards and letters I had not yet had time to open, and headed off into the country. There, basking in the sun and enjoying the sound of a little waterfall, I went through my post. Most of the cards were from sisters – from houses abroad as well as in England. They were hand-made, often exquisitely beautiful and all sharing some special verse or quotation that meant a lot to the sender. I was deeply touched by them. In many cases, it was the kind of sharing that forms a bond with another person because of what they reveal of themselves, and this was so even of those sisters from India and Africa whom I had never met, and would not meet till they returned for a furlough.

It was blissfully peaceful. I listened to the sounds of silence – those which actually heighten and intensify it. The musical waterfall, the paddling of a moorhen on the smooth-surfaced river a little distance away, the bees . . . I welcomed them.

"Feel free to share my joy," my heart sang out.

As though he heard, a blackbird flew down and hopped around me in a companionable way. So I informed him as to why I was so happy, and he fixed his beady eye on me intently, apparently taking it all in.

It was warm. It was peaceful, and I was very sleepy.

'He giveth his beloved sleep,' I thought, and dozed off.

The blackbird was still with me when I woke up and I held another serious conversation with him about the wonder of our creator. Then we shared my packed lunch.

The day flowed on in a great wave of gratitude, praise and prayer. I almost wished my retreat were not ending . . . it had certainly been one of the highlights of my life so far. But tomorrow – it would be back to the normal routine of the kitchen. And then, too, I had a dental appointment in the afternoon. The dentist was some distance away and we normally cycled there to economise on time.

'I wonder if it will be difficult in long clothes?' I thought. Certainly in my short twenty-four hours experience I had noticed a vast difference. The habit was so much cooler than the postulant's skirt and sweater. I could go without tights in a habit, too. That was freedom indeed.

I pottered about the kitchen in a rather dazed fashion the following morning, and simply didn't hear Sister Elaine asking me to do something till her fifth attempt. I was miles away on a little pink cloud! And, in any case, it would probably take a while to get used to a veil covering my ears.

My dentist blinked when I appeared.

"You weren't in those clothes last time you came, were you?" he asked.

"No," I laughed, seeing his unconcealed surprise. "I only received the habit two days ago. This is the first time I have appeared in it in public."

Sister Geraldine had asked me to get some stamps on my way home. As I left the bicycle against the kerb and turned to walk into the Post Office, I caught sight of myself in the full-length glass door.

That was me! I could scarcely believe it. Me – dressed in a habit. I felt terribly conspicuous and sure that people must be staring at me, fully aware that I was the newest and rawest novice.

They were doing nothing of the sort, of course. No one batted an eyelid, and no one would have guessed that I hadn't been a novice for several years. After all, the people of Wantage are used to seeing sisters walking round the town, mingling in the market place, queueing for buses, sitting in dentists' waiting rooms . . . as a normal, everyday occurrence. The Wantage Sisters – as we are often called – have been around in Wantage since 1848.

Leaving the Post Office, it was a temptation to linger on the kerb and have another surreptitious peep at my reflection. I yielded. I am, after all, a very normal woman.

6

WILL IT BE ALLOWED?

"There's this nun on telly, and she's leaving her convent and joining *Crossroads*,"[1] said a piping voice from across the waiting room as I sat writing letters. My train was not due for fifty minutes and I had reckoned to get through three letters at least in that time. But now I had to pause to respond to this fascinating disclosure by the nine year old girl opposite, who was fixing me with large solemn blue eyes.

"That's rather sad, isn't it," I replied. "She must have been unhappy." That was enough – nothing short of invitation, in fact. Immediately, the nine year old and two small boys moved across and knelt round me in a semi-circle to continue the conversation.

"Is it true that there are nuns who are shut up behind walls and never come out?" one of the boys asked breathlessly.

"And who say prayers all day?" added his younger brother.

"Yes," I replied. "But not perhaps in the sense that I think you have understood it. There are certainly nuns who enter what are called enclosed orders, where they do not normally come out except for very special reasons."

"What sort of reasons?" they demanded.

"Well, appendicitis might be one," I said. "Or tooth-ache. Or sometimes a nun is given special permission to attend a conference; but normally their calling is to stay put. It is their special vocation to lead very hidden lives of prayer, but in no way are they shut up like prisoners. And, yes, there is a sense in which they, and we too, pray all day. But it doesn't mean that they kneel in chapel all day saying prayers.

"Nuns don't say prayers, they are prayers, living prayers and they try to offer every day to God, and every part of the day as prayer. But, of course, there are special times for being in chapel too. It's a bit like your life. All life is a learning process for you, but you have set times when you actually go to school."

"Are they very strict?" asked the smallest child of all. By now the original group of three had been joined by four more children and I had quite an audience. They were at the station to do some train-spotting, but obviously nun-spotting made a nice change.

"Yes. I suppose you could say that the life is strict in the sense that training for a soccer player might be strict – if he's going to be a good player. If he is aiming high, perhaps at one of the First Division teams, then he'll happily accept discipline and advice from his coach. A nun wants to be the best she can for God, so she is prepared for discipline too. God needs spiritual warriors not flabby, milksop characters who only play at Christian discipleship."

"Do you have to wear those clothes all the time?" asked the original nine year old.

"Apart from in bed, we do," I replied.

"But what if, when you were away, you didn't, and your Mother Superior found out?" she continued.

"Well it wouldn't make any difference if she found out or not," I said. "When we received the habit, we agreed to wear it all the time, and if we don't, then we are being disobedient. It doesn't only become disobedience if we're found out in some wrongdoing."

"But, does your Mother come round to find out if you are doing the right things?" she pursued.

I laughed. "Good gracious, no. She's far too busy! Besides which, if we fail in some obedience we are sinning against God, not our Mother. We made our promises to him and he is well aware of all that is going on in our lives. Anyway, our Mother trusts us and treats us like the adult women we are."

"Look," I said, as they digested this, "there's a world of difference between being at school and being in a convent. All of us have thought it fun, at some time or other, to break school rules, especially if we could do it without getting caught. But there's no point in us, as sisters, deliberately breaking rules. We've all chosen to be where we are. We've all chosen to accept the 'rules' – if you like to call them that. Refusing to do what we've chosen to do, doesn't make sense."

"What about this nun on telly that's leaving her convent?" they pressed. "Is it very hard to leave?"

"Yes," I said. "Hard and sad. Sometimes a nun becomes very unhappy and the only thing to do is to leave because the cause of the unhappiness is not just a passing thing. Perhaps she needs the sort of help she isn't going to find in community. Maybe she made a mistake in becoming a nun in the first place. And sometimes little disobediences have grown and become one big disobedience, and she feels she cannot keep the vow any longer. Maybe the community hasn't understood her and given her enough love. There could be lots of reasons, but if she leaves, it is always a very hard decision, and a very sad one."

They continued to gaze at me enquiringly, so I carried on.

"And, of course, she can't just walk out. It isn't that easy. If she did, there would still have to be official permission given, what's called dispensation from her vows. When we take our vows it's a bit like a marriage. We are bound to God and our Community by love – like a husband and wife – but we are also bound by a contract, and, like any legal contract sealed with documents, it can only be broken through proper official machinery. The matter has to go to the Bishop and then the Archbishop."

"Have any sisters ever left your community?" asked the oldest boy.

"Yes. There have been some – even since I joined, and I haven't been in my community all that long. When it happens, it is still very painful – after all, we are losing a member of the family. But, you know, if it's hard to leave, I'd say it is even harder to enter."

"Why?" they asked, obviously astonished.

"Naturally no community would want to encourage anyone even to contemplate joining if it is obvious that it would not be right for them or the community. With us there are first of all several interviews and anyone seriously thinking about becoming a sister is invited to stay for a while at the convent as a visitor and find out a little more about the life at first hand. She would meet the Mother of the community as well as the Novice Mistress. She would be asked to give the names of several people for references – perhaps her parish priest or employer, or both. Then, if it still seemed right and she had received a satisfactory medical report, she could begin her training."

"And does she then become a novice?"

"No. Not at first. She enters the community as an 'aspirant' – someone who is aspiring to become a sister. This period may be just for a few weeks, and then if she wants to continue, she takes a further step into the life of the community and becomes a 'postulant' – someone who is asking a question, 'Is this God's will for me?' She may be a postulant for several months, even a year, and then if she feels ready, she is 'clothed' in the habit and becomes a novice."

"How long does she have to be a novice?" they asked.

"That depends. In our community she would have to be a novice for at least three years but she may want to take longer, or the Novice Mistress might advise her to wait a while before taking the next and final step which is called 'profession'. At profession we take life vows and it's tremendously important that no one makes that commitment till she, and the community, are absolutely sure that it is right for all concerned. A community wants to be as certain as it can be of God's will, because of all the heartbreak when mistakes are made. It's a wonderful life if it is the right one, but leads to great unhappiness if it's not."

"Are you allowed to have holidays?"

"And can you smoke?"

"And are your friends allowed to come and see you?"

The questions came thick and fast, and I was given no respite until my train arrived, at which point, rather thankfully, I put away my writing things and, escorted by the entire group, made my way to the train where they very sweetly found me a seat and stayed to wave me off.

In a way, the questions of those delightful children reflected the question most often asked in those months before coming to Wantage. I asked it myself. It was put to me over and over again by a variety of friends and acquaintances.

"Will you be allowed . . .?"

"Will you be able to . . .?"

"Is it permitted to . . .?"

Inwardly I often winced. It seemed from these questions that people viewed community life as a cross between boarding school and prison – full of negative, inhibiting rules that reduce freedom and prevent growth towards maturity. Much of it, I knew, was sheer perplexity that anyone could take such a step as I was taking, voluntarily. I knew too that mostly the questions were asked out of loving interest and a concern not to put me into embarrassing and painful situations where I would have to try to remain loyal to my new life without causing offence to friends of long standing.

Every religious order has its own Rule. It is perhaps an unfortunate word because inevitably it is associated with rules and regulations. The Rule of a community tries to express in words its spirit and special ethos. Some are based on the Rule of the Founder of an Order, as with St Benedict's Rule, or St Augustine's.* It sets out principles but tends to read more like a meditation than a code book of instructions. Often we might be tempted to think that life would be simpler if the Rule spelt out more specifically how

*Originally written as a letter, not as a Rule

we should act in every conceivable situation. But, on the whole, it doesn't. It points to the ultimate goal of loving God through, for example, reverence, silence, prayer, the vows, community of goods etc, but there is still much onus of responsibility placed upon the individual to respond appropriately.

For us, there are actual directives about such things as the minimum amount of time to be spent in prayer, reading and study. There is also an implicit understanding amongst us that we try to avoid extravagance or luxury in any way that would be inappropriate to those under a vow of poverty. But even there, it is more a case of following a 'spirit' of poverty. It is difficult to have general and inflexible rules when individual needs vary so much.

However, I tried to offer straight answers to my friends and give them the facts they needed. It was pointless getting defensive about the wording of the enquiries, even if it betrayed a lack of understanding, and an impression of the life as being negative and crushing.

When people asked us, as they frequently did in those days, "Will you be allowed to have this or that . . .?" I honestly didn't know what to say. My hesitations, due to ignorance, sometimes brought difficulties later on. Only with the passing weeks and months did I begin to see how some of the questions should have been answered.

Such questions as "Can you smoke?" which the children asked, were fairly straightforward. Poverty would rule that out, apart from all other considerations. It would certainly be a strangely incongruous sight to see a sister smoking.

"Will you be allowed holidays?"

"Yes." That had a clear answer.

But then, "Will you be allowed visitors?"

"Oh yes," I had said to all and sundry, "you'd be very welcome."

It was an embarrassment therefore to discover that there couldn't be an unlimited number of visitors, nor could those who came stay for an unlimited length of time. Sensing that she had a problem here, Sister Geraldine at first made the times very specific and fairly short. In any case, visits had to be fitted around my work schedules and in my early days in the novitiate there were no 'space days' or even half days as were later to be introduced.

The restriction on the number of visitors is partly for obvious practical reasons, as it would be in normal family life. It was also a form of protection. It can sometimes be very exhausting to answer endless questions. Worse still, it can actually hinder the Holy Spirit if we try to articulate too readily or prematurely, even to ourselves, those ways in which he is secretly at work in us, and, sometimes, albeit well-meaning questions can draw us out inadvisedly. All new plants need a degree of protection and that given to us, far from being repressive or wrongly secretive, was to give the newly growing vocation time to 'take' and put down roots in its new environment.

"Will you be allowed presents?" was another common question.

"It's lovely when presents are given that can be shared with everyone," said Sister Geraldine.

Certainly in the novitiate we valued the kind of gifts that could be added to our communal stock of art equipment for we were always making cards for some event or other.

Gifts are part of our community of goods as much as any money which we may happen to earn. One can see the wisdom of this, for some sisters have no families, or have been cut off by their families. It could lead to much inequality in possessions and therefore to jealousy if we did not have this understanding. Sometimes personal presents are given, and the sister concerned is asked if she needs it. If so, it is usually given straight back. The responsibility is then on the sister who has received the gift and not on the Superior.

One of the requirements of our life is an ability to move anywhere at any time. The prayer life is often likened to a desert journey, and for both these reasons one needs to be able to travel light. Hence we try to remain uncluttered. So showers of presents could actually become a hindrance in the work which we are called to do. They could ultimately lead a sister to become acquisitive, thereby breaking the spirit of having all things in common. Let me hasten to add that we do not speak of 'our' toothbrush and 'our' socks. Some essentials are given us by the community, but they are for personal use – and we don't hesitate to use a singular possessive adjective with them.

"Will it be allowed . . .?" presupposes limitations. Pruning there has to be, it is true. But pruning is for growth. The vows of poverty, chastity and obedience do not bind us as though we were in the grip of a boa constrictor. They are for freedom but it isn't always easy to show exactly how when people ask, "Will it be allowed?" We can only hope that increasingly friends will be able to recognise a growing freedom in us and then be able to make the connection between our new liberty and the binding of the vows we have taken, or are hoping to take.

There are three vows and yet, in a way, they are one. They are so closely inter-related it is impossible to separate them out at times. Nevertheless, the girdle worn by professed sisters in C.S.M.V. has three large knots symbolising poverty, chastity and obedience.

"What are those three knots for?" asked the small daughter of a priest during a visit, as she watched sisters walking to and fro, their girdles swinging. I told her. She thought for a while and then said, "If you are disobedient, would your Mother chop the bottom knot off?"

That's quite a salutary thought.

Much freedom is given to interpret for ourselves what God is asking of us under those vows. That does not mean, however, that we are given licence to do our own thing. That would kill true freedom. We all know how we can wriggle when things go against the grain. We may even be guilty of what Thomas Merton called the 'mutual gripes' but if obedience has lost its cutting edge a community is an impoverished community.

Obedience is not a powerful, crushing machine but an emancipation from slavery . . . it tackles the parasitic profusion of 'my own ideas', 'my own judgements', 'my own wishes' which encumber growth in the new life, and

99

exhaust its strength. Its objective is not to cut off every-thing immediately, like gardeners with the itch to use the pruning knife, but rather to purge and to put a new value on the natural and supernatural powers which are so often paralysed by selfishness. The divine Spirit respects and never does violence to the freedom of the creature.[2]

As time went on, I was able to meet the question, "Will it be allowed?" with a more adequate and positive response. For, really, "Would it be appropriate . . .?" is the better question. Would it be fitting to this new way of life? Would it be helpful to the life of prayer and that journey through the desert? Would it violate my integrity in any way?

The answers will not always be the same for every sister.

Some things which are perfectly good and enjoyable in themselves no longer appeal; they not only seem out of place in the new life, they are actually a hindrance. Already I had begun to sense that on the final cruise that I had made just before entering the convent. There were to be many other, mainly small, ways in which one became aware that tastes were changing, for example few of us can enjoy large and noisy crowds after having lived in an atmosphere of silence, even if we enjoyed these before.

We not only have to drop some things that have been part of our past life, we want to drop them – as much as a newly married man may want to drop some of his bachelor practices in order to spend more time with his wife and enjoying his home.

The Rule and the vows, then, offer a pathway to free-dom. They are not intended to trap people in infantilism but liberate them into a full maturity. That is the basic objective, but in practice the ways by which they confront us day by day can often seem far less sublime.

I once had a gift – something I had often wanted but never got around to buying for myself in my pre-community days. Now here it was – a guitar.

"We already have several in the novitiate," said Sister Geraldine. "Another one would be unnecessary."

"But we are not always going to be in the novitiate

together," I countered. "What about later on when we are professed and perhaps scattered in different houses?"

I could scarcely believe my ears as she told me to take it along to Sister Harriet Ruth who, as Precentrix, dealt with all matters musical.

"Oh what fun!" said Sister Harriet Ruth as I walked into her room. She was just closing a window as I explained why I had come.

"Forgive me if I don't find it much fun at the moment," I said. Still clutching the window pole, she turned quickly and gave me a penetrating look. She made no further enquiries.

"No, it can be very hard indeed," she replied gently, as I thrust the instrument in her hands and backed out of the room.

I had done what I was told – outwardly I was obedient, outwardly uncluttered by that particular possession. But inwardly? Not until three years later, when I was on the threshold of profession, did I really let go of that guitar, and the bitterness of yielding it up.

7

THE COMMON DENOMINATOR

What makes people resign their jobs, sell up their homes, abandon prospects of marriage and a family, or professional promotion, in order to enter a religious community? Why the madness? Why this waste?

"We need people like you in the world."

"It's so selfish, hiding yourself away so that you can enjoy a quiet, untroubled life."

There are as many reasons as people, and we all had to face this sort of comment without any hope of ever justifying what we were doing in the eyes of our critics, even if we tried. At the same time there is only one reason – love. It is love that draws and calls and puts that inner, insistent, urgent pressure on the soul. It is love that finally brings people to stand in front of a monastery or convent door, and knock and ask for admission. It is love that has followed them through their searchings and longings and questioning, love that hounded them down the nights and down the days, down the arches of the years, through the labyrinthine ways of the mind, sometimes through periods of darkness and uncertainty, sometimes through untroubled, carefree days. It is Love. And if the entering into a community is not the response of love to Love – then it is doomed to failure and disappointment from the start.

There are, of course, other factors behind each person's

decision and these vary from individual to individual, but in the final analysis, it boils down to only one supreme motive. That is the common denominator.

I doubt if any of us arriving somewhat tremblingly on the doorstep of our convent could have articulated our motives all that clearly at the time. We had all felt ourselves drawn irresistibly by some inner compulsion and mostly 'against all reason'[1] as Geoffrey Moorhouse so aptly put it; our own as well as other people's.

Miriam arrived with only the clothes she was wearing and a few essentials – a nightie, toothbrush, comb, Bible and fountain pen. And that was about all.

"How did you do it?" I asked in wonder. "What did you do with all your clothes and other possessions?"

"Got rid of them all," she said in her down-to-earth way. "You see, I sat at the back of my church and He said to me, 'Go'. So I came."

"Didn't you have any doubts?" I asked, thinking of all my own.

"Oh yes. I rebelled like mad. But he kept saying 'Go', so that was it."

"And your things?" I pressed. "You've got rid of all of them?"

"Yes – the lot," she said grinning. "Clothes, car, books, house – the lot!"

How different we were. Sister Geraldine had been most insistent that I should not sell my house before coming. I don't know if that was because she was less sure that I really had a vocation, or whether in her perception she could see that I wasn't sufficiently ready for that particular renunciation.

Whether or not we come as dispossessed as Miriam or arrive with all but the kitchen sink, or indeed, including the kitchen sink, as happened with one aspirant who hadn't been too successful in arranging her temporal affairs, the driving force is the same for each one and, in the end, the renunciations are equal for all of us. Only the timing is different. All are called to give up all for Christ, and that creates a very big bond between us.

Sometimes when I was still a postulant, from my seat at the back of chapel, I would look along the rows of sisters in choir and think what a strangely mixed bunch we were. When the media make films about nuns and convents, the characters always seem to be slim, fragile creatures with classic bone structure and beautiful skin and eyes like limpid pools – giving the impression of someone living on a cloud of permanent ecstasy. And then one compares that with reality. There seemed to be an unusually high proportion of very tall sisters at Wantage, some of them indeed slim, but there were also the shorter and more ample figures. Delicate bone structures, but also rugged, uneven features; some meticulously tidy in their dress, others who, despite all their efforts, looked as though their clothes were trailing rather reluctantly behind their bodies. There isn't one type – thank God. And interestingly, though our clothes are uniform, every sister seems to wear hers in a distinctly individual way that reveals a great deal about her. The habit may offer a certain blessed anonymity, yet we remain very much ourselves in them.

Musing from my vantage point at the back, I would also consider the enormous accumulation and variety of gifts and experience gathered under that one roof of chapel, thinking, 'And each one seeking to offer all.' There were the practical sisters – the craftsmen, the gardeners, the cooks, the needlewomen – some of them highly qualified and now pooling all their gifts and resources. There were those skilled in parish work . . . and some who were still in training for it. I thought of Sister Ursula pegging away at her books preparing for her Reader's[2] exams. There were the counsellors, teachers and scholars of no mean standing.

"We don't always appreciate the extent of our riches in community," said Sister Harriet Ruth one day, as Sister Paula passed us in the corridor, "but there goes someone who is actually 'quite' an authority on the Early Church Fathers."

Some had been nurses and doctors, some social workers. Their skills were thrown into the pool too, and still used.

A large proportion of the sisters sitting there had spent

years of their community life in one of our overseas provinces – or both. I used to amuse myself by picking out the 'Indian' from the 'African' sisters – and was usually right. Their missionary experience had left indelible marks upon them.

There were the trained artists and musicians, the homemakers, the cooks, the gymnasts and the dancers, the publishers, the secretaries, the accountants and the librarians, those who had been active members of political parties, weavers, printers, book-binders, dressmakers and embroiderers. It was hard to think of any walk of life that was not represented.

"No experience is ever wasted," Sister Zoe had once said to me. "It will all be taken up and used in community." It was hard to believe how at the time, but she was right. One sister many years ago claimed no special gifts or training. "I'm not particularly good at anything," she had said on arrival, and it had seemed that she was not being falsely modest. But then it was discovered that she was a superb rat-catcher, a gift which apparently in those earlier days of convent life was much appreciated. Yes, the cumulative experience was by no means insignificant. And yet, basically, we were all there for one reason, all pointing in one direction, all longing for one thing.

What makes a person throw up everything for this way of life? Since it is so difficult to put the mysterious call of God into so many words – and have no doubt, it is a mystery to us too – it has led to all sorts of peculiar impressions and phoney ideas. One of these is that convents are refuges for love-sick women – the jilted, the disappointed, those without hope of marriage fulfilment. Maybe there is a fractional shred of historical truth . . . that occasionally in the dim past, fathers whisked their daughters into convents for very unworthy reasons, and consequently some houses were peopled with frustrated and unhappy nuns. But that is an absolute caricature of the monastic life in general, and certainly of communities today.

"Have you ever been in love?" asked Sister Zoe in her very matter-of-fact way, when I first shared with her the inklings I was getting about God's call to me. I laughed. She was so direct about it – nothing coy about her.

"You see, it's important," she continued, "important that anyone contemplating taking a vow of chastity should have some understanding of what it is she is offering up. You need to have known what it is to be in love with a man before you can choose to renounce married love for celibacy."

There was great wisdom in what she said, and I am sure that I am by no means alone in having to satisfy a counsellor on that score.

It is of course much more difficult to be accepted even as an aspirant than many suppose. There is a curious notion that a Mother Superior sits like some large spider desperately anxious to draw likely young women into the monastic web. On the contrary, there is a very careful screening before anyone is encouraged even to begin testing her vocation.

"Why not let anyone come and try, if they feel God is calling them?" I once asked in a discussion. "At least if people try, and find out for themselves that it isn't right for them, they won't continually wonder if they should or shouldn't."

"Well, apart from the necessity of discouraging those who are obviously coming for the wrong reasons – hoping to find a private nursing home, or a more desirable alternative to unemployment than the labour exchange – there are others for whom it would still be very doubtful even if less obvious. We feel that it is better not to let people resign good jobs and vacate their homes if we know that it is likely to be only for a matter of months or perhaps a year. It might not be possible for them to find comparable employment and they would bitterly regret their action. Of course with everyone there is an element of risk. We cannot be sure that it is right till the vocation has been tested, and assessing a vocation is one of the hardest things to do," Sister Geraldine explained.

Even after the preliminary interviews, there are further reviews each year with the novice throughout her novitiate, to seek the mind and will of God through prayer, through discussion with the novice, through what the community has to say.

So – correction number one to any misapprehensions – our common denominator is not one of flight. The Religious Life is not a refuge from the world, but one avenue by which one comes to face reality starkly and painfully, abhorring all that is unreal in oneself.

Correction number two. The convent is not the place for the unsuccessful. Any Novice Guardian would want to be satisfied that an aspirant had successfully held down a job for a reasonable length of time and found some kind of fulfilment in it. Being unable to get a job or keep a job has been almost an instant disqualification (though with present unemployment problems, things must obviously be viewed rather differently). But in principle, no community would want to let someone who had just made a terrible mess of life test his or her vocation in the hope of finding an escape. It would have to look carefully at the reasons for past failures and ask whether or not the right lessons had been learned so that the failures were stepping stones rather than blocks.

Nor if there was any hint of running away from responsibilities towards elderly or dependent parents would an aspirant be encouraged to start. Nor if he or she were primarily fleeing from loneliness and looking for a support group. Doubtless for some, the community aspect of the vocation is stronger than for others, but for none should it be the primary motivation. On the contrary, it is more a vocation to a life which is a flight from the alone to the Alone, and one must be a lover of solitude.

Few if any people go through life without hang-ups about relationships at some point, but if these are a major problem to an aspirant the convent walls will be no protection and the life itself no solution. Far from it. Imagine the personal hell it would be if one couldn't relate to others, and the weight it would place on the community.

The idea of community life might tempt some to suppose that they would find the security that has so far eluded them in life. Every one of us enters the novitiate with some insecurities and, if we had not been aware of their existence before, we soon discover them under the arc light of the Religious Life.

For all of us there is a need to drop false securities and find our total security in God, but it can only be for love of God, and God alone. We do not set out to find security by entering a community. We set out to seek God, and in doing so he becomes our Security.

It is not altogether uncommon to receive enquiries from people who are emotionally unstable or in need of psychiatric help. The love and acceptance of a community are very healing – very healing indeed, as I was to discover (almost on a grand scale). But they are not substitutes for the professional help of a therapist, doctor or psychiatrist.

Of course, we all come with mixed motives, and we haven't enough insight all in one to be honest with ourselves, let alone with others. It sometimes takes quite a while before the wrong motives emerge – hence the need for a longish testing period so that both the community and the individual can see if it is a genuine vocation to the Religious Life, or not.

Poor Sister Geraldine! Sometimes it was her unenviable task to break it to a postulant or novice that it was abundantly clear that she hadn't got a vocation when she herself hadn't reached that conclusion – or she hadn't been able to face, at the conscious level, the truth which deep down she might have known.

Linda was a postulant when I arrived at Wantage, but she was a strangely discontented one. Most people have to go through trauma and pain in their early stages, but Linda's pain was different. She seemed bewildered and out of place. The life didn't really make sense to her and therefore she was highly critical (in a destructive way) of customs, traditions, and individual sisters. She was clearly not happy.

After a week away on holiday she said to me, "I don't know why I came back. They are such an odd lot. Do you

108

know, some of them eat their oranges with a knife and fork!''

I was intrigued. Having sought to keep custody of the eyes in the refectory, I hadn't observed these apparently strange practices. I was more observant after that and actually, in just over a week, counted ten different ways to eat an orange. But why not? Isn't variety the spice of life?

Linda went on pinpointing all the things she found unattractive in the sisters and spreading vibes of discontent. 'Moth and rust doth corrupt'.[3] Grumbling and complaining eat away at the very fabric of community life.

"Why do you stay?" I asked her one day. "You don't even seem to like the community."

"I don't want to go back to living alone," she replied. "I want to be with people."

But it wasn't enough. Even though she had set her heart on being clothed in the habit, Sister Geraldine had to tell her that it wasn't the life for her. At first Linda seemed to see the wisdom of this. In fact, I had the feeling it had come as a relief. She slipped away without fuss and we said very loving farewells. She returned, however, some while later, full of bitterness and suppressed anger, determined to hurt Sister Geraldine and others in the novitiate. We haven't seen her again but hope and pray she has found God's path for her.

It is one thing to make these discoveries in the early stages while still a postulant. It is infinitely harder if it is after three or four years as a novice. But throughout that testing time, there is the possibility that some trait will come to light that will indicate that it is not to be a life-long vocation.

"If God leads you back into the world," Sister Geraldine said to me on a number of occasions, "it will not be into a vacuum. He calls to, not from, and if he leads you out of the novitiate it will be 'to' some other form of service."

I was sure she was right, but never found it wholly consoling. Each time it reminded me that there has to be an open mind, and an open ear to God, all the way through, and the certainty as to whether or not it is a vocation for life cannot come until a novice has been elected by the community to make her profession and take life vows. I didn't find it easy to live with the uncertainty.

Even though we all recognise that God may well lead some back to secular life after a short period in the novitiate, a period which will undoubtedly have been rich in experience and teaching, it is nevertheless very hard if when the time comes to leave the decision about this is not mutual. No Novice Guardian can find it easy to ask someone to leave if he or she feels it is a totally wrong decision. Sadly, that can happen, and did, more than once during my time as a postulant and inwardly I was convinced that one day it would be my turn. 'Who is sufficient for these things?' I thought.

"How do you judge if someone has a vocation or not?" I asked Sister Geraldine. "You carry an almost frightening responsibility, don't you. You've got our lives in your hands."

"Well, not quite. I never act alone," she said. "But, yes, it is very awesome indeed. How do we judge? I think we look to see if a novice is flourishing in the life. That's a fairly safe sign. If she is flourishing at every level – in her work, her corporate life, her health, her appetite, her prayer . . ."

"Her prayer?" I interrupted. "How can you assess whether or not someone's prayer life is flourishing? It's a very personal matter."

"Well, novices do sometimes talk to me if they feel things are not right at the prayer level. Often they are unnecessarily alarmed and what they fear is a breakdown of their prayer life is usually a sign of growth – the next stage on in a contemplative vocation. But even apart from what is shared with me in confidence, it is very obvious if prayer is flourishing or not – by a person's body language, by their general behaviour, and of course by their work in general. For if one is in pieces inwardly, one is rarely able to cope satisfactorily outwardly."

The weeks passed and I was not asked to leave. I continued plodding on. There was no escaping the feeling that God wanted me right there in the novitiate of

C.S.M.V. Oddly enough, and in complete contrast to what some people believe about convents, for me the flight from reality would have been to leave. It was the pull 'to' reality that kept me there.

In the early days of monasticism, in the fourth century, the monks fled to the Egyptian deserts. Anthony, sometimes held to be the founder of Christian monasticism, considered this to be a straightforward continuation of the Apostolic way of life, i.e. the demand of the 'all or nothing' for Christ, particularly explicit in the teachings of St Paul. At the end of an era of persecution which had tested very poignantly the degree of all or nothingness in a Christian's commitment, the Church was in danger of growing comfortable, half-hearted and mediocre. To counter this laxity, martyrdom, the martyrdom to blood, seemed to give place to what became known as white martyrdom – the sacrificial way of a life of total renunciation in which there was a daily dying. This is at the root of the monastic life. Those early monks were accused of fleeing from the cities to the desert to get away from the evil influences of the world, to form for themselves a kind of spiritual ghetto where they would not be subjected to temptation. Nothing could have been further from the truth. They fled, not from the world but from the Church which had become too worldly and soft. They did not flee from evil and temptation but went out to face it head on – for the desert was commonly believed to be the chiefest haunt of evil spirits. The desert fathers were warriors entering upon the fiercest possible kind of spiritual warfare. When Anthony heard the call of God – actually during the reading of the gospel – he immediately responded with the whole of his being. No half measures for him. And he has been succeeded down through the ages by thousands of others who were not content to follow their Lord in any cosy, lethargic, undemanding way.

As Evdokimov has put it, "The Holy Spirit 'invented' the equivalent of martyrdom. The testimony that the martyrs rendered to the 'one thing necessary' passed to monasticism."[4]

Think too of the reckless generosity of Mary Magdalen.

111

She subjected herself to the taunts of the Pharisees as she came to anoint the feet of Jesus with her most costly gift. She probably minded their murmurings and reproaches, but that didn't deter her from expressing her love in this extravagant way. She has been the inspiration of countless numbers within the monastic life. She loved passionately. There wasn't anything she would not do for the one she loved. For that, she was prepared to be criticised and misunderstood. No gift was too costly. No gesture of love too embarrassing or silly. She was totally un-self-conscious. "What a waste!" the disciples said. How often has that been said since, as men and women have broken the 'alabaster box' of their lives over the feet of Christ. Is such love really so incomprehensible? I suppose it is. Yet we applaud the amazing sacrifices parents will make for their children, and husbands for their wives, out of love. And that is exactly what lies behind our apparent wastage of lives.

There is nothing new about parental opposition to the Religious Life, nor the misunderstanding of friends. Francis of Assisi was considered a lunatic by his parents and fellow townsfolk. Thomas Aquinas was content to be dubbed 'the dumb ox'. And in all fairness, there is a foolishness about it. The monk or nun takes a stand which may be considered an extreme. But such an extreme is a special kind of living at the edge of things.

Still today it is the call to the all or nothing that brings people aspiring to the Religious Life. Mother Teresa of Calcutta has a vast and growing community. A recent report spoke of over six hundred in the Novitiate. Asked why it was that young women flocked to join the Missionaries of Charity, Mother Teresa answered, "Because I ask everything of them."

Youth will stir to that kind of challenge.

However, the pull to the Religious Life today is not simply a movement of enthusiasm among young people. It is, I believe, the experience of many communities that aspirants are coming to them at a rather maturer age. When I arrived at Wantage, several in the novitiate were in their forties, two were in their fifties, the majority were in their early thirties, and two in their late twenties. Admittedly, the older one is, the harder it is in some respects – for one is already formed and has established patterns of life, manners etc that are not always readily malleable. On the other hand, it is valuable to an aspirant to have seen a bit of life, perhaps to have knocked around the world a little, and known a degree of independence. In our novitiate, as it happened, we had all trained or acquired some professional skill, and practised it. It sometimes leads to frustration and a sense of inadequacy if someone enters a community so young that she has not been able to complete any kind of training, pass any exams, or had the chance to take a driving test. A certain maturity is needed to face the testing of a vocation, though maturity is not of course necessarily coincidental with chronological age.

It takes maturity to be able to make a life commitment. Isn't it true that one of the reasons why many marriages break down today is that the marriage partners often enter into their new life together when they are too immature? Not having had time and enough experience of life to find themselves, and discover who they are, they can scarcely be expected to give this unknown, undiscovered self fully and unreservedly to another.

One of the attractions of religious communities, so we are told, is that here in a vastly unstable world there are people who vow themselves to a life of stability. Here, in a world where people know increasingly less about the meaning of commitment – whether it be to a cause, a job, a marriage partner, the Church, or indeed, to an international agreement – there are people who are prepared to make a total commitment to God. Here in a world where it is difficult to have any concept of permanence – where divorce is relatively easy to obtain and living together is often preferred to the binding commitment of marriage – there are people, ordinary, sensible people, who are actually prepared to take vows for the rest of their lives in this world. That has powerful appeal.

Novice Bronwen and Novice Celia were to be professed. It was to be my first experience of a profession service. By

113

way of preparation, Sister Geraldine went through the service with us and explained each section and its symbolism. Her face shone with joy and occasionally she got a bit misty-eyed. It was moving and beautiful, even in prospect. Why then were there these unaccountable waves of fear rising up inside me, bringing me out in cold sweats from time to time?

After their stripping, I couldn't but be aware of the deep pain they were both feeling at having parted with some very cherished possession. The fact that one wants to offer everything, and knows great joy in doing so, doesn't eliminate the pain. The two can cohabit without contradiction. They began their long profession retreat and all of us in the novitiate were preparing too – inwardly, by dwelling on the meaning of what they were about to take on, and outwardly, in all the practical details (of which there are a surprising number).

The day itself came. I was so nervous for them, I had a stomach upset. As we joined them in the novitiate room for the short ceremony that takes place there before going on to chapel for the profession they both seemed very composed and recollected. It was I who was shaking not them.

Receiving their candles from Mother, they moved off into the novitiate cloister, their fellow novices flanking them on both sides, as we began the Respond: "My Beloved speaks and says to me: Arise my love, my fair one, and come away."

Then came words which again struck me as being extraordinarily apposite for such an occasion, as they had done during the preparation class. No matter that they were originally written for the wedding of a Tyrean Princess – they expressed our own thoughts beautifully. "Hear, O daughter, consider and incline your ear: forget your own people and your father's house. The King desires your beauty: he is your Lord therefore bow down before him."[5]

Later, the Bishop was to preach a most memorable sermon on those very words.

The acolytes and banner bearers had reached the west door. Mother and Sister Geraldine processed side by side, and behind them came Bronwen and Celia – the candles reflecting a glow on their faces and lights in their eyes. 'But it isn't just the candles,' I thought. 'They are themselves absolutely radiant.'

The procession was ready to move in, we the escorts had finished the Respond, now it was the turn of the sisters, standing in readiness, to welcome their sisters elect. They did so by bursting forth with the Introit, "The King's daughter is all glorious within." My word! What a shout of praise and how beautifully they were singing.

The procession moved very slowly and with great dignity up through choir. The banner bearers and acolytes continuing up to the sanctuary, Mother and Sister Geraldine going to their stalls, the Novitiate headed by Bronwen and Celia moving forward to their seats on either side of the aisle. Then came the genuflection. We had practised this entry several times beforehand. Down we went on one knee in one perfectly timed movement like part of a dance and turned to go to our chairs.

Next came the thurifer, acolytes, priests and bishop.

"My heart overflows with a song of joy: I address my song to the King," continued the singers. They sounded as though their hearts were overflowing with joy too.

From where I was standing, I could only see Bronwen and she was positively 'enjoying' it . . . as indeed was right and natural. Moved as I was, I couldn't say that I was enjoying it. I was having to do battle with the waves of fear that had started rising up again. The Mass continued like any Sung Mass until we reached the offertory. It is at that point that the profession takes place. The sister seeks to give herself as a living sacrifice, through her vows and life-long commitment as part of the offering being made at this particular celebration of the Holy Sacrifice once offered. She is herself the offertory.

Each in turn knelt on the sanctuary steps as the Warden presented her to the Bishop.

"Father, I present Sister Bronwen, who has been elected for profession in this Community of St Mary the Virgin," he said.

"Sister, what do you desire?" asked the Bishop.
First Sister Bronwen, and then Sister Celia, replied,

> "I desire grace and mercy of our Lord Jesus Christ,
> to devote myself to his service
> in this Community
> in poverty, chastity and obedience,
> for the rest of my life in this world,
> and I pray you in the name of God
> to admit me to profession
> in this Community of St Mary the Virgin."

Then the Bishop addressed them with a series of very searching questions.

> "Do you understand that profession binds you in life-long covenant?
> Do you understand that this involves a life of sacrifice?
> Will you diligently follow our Lord Jesus Christ . . .?
> Will you strive to live in love and gentleness, humility and patience with all your sisters, in obedience to the Rule of this community, and in the Spirit of the blessed Virgin Mary?

> "I will," they each replied.

Then came a question to the community. "Will you the sisters of this community, welcome Sister Bronwen and Sister Celia into your family, and endeavour to live with them in a spirit of love and unity?"

The reply of the Sisters came back like a clap of thunder. "We will," they chorused enthusiastically. There could be little doubt about either their intentions or their delight as they received two more into the family.

Then as the Bishop prayed over the sisters, there came the lovely words ". . . May he accomplish his purpose in you, to the well-being of this community, and your own eternal joy and peace."

Both of them now prostrated on the sanctuary steps in a symbolic movement of total oblation.

It's strange how one movement can sum up and contain all the deepest longings of a human heart. I have explored the use of movement in worship for a number of years now and I find that the prostration has the power to do that more than any other I know.

The choir were singing the Veni Creator,

> Come Holy Ghost, our souls inspire . . .

I couldn't look at Bronwen and Celia. Nor could I sing. I was too choked. So I just closed my eyes.

After both had knelt before the Bishop to make their profession, they signed the community's register and we responded,

> Lord establish me according to your word, that I may live: and do not disappoint me in my hope.

saying it three times for each sister in turn. It was at that moment that my fear reached its peak.

"If I had seen two Buddhist monks douse themselves in petrol and set fire to themselves," I said to Sister Geraldine later, "I couldn't have been more horrified than I was at the point when those two signed their lives away."

And yet, strangely, I was also filled with admiration and longing. Their witness moved me deeply.

Then came the consecration of each sister – the setting apart. This is done through a long and most eloquent prayer in which the Bishop prays:

> . . . May she find all in you, whom she seeks to love above all . . .

Love had called them. Love had drawn them on through the novitiate years. Love had brought them to this act of covenant making. It really was a kind of wedding, even if we didn't go in for a lot of outward nuptial imagery. But then, what other human image is there, other than marriage, that expresses satisfactorily this response of love to Love?

The sisters now knelt before the Bishop to receive the insignia of profession, first the community cross with the words of Mary engraved upon it, *ECCE ANCILLA DOMINI. FIAT MIHI SECUNDUM VERBUM TUUM* – Behold, the handmaid of the Lord; be it unto me according to thy word;[6] then the girdle with its three large knots symbolising the vows of poverty, chastity and obedience.

Next the black veil of a professed sister in place of the white novice's veil which is whisked away discreetly never to be seen (on that sister) again. It is quite a dramatic moment. It marks visually the final severance from the novitiate.

When the black veils of Bronwen and Celia were securely in place, the rings were given.

"I am the bride of him whom angels serve, before whose radiance the sun and moon stand in wonder," we all sang for the 'brides' as they raised their right hands high and we saw the plain gold rings gleaming on their third fingers. Not quite plain though, for the ring is the seal of the sister's covenant with God and with the community. In token of that, the initials C.S.M.V. are engraved on her ring.

Finally the sisters were given their books containing the Rule and Constitution of the community and in which the Warden had written a verse of the sister's own choice.

"My soul proclaims the greatness of the Lord," we sang, as the sisters took up their candles once more and in turn were escorted by Mother to their stalls.

"My spirit rejoices in God my saviour; the Almighty has done great things for me: and holy is his name," and the joy on their faces confirmed that this was indeed true for them.

Sometimes one witnesses a scene, or participates in an act of dedication that is so powerful in its symbolism, one knows afterwards that one will never be quite the same again.

It was so for me that day.

If I felt emotionally wrung out, it was because I had been 'in' the experience with the two sisters, identifying, rejoicing, wondering, awestruck. We all had. For most of us still in the novitiate, it was a time of looking forward; for every professed sister, a time of memories and renewal of vows. For each one it was a cleansing experience – from the first notes of that opening Respond, "My Beloved speaks . . ." right through to the final Respond, sung at every profession,

Earthly Kingdoms and all the glory of the world I spurned, for the love of my Lord and Saviour Jesus Christ, whom I have seen, whom I have loved, in whom I have believed, whom I have desired.

The banner proclaiming its joyful message, "His banner over me is love,"[7] was carried by the bearers to the antechapel. Bronwen and Celia processed through choir till they stood beneath it, and one by one the sisters filed by to give the community greeting with its delightful blend of formality and restraint on the one hand, and spontaneity and joyful exuberance on the other.

Throughout the rest of the day, I gazed with awe at all the professed sisters in their black veils. Like Bronwen and Celia, they had all been through that experience of profession. They had each become living holocausts on the sanctuary step. Each one had offered herself as fully as she was able to him whom she had seen, whom she had loved, in whom she had believed, whom she had desired.

These thoughts were still going through my head that night at supper, as I sat in the refectory watching intently, quite unashamedly and in defiance of all good manners, as sisters moved to and fro. It was, I remember, baked beans and porridge on the menu that night, and suddenly the absurd thought flashed across my mind, 'How, after all that, can they sit there eating such ordinary food?' I suppose in my moonstruck state I felt that for them nothing but ambrosia and nectar were good enough.

8

THE SHELTERING GLASS

"Is it true that there are nuns who shut themselves up behind walls for the rest of their lives?" had asked the nine year old girl in the waiting room of Westbury railway station. Her great, round troubled eyes gave away the sheer horror she felt at such a thought – a horror that I suspect is shared by many adults. Perhaps more than anything else about our way of life, enclosure constitutes both the greatest mystery and the greatest offence.

To those who have never visited a convent, or had little opportunity of meeting sisters, brothers, monks or nuns, it probably seems like a form of imprisonment, an attempt to escape from the world of harsh realities, a flight from evil into a peaceful, secluded form of Utopia, and certainly an opting out of life and its responsibilities. There was a time when I thought like that myself. And what goes on behind those walls, anyway? If from one side people were granted an opportunity to peep over, would they find a whole lot of frustrated women longing to leap over from the other?

Before anyone can begin to test his or her vocation to the Religious Life, a medical examination is required. I remember the doctor who examined me telling me that I was a very healthy specimen, but why did I want to abandon my present happy life in order to become a nun?

"It's all very well now," she said, "but how will you feel in ten years' time? That's what worries me."

"How can I possibly know how I will feel in ten years' time about anything?" I replied.

"You are leading a very active, fulfilling and useful life at the moment and I fear for you. I suspect that, in time, you will become intolerably frustrated."

She went on to speak of people who were not particularly happy in their work. "I would have no worries about recommending them," she said, clearly aligning herself with those who mistakenly regard convents as clearing houses for people who have failed to make a go of it elsewhere.

"Nuns become so pale and develop all sorts of neurotic symptoms," continued the doctor. "They often appear anaemic, underfed and strained."

"Have you ever actually stayed in a convent?" I asked in astonishment.

"No – I haven't," she replied, "but I've seen some from the outside and they've looked forbidding and austere. And two or three communities send their aspirants to me for medicals."

I chuckled as I thought of the robust, energetic sisters I had met, many of them with clear skins, rosy cheeks . . . and surprisingly hearty appetites. Or perhaps not so surprisingly – for the life is vigorous and physically demanding and there is no nibbling between meals.

"You really ought to visit a convent," I told the doctor. "You'd get a good many surprises."

The conception that the majority of people have of the monastic life is largely shaped by the media. Earlier in the century, the gruesome *Tales of Maria Monk* were circulated, causing horror and revulsion. Then came *I Leaped Over a Wall* followed by *The Nun's Story*, and more recently *The Sound of Music*. These are not typical stories; for although some of the details may be authentic, they are generally not set in their true context. In recent days, some communities have allowed TV cameras inside their houses to film parts of their life and individual Religious have taken part in broadcasts. This may have helped to dispel some of the misconceptions, but still the mystique remains.

Any vocation or work that requires special conditions and an unusual environment is going to arouse curiosity and speculation. The Arctic explorer in his frozen wastes, or the research scientist in some remote desert area will attract enormous attention. The journal of an anthropologist living amongst a hitherto unknown tribe will make enthralling reading. Many people lap up details about the lives of members of the Royal Family. Explorers, scientists, Royalty . . . nuns. Ordinary human beings whose work or way of life necessitates an extraordinary lifestyle, who face fears, dangers and deprivation we may never have experienced, are the object of our fascination and tease our imaginations.

The life of a Religious requires certain conditions and an unusual environment. "Unnatural," some of my friends said, thereby denouncing it flatly in one word. There is perhaps a certain sense in which they are right (though it could be argued that the bustle, rush and noise of much city life is the unnatural life, and one of silence and stillness which co-operates with the rhythms and cycles of nature, the natural one). But where life in a convent may be thought of as unnatural – and certainly celibacy is not natural, though it can be super-natural – one could equally say, "Neither is it natural for men to be cooped up in a little capsule, wearing bulky garments, eating tabloid food and floating around in a weightless condition." They accept the unnaturalness of their surroundings for the sake of the goal – which is worth it all.

That is the clue. It all depends where one's sights are set. Saint Paul said, "Forgetting what lies behind, and straining forward to what lies ahead, I press on towards the goal for the prize of the upward call of God in Christ Jesus."[1] He forsook normal home life, academic status and financial security (all of which were good and could so easily have been his) for the sake of his burning desire to preach the gospel, particularly to the Gentiles. His peripatetic missionary life precluded the stability of a normal home, family life and career. He lived dangerously. But there was a burning zeal about his obedience to that heavenly vision he had received on the Damascus road. God calls for a total abandonment by some – even from those things which in the ordinary scale of things are his blessings. It is literally a case of leaving those things which are behind and pressing forward to the goal. The Religious Life is not a better or superior form of Christian life. Such an idea is a terrible distortion of the truth, for we are all called to total givenness, all invited to make a full oblation of our lives. No one way is better than any other. Obedience to the heavenly vision – that's the all-important thing for us. But it does seem that our Lord calls some to live out their baptismal vows through the gospel life in a very literal way by forsaking all things to follow him.

"He who loves father, mother, . . . son or daughter more than me, is not worthy of me,"[2] said Jesus.

Some of his disciples were called to forsake their nets, leave everything behind and follow him. Some, not all. Mary and Martha still had their home where they could entertain him. And there must have been many others scattered throughout Galilee and Judea in whose homes he and his disciples found rest, shelter and food in their journeyings.

"It was understandable in those early days of enthusiasm," some might argue, "but rather anachronistic and misplaced in our own age."

Why? The gospel call of all or nothing has not changed.

Perhaps a monastery in the middle of the Sinaitic desert or on a mountain exclusively set apart from monasticism – like Mount Athos – is just about acceptable, if mysterious. The distance and isolation combine to give a touch of glamour. But when it is slap next door in the middle of a busy town or industrial area with traffic roaring by and people hurrying to and fro . . . it is something of a threat, if not an offence. How can it be a valid way of life for healthy, strong men and women? Aren't they no better than religious drop-outs? Unless of course they are doing something 'useful' like teaching, or caring for the sick or cycling round the district looking after the elderly. Then they often become 'wonderful people'.

I knew, of course, when I went into my convent that I was not joining an enclosed order (see explanatory note in Introduction) – the technical name given to those communities which give themselves 'wholly to the work of prayer, standing before God in solidarity with all men and in the offering of Christ.'[3] The life of such communities is not incompatible with the offering of hospitality and the cultivation of a certain tradition of learning and spiritual direction, but on the whole they find this specific calling prevents them from a regular, active apostolate in the world. This is very hard to understand for many in the Church, let alone those outside it, but,

> the visible withdrawal of monks or nuns from the concerns of the world does not imply a lack of care for the world and its needs. Rather it presupposes a belief in the co-inherence of all men in Christ. It is built on the faith that, as a man offers himself to God in silence and obedience, in prayer and love, so the power of the Holy Spirit is able to work a transformation in him which is of significance not for himself alone but for all with whom he shares a common nature. It is in solidarity with all men for whom Christ died that the enclosed religious stands in prayer in union with Christ. Through his silent participation in the cross and resurrection of the Lord, the power of the Holy Spirit is made free in ways which are not insignificant, even though they are not easily to be discerned.[4]

The Community of St Mary the Virgin was, I knew, one which lived a mixed life – a term used of communities that combine a contemplative life of prayer and the regular saying of the Divine Office with some kind of active service. In our case it was services, for our outer works were, and are, very varied. Even though if professed we might eventually be asked to share in the community's more active apostolate and public ministry, it was important to know at this stage with deep conviction that the Religious Life was God's call to us and utterly valid in itself with or without that participation. For this reason, I knew that much of my early life in community would be spent 'at home' at the convent, learning to put down roots. It was difficult to imagine remaining in one place, under one roof, with the same people day after day . . . indefinitely. It was even more difficult in reality. Thelma and I both used to ache to get our hands on the wheel of a car again, and sometimes I indulged my imagination with thoughts of a free day, a sports car with a full tank of petrol and an open road.

There was nothing to stop us going for walks in our free time, of course, but so many other things seemed to have to compete for that precious time. Mine seemed perpetually swallowed up by my letter-writing.

Sister Frances asked me to do some shopping in Wantage one morning. We urgently needed some extra ingredients for the Christmas puddings. It was a very ordinary request, yet the joy that expedition gave was quite extraordinary – out of all proportion to what it actually involved. It was a lovely crisp autumn day. The sun was warm as I strode off down the Platt*. There were gorgeous colours in the turning leaves, several ducks were swimming up and down on the water and a cat escorted me in a companionable way, its tail raised in a proud question mark.

In itself the occasion was of no consequence, but what it indicated to me was.

'Isn't it extraordinary,' I thought to myself, 'the short walk into Wantage would never have stood out as a particularly memorable event before. Going into town to do some shopping isn't exactly my idea of a big thrill'. But here I was, revelling in the fresh air with all the autumn smells and sights and sounds, happy to be meeting and greeting people and much more aware of ordinary things than usual. Joy was given in and through simplicity. It was the restoration of something very good, something of my childhood that I had lost with all the accretions of age and sophistication. I recalled how I had loved the Somerset woods as a child – especially in the autumn with the smell of decaying leaves

*A lane running alongside the millstream in Wantage.

and wet earth. Now some of that simple joy was being given back. Pausing on the way back to pat a horse, I came to the conclusion that it was not so much the things that prompted joy that surprised me, but the intensity of my enjoyment. Too much of life had been lived as from a fast moving train with beauty flashing by. Now there was an opportunity for all looking to become a beholding, all listening to become a hearing, all tasting to become a savouring. It was a chance to deepen in awareness all round.

Even so, by the time I had been at the convent for two months, I was already beginning to feel restive. Admitting this to Sister Geraldine, I explained, "You see, I haven't actually stayed in one place for as long as eight weeks in the whole of my adult life. There have always been breaks – weekends away, conferences or holidays."

Those professed sisters who find their work keeps them travelling around quite a bit would, for their part, sometimes appreciate more time at home in the convent, or their branch house, with less interruption to their normal routine. I thought of Sister Zoe and the way in which she had travelled the length and breadth of the country to visit her oblates and their parishes. But she had so learned to interiorise her silence and enclosure, she could live a life of constant adaptation to different homes and routines without undermining the essentials of her vocation to prayer. In the early days of one's training, however, it is necessary to learn to feel settled and happy, to discover the discipline of just keeping going without those interruptions which could prove to be distractions or escapes. I, for one, began to feel slightly claustrophobic. The downs, which I could see all day from the kitchen window, called to me as 'deep unto deep' and the stability of convent life led to a feeling of being hemmed in. "How am I straitened!"[5] our Lord had said in his Passion, and I often thought of all the housewives who felt straitened, hemmed in, by the four walls of their kitchens and the need to stay at home with their young children. Even if there were possible escapes and distractions, many of them would never be able to afford to take them. The miner hemmed in by the coal face, the crew in a

126

submarine, the shop assistant behind the counter must all feel restricted at times . . . many and varied are our walls. We cannot deny them. Mostly, we learn to live with them, often happily and fruitfully. In many cases, we chose them in the first place, and in doing so, accepted the renunciations that went with them. The housewife would probably not choose to be single again even if it meant greater freedom and the submariner would probably re-choose the same profession if he had a second chance. The walls which perhaps none of us would deliberately choose would be those of a hospital bed, or a sick room. Yet how often have even those been transformed into blessings for the patient and for those nursing and visiting him.

At about this time, a wounded pigeon took refuge in the inner quadrangle between the novitiate cloister and the refectory. It trailed a damaged wing as it paced round and round in bewilderment. It was ringed, so we made a note of its number and tracked down its owner through the register of homing pigeons. He wrote to us that we could either crate it up, put it on a train and send it back to Stafford, or keep it until, hopefully, its wing mended and it could fly home. We kept it. I made a shelter for it on the door step of Sister Geraldine's office – a door into the quadrangle that was seldom used. It was a place where we felt reasonably confident the bird would be undisturbed. From then on we fed it on crumbs, and seed if we could get it. Ichabod we called him, for, in his flightless state, his glory did indeed seem to have departed.

I often watched him pacing round his enclosure. On two sides were the high walls of the north wing and on the other two the slightly less high walls of the cloisters. The chances of escape were about as good as those from Colditz. The great advantage was that he was safe from any attacks, either from cats, foxes, or other harmful intruders.

"I feel such a deep sympathy with Ichabod," I said to Sister Geraldine one day, as we watched him from her window. "He's become something of a symbol to me."

"There's nothing symbolic about the mess he is making on my doorstep," she said ruefully.

I made a mental note to scrub the step down from time to time.

"Why are you in such sympathy?" she asked.

"My heart goes out to him. I know what it is like to feel shut in, with no escapes or distractions, few visitors, a sameness about every day, and dependent on the community for the roof over my head and the food I eat. He must want to break out at times. He's known what it is to be free – to go wherever he likes, whenever he likes. Now we're both grounded. But if he can stick his enclosure, so can I." We laughed and watched him again. He had beautiful markings.

"And how are you going to feel if one day his wing heals and he flies out of his enclosure?" she asked.

"Please God, he will recover," I said, "but I hope by the time he does, I shall have learned more about the inner meaning of enclosure that lies behind the outward expression of it."

He stayed all winter – huddling in his little shelter during the cold, snowy weather, trailing his damaged wing round his quadrangle and happily accepting food and water. When spring came, we put out an old wooden chair hoping it would encourage him to get airborne for short distances. I regularly massaged and exercised the wing and gradually he began to flap it and move it for himself.

Now other pigeons joined him and drank his water and shared his food. One in particular showed special interest. Here was incentive indeed. Spring and a mate.

As I gazed out of the refectory window one tea time, I could scarcely believe my eyes. Ichabod was on the cloister roof. It was the first time he had flown for seven months.

He returned to his shelter that night, but next day he flew up on to the roof again, walking up and down in great excitement. Three days running this happened, his spouse-to-be giving him all possible encouragement. On the fourth day, he flew up and over the roof, and we never saw him again.

"Will you also go away?"[6] asked Sister Geraldine solemnly. The shaft went home as I recalled the original

128

context in which Jesus had addressed those words to his disciples. No – I wasn't going to leave. I was both sad to see my symbol go, but very happy for his new freedom. It was not too devastating because I also had survived several months of enclosure and was now beginning to find a new freedom. Ichabod's ministry to me was complete. Not finally and for ever had I lost those itching feet, of course. Most of us have to go on doing battle from time to time with longings that we think are dead but which rise up, under provocation, like a phoenix from the ashes.

Naomi and I were loaned a cottage on the Yorkshire moors for our holiday that summer. Oh! The joy of all that space – mile upon mile of it with no walls, no fences, no barriers of any sort. Just seemingly unlimited space. I revelled in it and wanted to stay out in it all day, every day, until the last possible moment. A car drew up alongside us as we picnicked one day, and the occupants got out with their dog – presumably to give him a run. What a paradise for a dog. But, to my amazement, it took one look at the immensity of the space and fled back into the car for refuge. It seemed so ironic, I just rolled in the heather and laughed.

The enclosure of a convent has its obvious practical purpose – that of safeguarding a certain degree of privacy. In that sense it is functional and should be no more offensive than the walls, fences and hedges surrounding the garden of any private house. Every family, communities included, needs some degree of privacy and a few sacred areas for healthy family life, and to us it is a constant source of deep concern and sorrow that so many people, particularly in the Third World, are denied this basic human right and forced to live in shacks or even drainpipes, as some do on the streets of Calcutta.

The enclosure of the garden and grounds of a convent is often preserved for another valid reason. If it is to be a centre of retreat and prayer – not simply for sisters but for the many visitors who come specifically to find quiet and refreshment – then it must be possible to provide silence for them. In the summer the garden is used a great deal for prayer and quiet contemplation. Enclosure for this reason is not a peculiar form of secrecy or exclusivism. It has the positive purpose of keeping something of value in order to be able to share it.

Enclosure in its deepest sense is, of course, not a matter of staking off territorial boundaries. It is an interior thing in which one seeks to deepen in one's longing and desires, concentrate one's energies and guard them for a single purpose. It is a single-mindedness, a unification, a guarding of the heart. And for that, limits have to be set on far-flung, widespread interests, in order to go deeper. It might be compared to the athlete who is a good all-rounder but who has to drop some sports in order to concentrate on the one.

All of us carry round within ourselves an inner enclosure, an inner chamber marked 'Private'. In current usage, the word enclosure usually refers to a pen, a fenced-in area, used for sheep or cattle, or the area surrounding a kraal, or a separate section marked off and reserved for Royalty and special guests at race meetings. In whatever context it is used, it indicates space – space marked out for a special purpose.

In the practice of ancient augury, the colleges of priests who were engaged in the art of divining, observed the flight of birds in a templum, a space marked out for the purpose. The templum, which could also be a circuit, was therefore, not only what we mean now by temple, but any enclosure made to encapsulate numinous powers.

It is from the same root that our word 'contemplate' comes, that word which denotes the activity in which one marks out a space in one's interior life and retires into it to fix one's whole attention on what is within, uniting oneself as far as possible with the numinous forces thus concentrated. This would be generally true of all forms of contemplation, but in specifically Christian contemplation we are, like King David, filled with a desire to "find out a place for the temple of the Lord"[7] – not just by building cathedrals and churches, but by marking out a templum, an inner space, within our lives and safeguarding it for him alone.

"You don't need to go behind walls to do that," you may object. Indeed not. There are many Christians, Religious included, who lead outwardly hectic lives but who have within them a deep inner enclosure which gives them powerful resources to carry into the office, the supermarket, the classroom, the Synod or whatever. They are able to do so however, because they have first learned to 'go deep'. They faithfully preserve and guard that templum and sacred space within, and often do so at considerable cost.

There are other people who find it almost impossible to mark out a place for the temple of the Lord – the demands of a family or a business seem to squeeze out that space. Nothing of course can substitute for one's own personal templum. We cannot live off the interior experiences of others. Nevertheless, the fact that contemplation is almost a full-time work for some means that those who have to struggle to find space to pray, don't need to go it alone. There are religious houses where the busy, the dispirited, the spiritually drained can come for replenishment. They are free to slot in to the ongoing worship, throw themselves into the river of contemplation and be carried along by it. If such places are to be available, however, there has to be a disciplined life of prayer going on all the time. It cannot be turned on and off like the central heating. The voice of prayer is never silent in such places because those who pray within them stand perpetually alongside all men in their various needs and offer themselves in solidarity with the world.

This is 'work' to be done, not an optional spiritual exercise. It is often hard going, unexciting and wearisome. Nevertheless it must be faithfully offered regardless of feelings or moods, for we are, after all, freed from many cares and responsibilities of secular life in order to be available for this work. It is therefore a very serious commitment. Perhaps one of the hardest things about it is that we are seldom permitted to see any results. Sometimes there are obvious answers to intercessory prayer for which we can all rejoice. But far more often one carries a great weight inwardly, a heaviness of spirit that seems to cause a real down-drag. At times it even brings an aching of head and limbs as though stretched to one's limits. Those are the dark days when faith alone keeps one on course, believing that in and through this passion there will be resurrection and joy. All too often we are aware that our battle is not one of flesh and blood but against principalities and powers, against rulers of darkness.

"What goes on behind those convent walls?"

"Warfare. Spiritual warfare," is a straightforward answer.

Nothing is visible to the eye, but at some time or another, battle rages in the inner enclosure of every sister.

"I will keep my strength for Thee,"[8] said the Psalmist and really he was speaking of an inner enclosure, a guarding of the heart, an enfolding of the energies to be kept for God alone. Far from being anything to do with walls that shut out, enclosure has to do with walls that shut in, that preserve and guard a gift – a gift to be cultivated in the innermost depths of secrecy of each individual heart but shared with all. The co-inherence of man puts no limits on the far-flung influence of that gift nor on the extent to which others may draw upon it. Quite early on we were taught that enclosure secures for us a certain personal freedom, yet its benefits are not for selfish enjoyment but for others. Like any gift, it has to be safeguarded by the necessary conditions. A garden is only beautiful enough to open to the public if it is tended lovingly and watered with care. So with us, the condition is a faithful, ordered life of worship, prayer and silence without which the gift would be squandered.

However it may appear from the outside, in no way is this a wish to put ourselves alone in a right relationship with God. Only as others come to share it with us do we realise how immeasurable is this gift that has been entrusted to us and how immense the world's need of it.

In the training days, enclosure may seem, as it did to me, to be a restriction of freedom. But with the passing of time I began to discover for myself what I knew theoretically from our teaching and indeed from commonsense, that it is actually an ingredient of freedom. To achieve a goal inevitably calls for sacrifices, and enclosure is both a gift and a renunciation – at times a costly and painful one. But a life without any sacrifices or boundaries is one of licence not of freedom. We offer some of the things which have previously delighted us in willing surrender to God because he wills us to give precedence to a particular work that he has for us to do on earth. This work requires a degree of detachment which can only grow out of a certain enclosure. We cannot possibly do it if we are constantly living on the surface of things. The retiring into the inner chamber and closing the door is an absolute priority.

How easily any space whether it be in our diary or in the larder, seems to get filled or cluttered up. It happens just as readily with the inner space we make – our enclosure – and then there is a battle for priorities. Our loyalties become divided and we are pulled about from one to the other; whereas enclosure, in its deepest sense, really has to do with singleness of heart, which in turn is a form of simplicity. In its literal sense, simplicity means a single pleat, or one fold.

"I will keep my strength for thee," I will be a 'one pleat' person, a single-eyed, single-hearted, one-purpose-only person – that is the aim of enclosure. It is a choice that involves many renunciations at all levels of life. It is the narrow way of which Jesus spoke, but it leads to life.

Metropolitan Anthony Bloom claims that it is "greed, fear and curiosity which make us live outwardly," and quoting a French scientist, he says

If you ask yourself where your personality ends you will see that the tongue of a greedy person is projected like tentacles towards the edibles of the world; the eyes of the curious person are like tentacles projected and attached to everything around; the ears of the eavesdropper become long and wide and go far far afield. If you could draw a picture of what you look like in those terms, you would see that precious little is left of you inside, because everything is extroverted. So that the first thing one must do is to detach the tentacles and bring them in. You cannot go inwards if you are completely outward.[9]

133

It is because silence is essential to this inward journey in which our awareness both of God and of the deep, inarticulate cries of the world is deepened that we seek to preserve it within and around us for, by doing so, we are loving and reverencing God and our neighbour.

A very wise and saintly old monk gave me, what seemed at the time, the oddest piece of advice. I had gone to talk to him during the course of an annual long retreat. I spoke to him of the agony of spirit which sometimes made me almost writhe physically. It was a form of pain I was beginning to experience in intercessory prayer and it was different from anything I had previously known. Particularly was this so if I had read the details of any kind of cruelty, especially to children. There were nightmares to go hand in hand with the praying too. "The trouble is," I told the old monk, "I know far more about the world now than I did when I entered the convent."

"Of course," he said, "and you'll grow to know it in a deeper and deeper sense the more you continue in the life of prayer." That was certainly true. For one thing, I was far more conscientious about reading the papers. And then, letters and prayer requests pour into convents daily giving a fairly vivid picture of the troubles and trials people are facing in every area of the world's life. These requests in our community are pinned on an intercession notice board, and the community goes to work in its prayers. Then too, we had sisters who were knowledgeable in current affairs and politically well-informed. They helped us to keep abreast of news, both national and international. By no means least were the daily intercessions at Mass. But above and beyond all that was a growing inner knowledge that came through the silence and greater time for reflection. While we had been training in the matter of enclosure, and the former outlets had been blocked off so that we could go deeper, our reflecting, thinking, imagining were all being directed one way – into prayer. With none of my normal creative channels open, my imaginative powers were certainly going into my praying, but having an unholy heyday.

The old monk seemed to shrink further and further down

into his cowl and remained silent for a long time. Finally he spoke . . . words which I am certain he had waited to receive from the Holy Spirit.

"I advise you to stop reading all newspapers, or watching the television news for a year," he said.

I gasped. Not read the newspapers! Not know what was going on outside!

He saw my horror. "I would think," he said, "that you have always been a person of powerful imagination and turbulent emotions."

I was stunned. Barely ten minutes ago we had never met, yet here he was uttering this amazing piece of insight. I had the tiniest inkling of how the woman at the well must have felt as she ran home to Samaria and said (of Jesus) "Come, see a man who told me all that ever I did."[10]

The papers were there. The TV was there and many sisters did, and do, watch the news. I steered clear of both for a year. It was, of course, only intended to be a temporary measure while I learned to keep the channels of prayer open and free from emotional blockage.

"For someone with strong imaginative powers, you don't need to have all the details of the world's evil, to know the evil itself," said the monk. "You will meet it in prayer in a stark, unadorned form without knowing the ways in which it has manifested itself in the world. Learn to meet it in the depths and not simply in its surface forms."

It was wisdom indeed. He was right – I do think very visually and would soon have been out of my mind with pain if I had gone on experiencing the mental movies in my praying.

Whichever way one turns in the Religious Life, the paradox of separation from the world and yet open-ness to it is there. The enclosure of the heart is safeguarded not just by an absence of distraction (ie that which literally dis–tracts, pulls us apart), but by silence. Silence is the natural air that the Religious breathes.

"I'm going to tell you something which you'll probably find hard to believe," said a Free Church Minister, as he introduced me to a congregation. "I went to Sister's convent for dinner one day and, we ate *the whole meal in silence!* I've never done that in my life before," he said. And he had clearly still not quite got over the shock. Those unfamiliar with convents do find the thought of silent meals rather odd; even alarming. We regard them as a gift.

Silence is not of course just an absence of noise, nor simply abstinence from conversation, and certainly not a matter of keeping rules. Silence is a living, vibrant thing. It is "no vacuum but a climate of listening to God."[11] Together with solitude of heart, it creates the atmosphere in which we can be receptive to God – like a vessel open to him, empty, eager to be filled, and then to be poured out again in offering for the world.

"I am the vessel: the draught is God's,"[12] said Dag Hammarskjold.

Through silence and stillness, distorted perspectives take on right proportions, greater clarity of perception is possible, new vision is given. The Religious is in a unique position to stand back and see things whole, and the world has a right to have its life reflected back from the stance of that detachment.

Whatever else people don't know about monks and nuns, they do understand that they are committed to some kind of search, a search for truth, for God, for what it is to be fully human. Not all realise however that the pathway to this is not via a set of rules and regulations, sacred formalities and ceremonies, crushing authority and hierarchical organisation. The chief means to the radical conversion, the re-birth, the total inner transformation to which we are all committed are silence, solitude, simplicity, penance, poverty, obedience, chastity, meditation, reading, liturgical worship and some form of productive work.

"There you go again," you might say. "It really is a cutting off from the world."

If we really believed that, most of us wouldn't be in monasteries or convents. It is in part because we love the world and care deeply about it that we are prepared to take vows of poverty, chastity and obedience with all that they stand for in terms of availability, freedom from the tyranny of self-will and possessiveness, identification with the have nots, the lonely, the dispossessed, the status-less, uninfluential poor of this world. If "God so loved the world that he gave his only begotten Son . . ."[13] how could we not love the world too?

Our life is, in some senses, a life of protest. Along with so many others who long and work for peace, we often ask, "What can one person do, or even one group do, in a technological society largely shaped by the mass media and seemingly bent on self-destruction? How can our pitiful little cries possibly help?" The sheer enormity of the problem of world peace is, I believe, one of the greatest contributory causes to defeatism. Our answer is that it must begin with the individual, with a total dedication to an inner transformation. For the seeds of violence, hatred, destruction, fear, and lust are there in all of us. Each of us is in microcosm the world. The weapons we, as Religious, try to take up to fight against the ever-increasing dehumanisation of man are those of the interior life – contemplation, asceticism, intercessory prayer, sacramental grace and, above all, personal renewal.

While caught up in the life of the world through our prayer in a deeply painful and costly way, there is yet another aspect of contemplation. Our life is a life of marginality. There are a number of senses in which the Religious lives out on the frontiers of existence. A frontier is a line of demarcation which implies not so much division as meeting – hence we speak of confrontation.

He is certainly out on the frontiers of spiritual warfare today meeting evil head on as did his predecessors in the desert. He is, or ought to be, on the frontiers of world issues – and indeed his voice is not infrequently heard in public places these days. In Old Testament times it was so often from the marginal life of the desert, with its own perspectives, that the prophetic voices rang out. That is still true. The struggle for peace, justice, freedom, human rights, fair distribution of the earth's economy and a reverent conservation of her resources are burning issues for the Religious. He may even have to confront power politics, ambition and greed very literally within his own local community. (For the Religious is free to participate in political action, to vote, write to his MP etc).

Deeply involved with the world and its problems as he is, there is yet another area of marginality, another frontier. Like his Lord, the Religious is in this world yet not of it. He or she is one who is on a pilgrimage out of this world to the Father. The fruits of his contemplation are to be shared, and his caring, compassion and political involvement point to the fact that he takes this world seriously.

In no sense is he just other-worldly. But he is also a sign of the world to come. Saint Augustine, in *Civitas Dei*, envisaged the City of God as a kind of heavenly archetype of the Roman Empire and spoke of the Christian dilemma of belonging to both. Every Christian finds himself in the same dual citizenship – temporary citizens of this world with our real citizenship in heaven for "here we have no lasting city, but we seek one to come."[14]

For the Religious, enclosure enables him to be a living sign of that world to come because his sights are set on the Kingdom of God. It is part of his calling to keep those perspectives, those special horizons of the desert, by which he interprets the signs of the times.

I still had my tentacles out on the world in many respects and there was a long way to go before I knew the meaning of the 'one pleat'.

"Lord I would follow you with an undivided heart . . ."[15] So we prayed at every clothing service, and on the anniversary of every clothing. They were words which stabbed me each time, and they articulated one of my deepest longings. Yet there were still times when I looked back over my shoulder – especially when feeling very insecure.

The announcement in a church paper or periodical that Naomi was speaking at this conference, or leading that seminar, or had written the following article, still had power to disturb me with regrets. Her letters told me that she lived with the kind of crammed diary that had once been mine. She was in great demand, her very obvious gifts were being used to the full, she was a well-known figure, mixing with interesting people. Her work was absorbing, intellectually stimulating, challenging. From outside, it all sounded very exciting and rewarding. And I . . . I was hidden, buried, probably forgotten. The work I did was humdrum and routine – certainly not noteworthy.

'But, hang on! Haven't you forgotten something?' I would remind myself. You chose to come here. No one pushed you into it. And if you so wish, you can choose to go back to your old life – go back to the over-full days, the travel, the exciting meetings . . . all those props that, for you, helped to build up your sense of worth.'

What a fool I was. Here a tremendous opportunity was being offered me, to find security in God, and God alone, and I was hankering after things I had voluntarily renounced. How could I seriously contemplate going back? I had embarked on a most exciting pilgrimage, even if it was through the desert, but the light at the end of the tunnel beckoning me on was like a pillar of cloud by day and fire by night.[16] God had called me – like Israel of old – out of much of my former bondage. He continued to call each time I reached a crossroads and had to make a decision. Faithful is the calling one.

Poor Naomi! Swamped as she was and inundated with demands far beyond her strength, and very obviously longing for some of the silence and stillness we have, she had actually been the object of my envy. In my mind, all unwittingly, I had fallen prey to the kind of thinking expressed by some of my friends initially, when they said, "What a waste!"

As symbols, candles seemed to play a large part in my life.

One day I was praying in St Mary Magdalen's chapel – one of our smaller chapels. On the solid slab of stone which forms the altar were two short, stubby candlesticks and in them two equally short, stubby candles. It was dark as I prayed, but suddenly, in a mental picture that came all unbidden, the candle on the left became alight. Its flame was flickering wildly, blown this way and that as it spluttered noisily. It seemed completely at the mercy of winds and draughts which came from all directions. 'Just like my life,' I thought. 'What wouldn't I give to be able to burn as a steady, living flame for God, but distractions and desires make me as vulnerable and unreliable as that poor candle.'

Then it seemed as though a shadowy hand appeared from behind the candle and placed over it a cylindrical, glass mantle – rather like the ones we used with our Aladdin lamps as missionaries. I shook myself just to make sure I was actually awake. Yes – the candle was still there protected by its mantle, burning now with a beautiful, steady, oval flame. It was an immensely powerful picture and I couldn't get it out of my mind for days even though its meaning eluded and teased me.

Some little while later, I came upon these words:

We must seek to deepen our silence – silence not only from empty words but from busy, anxious thoughts, restless movements, unnecessary haste; that silence which has been called "the sheltering glass of holy desire."[17]

That was it. The meaning of the picture clicked into place. The outward enclosure against which I had chafed at first, which had made me claustrophobic, and the inner enclosure of silence, the concentration of energies and curbing of the imagination, these were but a sheltering glass of holy desire, the pathway to the 'one pleat' and the undivided heart.

9

SKINNED ALIVE

Thelma had decided to leave. She stopped me in the corridor one morning and said that she didn't feel that she could carry on – at present, at any rate. She still wasn't sufficiently sure that it was the right vocation for her, but, even if it was, she felt she wasn't ready for it yet. Sister Geraldine had agreed with her and had advised her to take her time. If later she became more certain that God's call to her was to serve him in a religious community then the door was open for her to come back. In the meantime, she thought she would do some further training.

It isn't unusual for a postulant to leave, or a novice. The novitiate is, after all, a time of testing and there is always the possibility of comings and goings . . . and also of comings back. There were several in our Novitiate who had returned after a few years in secular life, and were now on their second round of training. Where a life commitment is involved there has to be flexibility and openness in regard to individual needs.

Nevertheless, I was sad at Thelma's announcement – naturally. We had been through so much of the initial fun and trauma together, it would seem very strange without her. Yet part of me couldn't be sad for her because she was doing a sensible thing. A wrong choice in this matter of vocation can only lead to great unhappiness.

"When are you going?" I asked.

141

"Later on this morning," she said, "I'm just on my way to the habit room to retrieve my suitcase and the clothes I brought with me when I arrived."

My stomach lurched. So soon! It was all happening so quickly. Yet once the decision is made, it is far better not to prolong the farewells. It imposes a tremendous strain on everyone but especially on the one leaving. I agreed to meet her again after she had packed her few belongings – just for a quick Goodbye. Thelma went in search of her case, and I took myself off to chapel in an attempt to digest the news. It hadn't come as a total shock. I knew Thelma had been feeling very unsettled, and her work had revealed it.

The corner seat in the back row of chapel was empty, and I stepped into it thankfully. I felt tucked away there. What a lot had happened since Thelma and I had arrived at the convent. Only a matter of a year ago, and yet in terms of new experience, it felt more like a lifetime.

"Why was Thelma leaving, while I was still sitting here?" I mused. There was still a long way to go before I could be certain it was the right vocation for me. Yet there had been some real pointers along the way, and I looked back to them and pondered them as I hugged the wall in my corner seat.

Yes. There had been a thread of certainty, despite all the turmoil. That sense of having arrived home, that had hit me with such force on my very first visit to the convent, had never entirely left me.

Then, too, there had been that first retreat day after we had become postulants. Everyone looks forward to a retreat day and, in those early days, I suppose I put far too high an expectation on them. It was a temptation to decide in advance that it would be a day of spiritual delights and mountain top experiences. Whereas, as my very wise Principal said when preparing us for our first college retreat, "It is a day that we give to God and it is up to him how he uses it. Like a day spent with a close friend, it may be just a very happy time of companionship, or, it may mark a turning point, a whole new stage in the relationship, with new depths of understanding, love and commitment. Either way it is up to God, and not to our strivings."

All the same, I was a bit frantic on that particular retreat day. God seemed to have absented himself completely. My mind was full of distractions and the Tempter whispered persistently that I had made a complete ass of myself in coming to the community at all. Since I was still reeling from shock, I seemed not to have the strength to say a firm, "Get thee behind me, Satan."

After a seemingly fruitless morning, my conscience dictated that I should at least 'try' to listen to God. So I took myself back to chapel and spent the afternoon in the back row. I gazed at the beautiful wood carvings on the stalls – the work of Oberammergau craftsmen. I stared at the east end window with its blues, purples and greens. And all the while I was consumed with a burning desire – not, I regret to say, for God, but for a Dry Martini.

By the evening I was feeling somewhat desperate. 'What a waste of a day!' I thought. At that stage, I was too raw in the Religious Life to realise any better. After supper I remember making my way back to chapel and, almost accidentally, picking up a booklet from the windowsill in the cloister, on the spirituality of Mother Julian of Norwich. It contained several well written articles with liberal sprinklings of quotations. I remember nothing about it in detail. What remains as vividly clear to me now as on that evening itself, is the mental picture I was given as I prayed, of a long, rugged, dark tunnel, and at the end of the tunnel, a light. Not a harsh, brilliant light, but a soft, mellow, warm light like that of a candle.

There was no doubt in my mind that it symbolised Christ, the Light of the World beckoning me on down this path. Like the pearl merchant who glimpsed the pearl of great price and, thereafter, could be satisfied with nothing less, I too had caught a glimpse of what lay ahead and it was compelling. If the tunnel was the only way to that Light, then that's the way it would have to be. Sometimes that pinpoint was to be my only light in a journey which often seemed alarmingly long and frighteningly dark. But, like Paul when he had seen a Light which blinded him, I could not be disobedient to the heavenly vision.

That, I realised, was why I was still sitting there in chapel, rather than packing my bags with Thelma.

It was not the only pointer, of course. Certainty that it was right to continue the testing grew steadily despite periodic doubts, and even though reason often jolted me by saying, 'Get out whilst you still can,' I couldn't. I was held.

The fact that I had to withstand a fair bit of pressure to leave from well-meaning friends actually ended up reinforcing my choice to stay.

"Give her six months, and she'll have got it out of her system," some had said when I entered. Six months went by. Not only was there no hint of my coming out, but plans were afoot for my clothing – a step further in. They began to get troubled. Letters arrived with alternative suggestions.

'There's a vacancy . . . you ought to be applying.' Or, 'I'm on the governing body,' wrote one, 'and I am sure that if you applied you would stand a very good chance . . .'

I was faintly annoyed that friends were beginning to mount rescue operations. To one who was certain that he knew God's will for me, I wrote saying, 'I wonder how you would feel if you received a letter from someone telling you he was certain God had revealed his will for your future to "him" when he hadn't thought to ask if God had perhaps given you a few clues yourself? I wonder if, like me, you would consider it rather presumptuous?'

Yet I knew it was meant in love and out of genuine concern for my welfare. Love would not permit them to sit back and do nothing to try to prevent me making so gross a mistake, as they felt this choice to be. Or would it? Would it be sufficiently disinterested to allow the other that freedom?

'We feel sure you were right,' wrote others, 'to have this time of complete rest, ("Oh, if only they knew," I exclaimed as I read that), but God gives these times of withdrawal for refreshment and learning so that you can return to the world and enrich others. We long to share your discoveries.' No matter how I answered that one, I was sure it would sound terribly selfish.

A car drove up to the convent one day and out bundled three other friends, grinning from ear to ear.

"Hullo," they chorused. "We thought we'd spring a surprise on you."

Surprise. I was staggered. What an embarrassment. Not knowing they were coming, I hadn't booked a room for them. There was nowhere available to take them. Sister Geraldine was out so could not accommodate us in her office. I couldn't even offer them tea. What's more, I was on my way to an appointment. But how could I not stop when they had come such a long distance? I could see exactly how their thinking had gone and what fun it had been to hatch this plot to surprise me. But how could I tell them that with our fairly tight timetables we need advance warning of visitors so that work schedules can be re-arranged if necessary? Somehow there is a wildly false notion around that sisters don't really do anything except pray from time to time.

I tried to chat naturally but was totally unprepared for the real reason behind their visit.

"We've come to take you back with us," they said.

Bless them! They had really believed that the sight of a car and a minimum amount of pressure would be enough to persuade me to hop in and escape.

"The community can send your things on later," they assured me.

"Look," I said, trying not to get in a panic. "I am NOT here under any duress, or against my will. In no sense am I being held here as an unwilling captive . . . even if I did appear at first to be a rather reluctant postulant. I can't leave unless God makes it quite clear that I must. I am here out of choice."

They gaped disbelievingly and it took a while to convince them. No. On reflection, I don't think they were convinced but they accepted that they weren't going to carry me off in triumph.

145

After waving them off, I stumbled into the novitiate and dropped into a chair feeling quite weak.

When a few days later I got yet another well-meaning letter from a friend announcing that he would arrive at a certain time the following Saturday and that if he wasn't allowed to see me, he would go 'straight to the Reverend Mother,' I groaned in despair.

"Oh no! I can't cope," I wailed, and took the letter to Sister Geraldine.

"What am I going to do?" I asked. "This bombardment is really upsetting me. I almost wish I had gone into a strictly enclosed order."

"Would it perhaps help if you were to write a very loving letter," she asked? "Maybe you could get it duplicated and circulate it to all your friends. Remind them again why you are here, what lay behind your choice in the first place, and why you choose to stay. Be very gentle and ask for their prayers and support."

In a curious way, although I had found it distressing at the time, that burst of pressure had actually strengthened my conviction that I was where God wanted me to be – not out of obstinacy, but it forced into the open some of the clues which till then had been partially hidden from me.

Of course there had been the great confirming experience of the clothing itself. The peace, the sense of rightness, the joy, the acceptance by the community – these were not figments of my imagination. They were very real and convincing.

"I will seek him whom my soul loves"[1] had been the verse especially chosen for my clothing and it summed up perfectly the love affair that the Religious Life is. It is sometimes referred to as a search.

Not that we are hunting around for a God whom we have not yet found and who has never found us, for it is he who meets us every day who will meet us at the end and be the reward of our search. Rather the expression implies an ever deepening longing and love for God. Curiously, it is a longing that is never satisfied, for we can never have enough of him. As Gregory of Nyssa puts it: "The soul's desire is fulfilled by the very fact of its remaining unsatisfied, for really to see God is never to have had one's fill of desiring him."

"What is the hardest thing about your life as a novice?" I was once asked.

There was a point at which I would have said, "Renouncing my independence." But before long, I knew that was no longer true. I came to see that in all that so-called freedom in which I had previously gloried, I had never really known true independence, nor indeed true dependence.

"What is the hardest thing about your life as a novice?"

As time went on, the answer I would have given (to myself, at any rate) would have been different. "The stripping," I would have said. Oh yes – there was the stripping of material possessions before my clothing. But this stripping was infinitely more painful and sometimes utterly devastating. It is not programmed or engineered by any human being, certainly not the Novice Mistress. It comes in God's good time as the direct result of the silence, the waiting upon him, exposing oneself to the rays of his love, the opening of one's heart to the penetrating light of the Holy Spirit, who is after all the Spirit of Truth. He sifts and searches the inner recesses and hidden motives, until one can no longer sit back comfortably in all one's protective masks. Slowly and painfully they are peeled off.

Towards the end of my novitiate when I spoke of this to a priest friend, he said, "I'd be terrified if that happened to me – terrified that when all the skins had been peeled away, I'd eventually find there was nothing there . . . just an emptiness."

Exactly. Isn't that the fear of us all, that when all the masks have been removed . . . there will be nothing – the 'existential dread' as Kierkegaard called it?

In the search for reality, which will ultimately unite us to God who is Reality, all that is unreal must go, including the masks. We all wear them – many of them. We often hide behind them out of fear – anxious that people should be favourably impressed by our outward front and dreading

lest they should detect the inadequacies we feel underneath.

Many and varied are the reasons why we are afraid to be
seen and known as we truly are.

"Why am I afraid to tell you who I am?"[2] Why indeed?
Probably because I can't. I don't know who I am. I have not
yet found my true identity.

When I reflect on the life of Jesus, it is his wholeness that
I long for. He was on the outside what he was inside. There
was no sham, no hypocrisy, no pretence. He was completely at unity within himself, never needing to wear
masks. His through and through integrity, utter trans-
parency and ability to be his true self meant that he could
always stand over his words and actions without fear of
being caught out in some deception or uncharity. He never
vacillated, taking on the colour of the group he was with for
reasons of popularity or approval.

We long for that kind of inner wholeness but it comes
only after a dying and a re-birth.

Nicodemus may have asked with incredulity, "Can a man
be born again?"[3]

The answer is most certainly, "Yes – indeed, he can . . .
and must, for growth implies a whole cycle of deaths and
re-births."

The novitiate is rather like the womb of the community –
a place of formation, growth and re-birth. Very literally for
some. For, under the guidance of the Holy Spirit, what
sometimes happens over a period of years under primal
therapy or analysis, can happen very much more rapidly for
novices.

"Why is it," a priest once asked me, "that people seem to
regress into childhood when they enter the novitiate of a
community?"

It is possible that some may abdicate personal responsibilities in such a way that they become childish. But by far
the more likely reason for what appears as regression is that
a novice is having to relive very literally and sometimes
cruelly certain parts of his or her childhood.

None of us has come through life undamaged, but some

are more badly scarred than others by childhood, and indeed by adult experiences too. Once masks have been stripped away they may reveal fears or wounds that reach right back to babyhood. And, if there is ever to be wholeness, healing must be received, progressively, as each layer comes off and before the Holy Spirit can remove the next.

Transactional Analysis speaks of the 'parent', 'adult' and 'child' in each of us. We all have all three and, diagrammatically, one might think of the child-self in the cellar of one's life, the adult-self in the living space and the parent-self in the attic. We may prefer to forget the child-self (or indeed children, for there are usually many of them down there) or maybe not know of their existence in the cellar until they clamour relentlessly to be recognised, owned and loved.

Our child-self has done much to make us what we are now in the present . . . and, perhaps more importantly, to make us what we are not. Inevitably, if we are to see ourselves whole, we have to take our child-self into consideration, examine its needs and hear what it is saying. Equally, of course, it is important to listen to our 'parents' in the attic who might possibly be laying a heavy judgemental finger on our lives thereby crushing initiative and joy.

Meeting up with our children, or the part of our child-self which is split off from us and repressed in some sort of cocoon, can be very traumatic indeed. In fact, it can be quite dangerous to go down into the cellar alone. One really needs a trusted friend and wise counsellor to take one by the hand and be there at the meeting. For we are not just encountering a stranger, though it may feel like that at first. It is the reunion of part of one self with oneself in truth. "The truth shall make you free,"[4] but not, perhaps, without considerable cost.

"Is it really necessary to go through that kind of stripping?" some might wonder. For those with unhealed wounds it is, if there is to be a growing inner freedom and any future in community. For living cheek by jowl with people day in and day out, is just the kind of situation in which a long-buried child will rise up, do a take-over bid and start hammering other people's children.

It is a curious thing. Community life will sometimes trigger off memories which cause our childhood to surface and clamour for attention. Yet, it can also provide the loving, healing, therapeutic environment that fosters real growth towards wholeness. Where wounds are ignored and unattended, they can wreak havoc. A sister, or anyone else for that matter, may be trapped at a certain point of growth. Unable to move in any direction, she puts on a massive cover-up and becomes hardened. Then, sadly, few people are able to penetrate the encrustations and meet the real person. But once one has met up with one's children, and parents too, and they have been owned, accepted, healed and loved, they can become integrated into the adult and no longer manifest themselves as problems. They will always be around and part of us but they will not dominate on the one hand, nor drain on the other.

There is little hope of fruitful relationships within a religious community if a sister has no real foundations of trust and security. But she may start her life in community with very little of either and find that it is within and through her community life that she is given both. Unstable backgrounds, broken homes, violence, rejection . . . these kinds of thing leave deep and terrible wounds. The damage can never be undone but it is the testimony of many that it can be transfigured – and for some, their vocation to the Religious Life has been the means to this. The community, under God, has been the healing agent, "putting love in where love was not," restoring "the years that the locust had eaten."

I had to meet up with my child in a most unexpected and traumatic way. Having been something of a dare-devil in earlier years, very keen on every kind of sport and fond of crazy exploits, I thought I didn't know much about fear from personal experience. But I was reckoning only with physical fear. Little did I realise how deep-seated can be the fear in all of us that lurks behind such masks as apparent confidence, competence, efficiency and social ease. It is a terrible shock when, eventually unmasked, we are faced with naked reality about ourselves. Sister Geraldine and I sometimes used to discuss my child-self (almost as though she was sitting on the floor between the two of us) in a kind of adult to adult analysis of her problems, where were not inconsiderable. However, one cannot always be dispassionate, objective and adult during this kind of self-encounter. Sometimes one must actually be the child and rage and stamp and shout, and even cry. There is precious little point in re-living the pain of the past unless one is able this time round to articulate what previously one could only bury.

To stand alongside people in this kind of healing of the memories is extremely demanding not only in terms of wisdom, but in time and energy too. For Sister Geraldine there had to be immense discernment, for while she rightly accepted and shared all that came up from the past there were the demands of the present too. It was her duty as Novice Mistress to face us with the challenges of our new way of life and see that we tried to meet them. Her primary concern had to be the fostering and nurturing of our growing vocations, and the mothering of our damaged children had to take its rightful place within that context. As human beings we can be very selfish about our needs. Sometimes they seem all important and must be met – now. They can make us demanding, inconsiderate and unreasonable at times. We were certainly not above reproach. The healing of past wounds is, I am convinced, essential if one is to grow towards wholeness and fullness of life. But the re-enactment along the way of sibling rivalry with all its attention-seeking measures, can be very trying indeed. The community is usually enormously patient and trusting, but then, I suppose, most of the older sisters have seen this kind of autumn and winter in the lives of postulants and novices – indeed have known it themselves – as the skins start peeling off. They wait quietly, knowing that suddenly there will be signs of change and springtime in the vocation of the novice.

For me it was a very long haul. Acknowledging the

feelings of insecurity, of 'not being wanted', that without my consciously realising it had haunted me from babyhood, was humiliating in the extreme. I had to go back to square one and learn a basic lesson in trust. When this stripping started, soon after my clothing, I was appalled. Yet, whether we want it or not, the Holy Spirit the Revealer, brings these areas to light. They are forced to the surface, if one truly remains open to him; there is no possibility of resorting to repression as an escape route.

There came a point when I did want to escape. I knew that either I had to turn back there and then or it would be too late. In this work of healing there comes a point of no return when it would be highly dangerous not to complete the journey.

It was up to me. I was free to choose . . . and yet that is only a half truth. The Holy Spirit seemed to have it all well and truly in his hands. He never steam-rollers over our wills, always preferring to ask for our co-operation, but I certainly couldn't resist his pressure.

One day I panicked and fled to Sister Geraldine after breakfast saying, "It's no good. I can't go through with it. May I have leave of absence?" Even at that point, I didn't think of giving up in the sense of leaving the community altogether. I simply felt desperate for space to come to healing without all the other pressures of novitiate life. Yet it had been in the context of the Religious Life that this particular work had begun.

Sister Geraldine fully understood the reasons for my request and was certainly not unsympathetic, but as we talked it over we recalled the immense healing that had already taken place and it seemed that we now needed to grasp faith firmly by the hand and lay the whole matter open to God. He who had begun a good work would, we knew, thoroughly finish it, but where? That was the question to be decided. For both of us it was a considerable act of faith to believe that it could be accomplished by continuing in the novitiate. It might be that God's answer would be to have some time out of community. The important thing was to be completely open either way. For my part, I feared that if I didn't get away it might lead to a breakdown, but as has often been said breakdown is not necessarily the same thing as disaster. It can be the means to break-through.

"What if I go out of my mind?" I cried one day.

She was very firm about that – very firm indeed. "Now you are to put that right out of your head," she said. "That is unmistakably the Devil at work. He nearly always tries to unsettle novices with that fear. But he is the father of lies, and you are not, and will not go, out of your mind."

She suggested that I spend the following day in retreat, waiting upon God to know his will. We would both make it a special day of prayer for this purpose. Early next morning, before Lauds, I sat alone in one of our smaller chapels, and the words that came into my mind and repeated themselves like a kind of mantra were: "Lord, establish me according to your word, that I may live: and do not disappoint me in my hope."

Then I found myself quietly singing them. 'Of course – they are the words we sing at the profession of a sister,' I thought. They had, I was sure, been given to me, not for assurance about the future, but for comfort (in its literal sense) in the present. 'Establish me' – there's something very strong and rock-like about those words, and they strengthened me. I moved on into Lauds feeling very hopeful about the day.

Sister Geraldine and I had arranged to meet at midday to pray. After we had spent quite a while in silence, she said, "There are some words that keep coming to me and I feel they are right for you. You'll probably recognise them as words from a psalm that we use at our profession services. They are . . .

(I could scarcely believe my ears – I knew what was coming.)

. . . Lord, establish me according to your word, that I may live: and do not disappoint me in my hope.

153

Practically quivering with excitement, I said: "I've already been given those very words – first thing this morning."

She had no idea. It was one of those occasions when one knows that, without a shadow of doubt, the Holy Spirit is around and at work.

The really healing thing in community is that there is an ongoing relationship of love and support, and an environment of prayer and silence which are probably the greatest healers of all. Healing, counsel, guidance may be mediated to us through one particular person, and perhaps different people at different stages in our lives, but always the sisters engaged in such a ministry are the instruments of God and the representatives of the community. Both God and the community have ways of dealing with an over-dependence on any one human being, and if at any point there has to be dependency, as does quite properly happen from time to time, it is nevertheless seen as a temporary thing.

Sister Geraldine had been appointed as guide and counsellor to those of us in the novitiate, but there were, of course, a good many others involved in the pastoral care of sisters. Obviously it was an important part of the work of Mother and her Assistant and all who held office as Superiors of houses. And God uses others in the ministry of sister to sister.

Were it not for this ongoing growth within the community in general, there would not be a healing ministry to offer to those who come to stay or whom we meet in our public ministry.

Despite the fact that I had survived my particular panic, the emotional upheavals took their toll on nervous and physical energy. By this time, I was working on the infirmary wing and not coping at all well. I tried. I tried very hard indeed. I endeavoured to show initiative and enthusiasm and was genuinely puzzled that my work seemed not to give satisfaction. Increasingly I was unable to cope with the monotony of the routine, and grew depressed by the lack of encouragement (What was there to encourage? Apparently I was a pain to all and sundry). I felt a complete failure.

Now that was something my child could never afford to be – a failure. Success, achievement . . . these had been essential to a sense of well-being, of being wanted, respected, loved. It had been one of the hardest things to accept about my past – the knowledge that I had spent so much energy in my childhood years trying to win my parents' approval, and never feeling sure that I had succeeded. And how I had despised my child for it. It was Sister Geraldine who had shown her compassion and understanding – not I. But gradually she had persuaded me to do so. Now here was the infant Kirsty again, rearing her fair, curly head with her insistent and terrible need to be successful. And I, her adult, was a total failure.

The one bright spot on my horizon at this point was Sister Clemency. She was small, frail, very infirm, and permanently in bed. But she was so 'alive', full of fun and uncomplaining. We used to compete for the joy of taking her meal trays to her. I used to tease her about her pills which were an unusual hyacinth blue colour. Always her eyes would crinkle into a wonderful smile and she would laugh heartily. One Good Friday she was suddenly seized with violent pains, and was obviously in great distress. I found her soon after the attack had started and, although she was in agony, her great concern was that she shouldn't disturb other people's silence. She clung to me until the infirmarian came. Very shortly after that she died – and with her death a light went out for me in the infirmary. From then on, things went from bad to worse.

The monotony, the misery, the exhaustion eventually ended in a breakdown in my health. Everything in my body seemed to go out of working order all at once. Never will I forget the doctor's face as I worked my way through the catalogue of woes. He listened seriously enough at first, but suddenly threw down his pen and burst into helpless laughter.

"You're just falling apart at the seams, aren't you?" he said. He confirmed that each of the disorders was genuine enough, not just in the mind – but of course we are so constructed that the mind and the emotions interact upon the body. I was not fooled as to why I was cracking up.

"But you see, Doctor," I urged. "You've got to pull me out of this mess or they will all say it's the sign that I haven't got a vocation."

I blush now to admit such arrogance. For God is able, and sometimes does, speak through such warning signs of health, as through any other channel, and it might have been his way of saying, "Thus far, but no further."

Amongst my disabilities, I had my foot in plaster and under obedience was going to bed early each evening. One night when I was toying with my supper, there came a knock at the door and in walked Sister Harriet Ruth. It had been a ghastly day and I was languishing in bed, just one great lump of misery.

"You are not feeling so good, I hear," she said, and sat down. "What is the problem? Is it the foot playing up?"

No. That was possibly the least of my problems at that point. I talked . . . at considerable length. And Sister listened – very intently and without a single interruption. Really good listeners are a rarity, but she is one. The trouble is, good listening draws more and more out. With incredible patience she heard me out, bore with my hot, stuffy room and unfinished supper tray, and then began to ask some very searching questions. I knew she was bound not to agree with all I had said, or at least she could see another side to the picture. In a way, that wasn't important. It was the caring, the generous gift of time, the complete attention that was so comforting. "I hear you," she said, and I knew that she had also applied shrewd judgement to that hearing.

Bit by bit health returned, but it was a very unhappy period of my novitiate. Part of the trouble had been that I was leading a double life. My work was one thing, and my prayer another. It was always a relief to get away from the infirmary to chapel. The two had not yet come together to form a unity in my life. Indeed it was to be some while before that began to happen.

Being a failure made me very angry, and anger was something I had always feared both in others and in myself. Consequently, I had not learned to express it – and dammed-up anger, as we well know, can lead to depression. Add to that the fact that a vast amount of creative energy was also blocked, not yet having found appropriate outlets, and you'll get the general picture of my wretchedness.

Almost every session that I had with Sister Geraldine ended with her words of reassurance: "It really is all right, you know."

And it was. Despite all the pain, there was a steady healing going on, of the memories and of the body. Trust was built up, and though it was very fragile at first, I could actually believe myself loved not after I had ceased to be a failure but *while I was still a dismal one*, while I was apparently useless and weak . . . for at that point I was hobbling around on crutches.

There was still a further test. Could I be angry, even express that anger, and still feel accepted? Of course, I hadn't articulated this question even to myself. But I realise now that there was a great inner need for assurance on that one. In my evangelical upbringing the emphasis had been on restraint. "The fruit of the Spirit is . . . self-control" had been taught almost to the exclusion of that other fruit, meekness, which is really knowing how to be angry at the right time, in the right way and for the right reasons. I had certainly not been used to angry outbursts at home.

Then one day it happened. I was working in the pantry at the time and on that evening it seemed that the stream of sisters storming in to complain about this and grumble about that had been more steady and more bitter than usual. The 'oughts' and 'musts' flew at me from all directions, doubtless much of it deserved. But the pantry was also a useful and central place where people could, and often did, vent their feelings, whether or not it was directly the pantry sister's affair.

Each sister charged in more wrathful than the one before. Each one shattering my nerves just a bit more. Finally, driven beyond endurance, I fled to the refectory to wash down the tables. But inwardly I was so furious, it all exploded. Picking up a rather revolting dishcloth, I hurled it the full length of the refectory with a throw that would have earned me a round of applause in my former cricketing days.

"If that's community life," I shouted at the top of my voice (in the middle of what is a silence place), "you can stick it on the wall where it belongs."

Silence. Then slowly the door opened; a face appeared round it. It was one of the younger sisters. She showed no surprise – certainly no shock. She took in the situation, 'Just a novice having the atmospherics,' her face seemed to say, and withdrew without a word.

Later when I went to apologise, she laughed about it so uproariously with me, that I knew she had actually rather enjoyed the moment. At any rate she fully accepted the anger as normal. That was a revelation to me.

One outburst was not enough to bring total conviction of course. Nor was it sufficient simply to know that when other novices became angry, they weren't shown the door. I had to know that I wouldn't be either.

The next occasion when I erupted was, as it happens, very justifiable. A sister had been outrageously interfering in the department for which I was responsible at the time. She wouldn't have dared take such liberties with a more senior sister. Even so, she must have been wholly unprepared for the vehemence of my explosion. Sadly, I seem to be far more articulate when I am angry than at normal times. The words poured forth like lava from a volcano. When eventually I stopped, I went as white as a sheet and fled outside, where I stood by a row of dustbins trembling all over.

'That's that,' I thought. 'All these years of training and the pain I've been through . . . it's all over in four minutes flat.' And I seriously believed that once my misconduct had been reported I should be asked to pack my bags and go.

Imagine my amazement, therefore, when not only was I not required to leave, but the response from my superior was, "Thank God. You are actually learning to be angry at last."

"Isn't this a terribly slow process," I complained to Sister Geraldine one day. In fact, by normal standards of therapy, it was by no means slow.

"God chisels away very slowly and carefully," she replied. "He has all the time there is for his healing, transfiguring work."

"Hasn't he heard of high-speed drills?" I said in some exasperation.

"He prefers the slower, safer methods," she said quietly. "He never does violence to a person through impatience."

It is difficult to say how, or when, but eventually I began to emerge from this period of darkness, and as I did so started to feel more real, more myself. It would have been surprising had it not been so, for if prayer is not leading us into deeper and deeper reality there is something amiss. At first, I used to get very worried at the amount of time I seemed to spend looking in at myself. This was the exact opposite of what I had always believed prayer to be. It was a necessary stage along the path, however.

"Don't try and escape it," my confessor had said. "Your prayer at the moment is to stay with the pain and let God throw the light of his truth on to those inward parts. After all, it isn't only God who desires it. We all do, don't we?"

"How do you see contemplation?" I asked Sister Frances one day as we went for a tramp in the country.

"How do you see it?" she replied.

"Basically, I think of it as looking at God and loving him," I said.

"To me, it's much more a case of being looked at by God and being loved by him," she answered.

In time, I came to see what she meant. The story is told of the visit of Yeshi Dhonden, the personal physician to the Dalai Lama, to a hospital in Connecticut. The notice was posted saying that at 6.0 am next morning he would make his rounds and any doctors were invited to observe him.

Promptly at 6.0 am the next morning he appeared in the room of a woman patient to examine her. Only one member of the staff knew the diagnosis of the patient. There were no signs or obvious symptoms to give the clue to the nature of her disease. Dressed in a sleeveless saffron robe, the short, tubby man whose only visible hair was his eyebrows, stood and looked at the patient for twenty minutes. Not a word was spoken. Not a soul moved in the room. Then Yeshi Dhonden moved forward to the bed, took the woman's hand and with head drawn down into the collar of his robe, he closed his eyes and listened to her pulse for half an hour.

One woman doctor observing said, "All at once, I began to feel envious – not of Yeshi Dhonden and his skills, but of the patient. I wanted to be held like that, touched so, received."

As the Tibetan reached the door, he turned and bowed to the patient. Still no word had been spoken, but at last she broke the silence, "Thank you," she called out. "Oh! Thank you."

In the conference room next door he was asked for his diagnosis, and speaking in Tibetan through an interpreter, he told of winds coursing through her body, vortices in her blood. Between the chambers of the heart before she was born a wind had come and blown open a deep gate that must never be opened. Through it were charging the full waters of her river, as the mountain stream cascades in springtime, battering, knocking loose the land, flooding her breath.

I doubt if any of them had ever heard a diagnosis like that before. Turning to the one physician who knew the nature of the patient's condition, they said, "What is her illness?"

He replied, "Congenital heart disease with interventricular septal defect with resultant heart failure."

Yeshi Dhonden for all his poetic language had been absolutely right and all he had done in his examination of the patient was to look at her and listen to the murmuring of her heart, and he knew her exact condition.[5]

This, then, is the activity of God in contemplation. He has but to look at us and listen to the murmurings of our hearts and he knows us through and through.

Looked at by God, and loved by him.

William de St Thierry wrote:

O Lord, I dare not look upon your face against your will lest I be further confounded. Needy and beggared and blind, I stand in your presence, seen by you, though I do not see you. And standing thus, I offer you my heart full of desire for you, the whole of whatever I am, the whole of whatever I can do, the whole of whatever I know, and the very fact that I so long and faint for you.[6]

That, then, is the outcome of the peeling off of the masks, the being skinned alive – a greater reality. Thomas Merton actually equated sin with the identity-giving structures of the false self. For him, sin was not so much an action as an identity – "a fundamental stance of wanting to be what we are not, . . . an orientation to falsity, a basic lie concerning our own deepest reality."[7]

Looked at by God and loved by him – unconditionally and without having to earn that love by good works. Thus we enter into that liberty of his children that allows each one to be himself, to be real.

"What is REAL?" asked the rabbit one day, when they were lying side by side near the nursery fender, before Nana came to tidy the room. "Does it mean having things that buzz inside you and a stick-out handle?"

"Real isn't how you are made," said the skin horse. "It's a thing that happens to you. When a child loves you for a long, long time, not just to play with, but REALLY loves you, then you become Real."

"Does it all happen at once, like being wound up," he asked, "or bit by bit?"

"It doesn't happen all at once," said the skin horse. "You become. It takes a long time. That's why it doesn't often happen to people who break easily, or have sharp edges, or who have to be carefully kept. Generally, by the time you are REAL most of your hair has been loved off, and your eyes drop out and you get loose in the joints and very shabby."[8]

10

A NEW SONG IN
MY MOUTH

There were two hours to wait before my coach left Victoria. It was too cold to sit in a park so I made my way to Westminster Cathedral in the hope that I would be able to find a quiet corner somewhere to pray. As I entered by the west door, I found the choir processing in from the east. They were about to begin Terce which would immediately be followed by Mass. I sat in a pew at the very back of the cathedral completely unaware that this was to be for me a major conversion experience.

I knew even before I had gone to Wantage that one of my big battles was going to be on the music front. The community is one of the remaining strongholds of plain-chant, and, at the convent at any rate, plainsong is sung at Vespers each day and at all festival Masses. On my very first visit, I had found it hard on my untutored ears, and even successive visits and my years as an oblate had left me with no taste for it. Living in Zaire had given me a love of rich harmonies for, as in most African countries, the people never sang in unison, not even as small children. Plainsong was not only unison singing but seemed to me, in my ignorance, to wander about with little sense of direction. Of course I had weighed up this factor before coming to the community. Singing is a very important part of our life and I realised this might well be a stumbling block for me. The question was, 'Could it be surmounted?'

Sister Rachel had laboured painstakingly in introducing Thelma and me to the rudiments of plain-chant. It was not her fault that I was so slow to grasp things. Blame could not be attached to anyone. It was just that this was a musical language which was foreign to me and, up to now, unattractive.

As postulants, we now attended the general singing practice for all sisters as well as having our own classes. Sister Harriet Ruth had taken over from Sister Rachel. Gradually I became less sceptical because I could see how much she valued it – but still I had no liking for it.

Sister Geraldine looked pained beyond words – almost as though I had committed sacrilege – when I voiced my discomfort. She clearly loved it. I went off disconsolately to Sister Philippa to moan about this particular hardship and ask if it was going to be possible to endure it year after year. That was even worse. She was a greater devotee than Sister Geraldine and turned out to be not only extremely knowledgeable, but a recognised authority on the subject.

Obviously, I wasn't going to find much sympathy. Why, I wondered, were sisters so enthusiastic? What did they find in this form of music that was clearly such an enrichment to their worship? Why were they prepared to put in so many hours of hard work in order to offer worship as perfectly as they could? At that time plainsong seemed to me so restrained, so lacking in emotion, so unrewarding. Practices were sheer boredom, and individual singing lessons downright misery. I shocked one sister to the core when I admitted that at Mass I longed to reach the offertory so that we could begin to sing 'proper' music, ie hymns.

Then I wandered into Westminster Cathedral that morning . . . a seemingly chance decision to get some prayer time before continuing a journey, an 'accidental' timing that led me to arrive at the same moment as the choir. And the outcome? A revelation, and a total conversion. I was reminded of the words of the Psalmist:

"Then I thought I to understand this: but it was too hard for me, until I went into the sanctuary of God . . ."[1]

Terce began. I sat completely entranced. There were very few visitors in the cathedral at that time in the morning, and I was, if I remember correctly, the only member of the congregation. Or was it perhaps that the experience which so rapt me made me oblivious to others?

Mass followed straight away and I listened with ears that seemed to be hearing for the first time. It was magnificent yet had great simplicity. Only the men were singing, the boys being on holiday, and their voices rose and fell in beautifully rounded cadences. They were singing 'our' Introits, 'our' Graduals, 'our' Alleluias. I recognised them all – the same music that I had been struggling to learn and appreciate but it sounded so very different as it soared and echoed all round that vast and mostly empty cathedral.

For the first time, I heard the shape of the chant.

It was so obvious really, yet up till now it had eluded me. I was vividly reminded of the movements of gulls wheeling over cliffs, tumbling and rising on the offshore air currents. In fact, I could almost see them in my mind's eye and hear a lone voice singing a haunting celtic folk song.

I wonder why it hadn't struck me before? The lilt, the flow, the rhythm, the risings and fallings, the haunting quality of plain-chant – it is the music of nature using the aeronautics of birds and the natural tones of the voice. There is discipline in it, but also the freedom of a bird in flight. The voices of the men away up there in the choir were free and unforced. It was the vocal equivalent of free dance. In fact, my whole body longed to get up and dance.

The music of the Mass seemed to evoke a whole series of memories. I went back in my mind to the synagogue I sometimes used to visit as a student. In the lamenting quality of the Gradual the Westminster choir was singing, I heard again the Jewish cantors. I don't think I have ever known human voices so able to convey deep yearning as those in the synagogue. I rarely understood the words they were singing, but their voices seemed to utter a haunting cry releasing that cumulative longing of Israel through the ages.

"How long, O Lord? How long?"

I remembered, too, that Sister Harriet Ruth had told us that some of the music of our plainsong could be traced back directly to the worship of the Temple at Jerusalem, so that my mental link-up with the Jewish cantors had historical foundations. "Even today, the melodies used for chanting the Psalms – the eight Gregorian Tones – have their recognisable counterparts in Jewish practice."[2]

Perhaps strongest of all the pictures that came to me as the Mass continued, was that of a charismatic festival. In memory I saw again a huge cathedral, packed to the doors one Saturday, with five thousand people singing in the Spirit. It was the first time I had heard such singing. It began almost as a hum which gradually swelled in volume till, like 'light fracturing through unquiet waters', it broke into beautiful melodies, weaving in and out of each other, separate yet related, rising and falling, controlled and yet gloriously free, engaging the emotions and yet disciplining them.

I had taken Sister Zoe along with me – for at that point I was an oblate of C.S.M.V. With her typical freedom and utter unselfconsciousness, she was singing away completely caught up by the movement of the Spirit. Nowhere amongst that vast crowd was there any hint of the unrestrained unleashing of wild emotionalism people sometimes fear on these occasions.

That morning in Westminster Cathedral brought to an end an eighteen month struggle. At last plainsong began to make sense and I was transported into a new dimension of worship. Here was a vehicle of praise that looked back to the Temple (presumably Jesus had heard and sung this kind of music?), forward to freedom in the Spirit and the singing of that great throng around the throne in heaven, yet all the time using the natural flow and rhythms of the voice.

This was worship devoid of a wrong kind of individualism (any choir knows the curse that can be), that exalted corporateness and unity, and in which discipline and restraint cleansed away any tendency to mushy sentimentalism and self-indulgence. Here was praise that was not without emotion yet did not pander to sensuous enjoyment. I began to understand a little more why Dietrich Bonhoeffer could speak of unison singing as the purest form of worship[3] – a view which I had never previously been able to share.

No more did I groan at the thought of singing practices. Naturally I was going to have to put in a lot of spade-work before I would know the kind of freedom in singing I had heard at Westminster, and now heard in my sisters. I was still a mere beginner. Just as with gliding there are all the technicalities of winches and tow ropes to be suffered before the plane can get airborne and swoop and glide effortlessly in the air streams, so there were many technicalities to be mastered in singing. But I had caught the vision, and although this form of singing in the Spirit does not by-pass hard, faithful practising, or offer short cuts to skilled musicianship, once one sings from the heart the freedom begins to come.

There and then I quickly wrote a note to Sister Harriet Ruth telling her what had happened and sharing my joy that "whereas I was blind, now I see". She couldn't have guessed how radical a conversion it had been, for I had never before ventured to tell her how I felt about plainsong. But as I popped the letter into the post on my way back to the coach station, I knew my stumbling block had been removed. The voices of those choirmen had been the instruments of God to lift me into the heavenlies and I was excited beyond measure. This I dare to believe is the kind of music some of those who have had near-death experiences have claimed that they could hear from the other side.

Although this had been perhaps my biggest and most daunting block in the realm of worship, it was not the only one.

166

At the heart of our life and prayer is the daily Eucharist. Our day, like the Jewish day, begins at sundown, ie with Vespers and continues till Vespers the following day. By this reckoning, our Eucharist is at the centre of our day, even though its actual time GMT is 7.00 am.

The Eucharist itself was not a new experience for me; I had been a regular communicant since early teens. But never before had it been possible to receive communion daily, and it was an untold privilege. I must admit that, just at first, I had a niggling fear that perhaps the frequency of reception would lead to over familiarity and rob it of some of the mystery.

What I discovered, however, was a shift in emphasis which, far from impoverishing, greatly enriched the Eucharist for me. It seemed that the words of Jesus, "except ye become as little children," began to apply in a new way. Maybe they are strange words to put in juxtaposition to one's liturgical experience but, remember, I had entered into this heritage from an evangelical background. To my joy, I found that the symbols, the imagery, the ritual acts made an impact without my having to make sense of it all. By that I do not, in any way, suggest that they were non-sense, or that I approached the sacrament less seriously than before, or with less reverence. On the contrary, my eyes were filled with new wonder and I opened myself to the power of the symbol as a child does. We tend to think that 'child's play' means something easy, to be tossed off with the flick of the wrist. But that is just what it is not. We are saddened sometimes when we feel we have

lost something quite irrevocably, the direct contact with experience that is the most striking aspect of being a child. When we were children, we could be held spellbound by things, by events and sensations, and so completely absorbed in that experience outside us that we did not glance back even fleetingly at ourselves. We were whole and undivided, and as such very close to something, whole, single and undivided. At such times, it did not even occur to us to account for or justify anything.

We were simply there, completely given up to that overwhelming experience with our eyes wide open.[4]

"Lord I would follow Thee with an undivided heart," was an aspiration that could equally well be uttered of worship as of other desires.

A child totally absorbed in some drama or story does not continually interrupt to analyse the myth or interpret the symbol. He allows them to speak with their own powerful immediacy. "Although small children are much given to metaphysics and rudimentary theology, unlike those who are older they do not let ideas get in their way," and while acting the story out they are lost in it. "That, after all, is what we often envy them for."[5]

In the past I had always felt that I could only participate in something if I understood its meaning – or thought I did.

"What does it mean? Why do we do that?"

Always it had to be reasoned out first. But as Dag Hammarskjold said, sometimes we have to, "dare our 'Yes,'" and then "experience the meaning."[6] Liturgy is the playtime of the children of God and I had been guilty of turning it into a theological exercise. Now I stopped making such hard work of it. Theology is the homework one does beforehand, but when one comes to the liturgy itself one celebrates – abandons oneself to it, enters into the story, becomes immersed in it in wonder, love and praise. The story has its roots in the past, it points to the hope of the future, and is interwoven with the life of today. It is the redemptive story and my story. It unites me to all who are caught up in it, my sisters next to me as well as that vast company which no man can number.

All this is probably self evident to those who have grown up in the Roman or Anglo-Catholic Churches, but not perhaps for those from the Protestant tradition for whom understanding is important and fear of anything veering towards superstition still very deep.

I was thrilled to discover that my growing experience tied up with that of the Catholic theologian, Romano Guardini, when I read his words:

The liturgical life speaks measuredly and melodiously; it employs formal, rhythmic gestures; it is clothed in colours and garments foreign to everyday life; it is carried out in places and at hours which have been co-ordinated and systematised according to sublimer laws than ours. It is in the highest sense the life of a child, in which everything is picture, melody and song.[7]

Candlemas is one of our big community feast days because of our particular dedication as the Community of St Mary the Virgin. I shall not easily forget my first experience of this feast at the convent – not so much for the special touches like the small vases of snowdrops on every cloister windowsill, or the customary invasion by an army of our associates who kept this as their annual day of dedication and thus packed out the ante-chapel for the Sung Mass. No. I shall remember it for something very simple and very beautiful.

There wasn't room for the four of us who were postulants to have seats in chapel – it was too full. So we had chairs just outside the west door. Also gathered in a small group at that entrance were some of the women who, at that time, lived at the convent and shared in our domestic work. For some of them the convent had been their home all their adult lives, for in their simplicity they would always need a degree of protection. If they were backwards in some ways, their innocence and deep devotion put them streets ahead of most of us. No wonder the Russian Orthodox Church calls them the 'holy ones'.

Grouped as they were, the glow of the candlelight playing on their faces seemed to highlight their joy and wonder. In particular I was struck by Emma, whose face shone with such radiance that I was at once reminded of the Israelites feeling the need to cover the face of Moses, when the glory of God reflected on it was too great for them to bear. It was so with Emma. I saw, and I looked away, for to gaze would have been an intrusion into something not meant for other human eyes. But I shall never forget that fleeting glimpse I had of her holding her candle aloft worshipping with a childlike delight, helped perhaps by the fact that her intellect probably raised few barriers for her.

I held my candle aloft too, no longer feeling inhibited by this unfamiliar practice. I had seen the joy of the occasion through the eyes of a child. Brakes had been released inside and 'I' was now celebrating – not just looking in from the doorway as a spectator. I could have hugged Emma for her innocence. She was completely unaware that she had actually been a living illustration of what Plato pointed out in *The Laws*, that play is the holy condition, and the right way to live is 'playingly'.

Occasionally I had a few guilty hang-ups wondering whether or not I was being untrue to my past, turning my back on things I had formerly cherished, doing a *volte-face* on doctrinal tenets I had once held. I even felt embarrassed and apologetic from time to time when evangelical friends came to visit and joined us in the chapel for worship.

'Am I at all lacking in integrity?' I wondered.

Apologies were quite unnecessary. In the main, they were as moved and impressed by the worship as I had been on my first visit – a visit which I had fully expected to be a one-off affair.

Increasingly it became clear to me that this was not so much a change of direction as an expansion. Nothing from my past had been lost. It was filling out and flowering in a different soil, but in no sense was there a denial.

"What worries me most about your becoming a sister," said Donna, a very dear friend, "is that you will have to say the Office every day." Before I could protest, she added, "I think after a while you will be crawling up the wall with boredom. It is so repetitious and dull."

I had been a novice less than two years when, in all kindness, this remark was made, and it would have been arrogant to have waved it aside as an insignificant, unimportant objection. For, how was I to know, at that stage, if the time might not come when the Office would pall? Two years as a novice and nine months as a postulant were not all that long a test when one thought of the years stretching ahead.

We were sitting in a car overlooking a pretty bay. It was sunny and some yachts were out on the water cutting cleanly through the choppy waves, their brightly coloured spinnakers billowing out in a stiff breeze. 'A lovely day for racing,' I mused. 'I wonder if I'll ever sail again?'

Despite the temptation to give my whole attention to the sea and the sailing, I felt I had to ponder Donna's challenge and at least attempt to articulate what the Office had come to mean to me. Yet even before starting, I was doubtful that I could succeed, for in making an offering, one is not usually primarily concerned with what it 'means to me'. The Office is part of our sacrifice of praise, and maybe there would be days . . . 'Yes, I'm sure there *will* be days,' I thought, 'when there will be more sacrifice about it than praise.'

'How far could one slip into mere routine? Was it possible simply to become conditioned?' I wondered, not for the first time.

"What if you hit a patch where the words mean no more to you than 'Rhubarb, rhubarb, rhubarb'?" Sister Frances had challenged me shortly after I arrived at the convent. "It could happen, you know."

At Wantage we had a five-fold Office. The day began with Lauds at 6.30 am. Later in the morning came Terce, and before dinner, Sext. It was at these Little Hours, as they are called, that we followed a systematic Biblical lectionary. Vespers were sung each evening at 4.30 pm and the last Office of the day, Compline, at 8.45 pm.

Psalms form the major part of each Office and are sung in a regular cycle. So Donna had a point. There was going to be a lot of repetition.

The Office was not totally new to me, of course. As an oblate I had said Lauds and Vespers each day for four years. It had been an important part of my prayer life, but it would be hard to say why, even to a sympathiser. With my limited experience I doubted if there was anything I could say, at this stage, that would allay Donna's fears, or counter her seeds of doubt. We lapsed into a thoughtful silence. Still relatively new to the full Office, and only on the threshold of discovering its riches, I needed time to consider how to express my growing conviction.

'There are bound to be times when we feel tired and the rhythm of Office all but lulls us to sleep', I thought. Everyone must experience distractions, and know those times when one reaches the end of a psalm with little recollection of what one has been saying. But it doesn't happen to everyone simultaneously, and in such moments of weakness one is carried along on the corporate stream of worship like a dead twig on a river.

Words are of course important, but there can be a danger of attaching undue weight to their meaning. If, in saying the Office, we expected every word to yield its maximum meaning – we would never keep up. That had been my problem when I started.

The steadiness of the rhythm is important too. It is, after all, the 'recitation' of the Office. The unity in choir matters greatly – and it is in choir firstly and most glaringly that any disunity in our midst manifests itself. Above all, we are there to do a piece of work – to offer the public prayer of the Church. We are commissioned to do that, and set free from a lot of other cares and duties in order to be able to do it. So naturally it will have its cost too. There are very few people whose work does not at times bring some monotony. But monotony is not necessarily the same thing as boredom. I knew from the experience I already had that there are many times when part of an Office will light up with meaning and provide nourishment for weeks. While our saying of it is not for what we can get out of it, the Lord who is rich in mercy still supplies us with food for the desert journey, as he did his people of old. And, like them, we are faced with the same inescapable challenge of those words: "This people honours me with their lips, but their heart is far from me."[8]

"That is the secret," I thought, "for where your treasure is there will your heart be also."[19]

The mind and the heart are together bent on offering praise and worship, not just in outward conformity, not in a mere ritualistic participation, not simply in the ceremonies of collective worship (all of which could be capable of stifling our freedom and stunting our spiritual growth), but out of a deep interior commitment that springs from a personal love of our Lord.

"Great is the Lord and worthy to be praised." That is the raison d'être of our Office.

"Let the people praise thee, O God . . . then shall the earth bring forth her increase and God, even our own God shall give us his blessing." Praise first. Then blessing. And through praise, the Spirit is sent forth to renew the face of the earth.

Was it hopelessly idealistic to suppose that the sense of being caught up in God's recreative, renewing work, in and through our Office, would redeem it from boredom?

After what must have seemed an age to Donna, I began, very falteringly, to share some of this thinking. Simply holding convictions is a very different thing from having them tested and tried over many years and, conscious that my beliefs were not, as yet, born of long experience, I was very anxious not to give Donna seemingly easy and slick answers. Yet I could honestly testify that even at those parts of the Office that still left me mystified and questioning, I was able to say, "Lord, I believe. Help thou mine unbelief."

"Would it make any vital difference," I asked Sister Geraldine, when I got back to the convent, "if as a community we gathered five times a day for extempore prayer, or prayers led by different sisters?" After our discussion overlooking the little bay, I felt I had to ask if the actual unchanging content of the Office was of its essence.

"Ah! Yes – it certainly would," she replied. "I'm glad you've asked that."

"How would you explain the fundamental difference then?" and I told her about my conversation with Donna.

It was not that I seriously considered the alternative of extempore prayer. That certainly has its place and we were familiar with it in some of our prayer groups. But I needed to be able to spell out the essential difference.

Sister spoke of the objectivity of the Office as it has been handed down to us with language and content able to bear the weight of continual repetition. Whatever personal nourishment it may give us, the Office must focus and realise something which characterises the whole Church, the whole worshipping Community. It must be able to voice the praise of the whole Church, and do so continually on behalf of those who, dispersed in the world, can express it only with difficulty. For, acting representatively, it ought to be possible for any Christian in any part of the world to hook on to our prayer at any time. The worship is theirs as well as ours, and on their behalf we offer it.

The structure of the Office is such that the Psalter is our main way of praying. Every aspect of human experience finds expression in the Psalms – joy, praise, adoration, fear, depression, guilt, penitence, anger, desire for retaliation, doubt, mistrust . . . it's all there. And expressed in a way that could scarcely be bettered. The Psalms have a clean, objective ring and save worship from becoming too inward looking and subjective. Partly this is because they have been handed down from age to age, each generation hallowing them a little more by their use of them. There is about them an ancestral sure-footedness that makes them safe and full of wisdom. More than anything, of course, they are hallowed by our Lord's own use of them.

I thought back to my day with Donna. "Could I, even with all these convictions, still find myself one day crawling up the wall with boredom?" No one can give an answer to that in advance, but we are not left without signposts – living signposts at that. They were my sisters. Many of them had been saying the Office faithfully thirty, forty, fifty – yes, even sixty years – day in and day out, previously when it was an eight-fold Office, then later when it became five-fold. Some of them now very old and infirm still struggled to chapel every day. Others faithfully prayed it from their beds in the infirmary wing.

A Religious never becomes redundant, never retires. For the work of the Office can be carried on long after one's body has begun to fail. The shining example of the older sisters, their loyalty, devotion and sheer steadfastness were and are of incalculable value. It is not without significance that the oldest in community years, and the youngest are brought together at the Mother House where, in those nearing the end of their lives, one is often confronted by the visible testimony of what the life of prayer, and not least the Office, can bear in terms of fruit. Most of the older sisters are far too humble to realise what their example means to those starting out on the life, but they provided for me an answer. Such fidelity leads not to boredom but holiness.

Nor is it only the living saints who help us on our way. Some of them "being dead, yet speak". The Office book of a sister, long departed, came into my hands during the course of my work, one day. The notes that she had made were not only extremely informative about various feasts and saints, but I caught a glimpse of her devotion through the aspects of the Passion which she had noted down to be remembered at each of the Hours. I felt I was on very holy ground. On the fly-leaf of her Office book were words which I had not met before, though I have sometimes heard them quoted since. They made such sense to me, I copied them into 'my' Office book, and frequently bless her for them.

The choir should be to the Religious what the altar is to the Priest. Over the altar the Priest offers the Body and Blood of Christ. In Choir, the Religious offers the Mind of Christ as expressed in psalms and hymns.

It is thy great and bounden duty. Thy stall in Choir is thyne altar, see that thou offerest thy sacrifice there with carefulness, reverence and thoughtful preparation.

Love your Choir and your Offices. Study them and seek to perfect yourself in them. Let your sacrifice be the best you can offer, and keep your offering very fresh . . .

11

THE SIMPLE VISION

What does it mean to be a contemplative in the twentieth century? That is a question that could receive many answers, but I believe all of them would say something about our vocation to live life to the full. They would speak of the search for a fully authentic human existence.

The secret of this is the complete gift of ourselves to God, and is by no means confined to religious communities. There is much to challenge us in both the lives of individual Christians and the witness of the different lay communities that are exploring the meaning of community in terms of twentieth century society and possible alternative life-styles. They too are often extremists in their commitment.

There can be no fixed answer to the question, and the monk or nun is continually questing, searching, trying to ask the right questions about life, and, because the Religious Life is dynamic rather than static, is continually reassessing its values, reviewing and renewing his or her commitment at ever deeper levels. It is not a restless search but one prompted by the Holy Spirit who urges all men to seek the Truth that will make them free. That search is work to which the Religious is committed, for out of his silence, and from the perspectives given him by his enclosure, he ought to have eyes that see, and the prophetic voice of the seer.

He will not always be appreciated for this, any more than

were the prophets of old. He has always to accept that in the terms of a technological society, he is useless. That is to say, his most central functions of adoration, contemplation, penance and intercession are unproductive in material terms. But probably one of the major contributions of religious communities to society today is the willingness to stay with this seemingly irrelevant role. Amongst young people particularly there has often been a reaction against Super-Efficiency and Technical Skill, those twin gods set up by society to which every knee must bow. There has been a longing to replace them with Awe and Mystery. Hence, the great interest in the 1960s in the occult, in way-out sects, in Eastern forms of mysticism, in drugs, pop and psychedelia and all the other manifestations of the whole American sub-culture.

How often was this in fact an expression of a deep yearning for God? He might perhaps have been a God without a face or name for many of them, but the God-shaped gap in their lives left them searching and hungering for the One who alone could fill it.

"Thou hast made us for thyself," said St Augustine, "and our hearts are restless till they find their rest in Thee."[1]

A number eventually looked in the direction of religious communities. Some even joined them.

What were they really looking for in that quest of the sixties, and indeed in the decades since, and what did they hope to find?

For some it was undoubtedly a search for an experience of transcendence – not simply self transcendence but of the *mysterium tremendum et fascinans*.[2] It was a desire to restore a balance to life ensuring a right place for the contemplative element, which is all too easily squeezed out by our highly materialistic society. So they took their trips and tracked down their Maharishis and gave themselves to transcendental meditation. This was a serious search but what really lay behind it was often not heeded by the older generations as a whole, including the Church. Some were critical without even being aware that young people were actually making a valid statement.

Perhaps they could not hear because they were unhappy at the way in which the search was being conducted. It may have appeared to the critics amongst them that young people were prepared to jump on the bandwagon of any sect that offered an easy path to heightened awareness, and instant spiritual experience of a novel and sensational kind – spiritual experience that remained at the feeling level and seemed neither to affect the mind nor impinge on the will. It was the uncritical character of the new upsurge of religiosity that worried some in the mainline churches. Its followers seemed too easily satisfied with experience which lacked doctrinal foundation or personal discipline.

We have much to learn from Eastern mystics in terms of dedication, single-mindedness and self-denial, but one cannot be as selective in one's learning as some seekers from the West tried to be.

A young Taize brother (an Indian) was asked why it was, in his view, that worship at Taize appealed to thousands of young people who were disenchanted with the churches in their own countries. He claimed that the opportunity for contemplation was one very major reason, and admitted that there was an Eastern element in the worship of the community but not a deviation from the basic form of liturgy that had been there since its foundation. He said,

As an Indian, I am disturbed . . . The need (for contemplation) comes from a two-fold tendency in European society: on the one hand the search for an emotional outlet in face of the growing rationalism of industrialised society, and on the other the subjectivism, the desire to experience everything directly. What scares me most of all is that in the West, Eastern mysticism is not integrated within the existing culture, as it is in my country. People take a slice of the cake – the direct religious experience – and leave all the rest. This creates a sort of alienation. You can't separate the experience from the rest just like that. You can't do without the backbone of mental substructures that accompanies the mysticism over there. I would much rather see European young people rediscover their own monastic tradition.[3]

One could add – rediscover the Christian tradition as a whole, for the answers to much of what the counter-culture threw up could have been found there, had not young people been sickened by what seemed trivial, bourgeois and hopelessly out of touch in much church life. So we have ended up with an anomaly, as Carl Braaten points out, of not so much a "Christianity without religion," as a "revival of religion without Christianity."[4]

What then were young people searching for as they sat in their lotus positions, learned breathing techniques and studied methods of contemplation? Seeking an experience is a very far cry from seeking God, and some of the manifestations of the counter-culture were positively dangerous. Attempts to empty the mind and create an inner vacuum can be an invitation to invasion by undifferentiated spiritual forces with disastrous consequences (cf the gospel story of the house swept clean[5]). In Christian prayer the emptying is to mark out a space for God, "to find out a place for the temple of the Lord."[6] So, it is no ego trip.

There are certain signs of a growing contemplative vocation and I think each of us novices, without in any way deliberately cultivating them, began to detect them in ourselves and in one another. From the ever deepening hunger for God comes a desire for greater simplicity, a deeper harmony with one's environment, a new and growing reverence for all things, and a developing sense of the importance of genuine community. It was the very lack of these elements in society that precipitated that explosion of religiosity and religious revival twenty years ago and which has continued, perhaps less sensationally, ever since.

A few years ago a Pop Festival was held not very far from Wantage. A group of sisters went along each day to mingle with the young people and talk to them, but chiefly to listen to what they were saying. Pop was the object of the gathering, but not the only reason. Many were panting to leave the air and noise-polluted cities and get into the country for a while to enjoy the genuine 'community' of a shared interest (pop), shared food, leisure, discussion and the opportunity to articulate political hopes and religious ideals, a shared desire for the natural things of life, eg the earth, trees, stars, wind and even rain. The sisters met with strange sights, new customs, unfamiliar vocabulary, unusual foods, different clothes . . . and sometimes no clothes . . . long hair, no hair, employed and unemployed, socalled drop outs and eager go-getters . . . they all came together for a week.

Despite the fact that their primary purpose was to enjoy themselves, in all sorts of ways they were voicing a protest about the distortion of life as it is lived in the concrete jungles of our cities, in the stifling pollution of industrial areas, in the midst of exploitation, unrest, unemployment and all the dehumanising factors of modern life. They wanted the good things of God's earth – not just pop. For some, one suspected, hardly pop at all.

Our sisters recounted to us the kind of conversations they had, the contacts made, the questions asked. It seemed that no one felt it out of place that they should be attending the festival. Maybe without actually realising it, the pop lovers recognised that they had much in common with our search. For as Harvey Cox has written, "Man is more essentially religious than many of us have assumed. He thirsts for mystery, meaning, community and even for some sort of ritual."[7]

Many involved in the search for a spiritual dimension in life seemed to be looking for the same things that we found growing out of our prayer – simplicity, harmony, reverence, and community. Secular society has seemingly simplified life in the many material areas where we can 'leave it to the machines' – and made it profoundly complex in others. Yesterday's world is today's global village and a seemingly innocent remark made in Washington can resonate in Moscow in a matter of minutes and have the power to affect the economies of every major country in the world. Everything seems to have escalated in importance, influence and, indeed, price . . . except man himself. He is having to struggle against the tide of mass everything – mass media, mass meetings, mass production etc. Hence an almost neurotic stress on the importance of the individual today. Much of it is reaction to urban society, with its vast sprawling housing areas, and technological society where a sense of identity can so quickly be threatened by size and uniformity.

Of our three vows, poverty seems to speak most strongly here. Poverty is a much misunderstood word and, with the enormity of the economic problems of the Third World, can only be used relatively. But poverty is not the same thing as squalor. "Let us get rid of squalor and cultivate poverty," Gandhi taught his disciples.[8]

When we discussed poverty in the novitiate, as we frequently did, we often times agreed that the word simplicity more accurately expresses what we understand by that first vow. Indeed we tended at times to feel embarrassed by the word poverty for, as Religious, we are not deprived of the essentials of physical well-being as so many in the world today are. But we do aim at simplicity.

We are exhorted by our Rule to omit any articles of luxury from our houses, to attempt to let our needs be simple and our possessions few. But it is surprisingly difficult to sustain even that degree of simplicity. It seems to us, however, of immense importance that our life should be an expression of contentment with the bare essentials, and rejection of excess, if we are to cultivate poverty as Gandhi urged. Young people are rightly concerned about poverty in view of the appalling economic imbalance in the world today where two-thirds of the world's population lives on the verge of starvation. Our desire too is to identify with those in dire need, by personal denials, however small, insignificant and valueless they may seem to be in the face of the immensity of the problem. There is an important place for such gestures of sacrifice, if only to focus our concern.

Self-denial, however, can take many forms, and poverty (or simplicity) in the monastic sense has a meaning other than a material one. It has to do with acceptance – the simple receiving of what comes each day through the changes and chances of this life, the acceptance of the circumstances, the interruptions and the 'blessed inconveniences'.

Sometimes it is easier, and more satisfying, to make the grand gesture of self-denial than to accept the provisions made for us. Simplicity implies the grateful acceptance of a roof over our heads, clothes to wear, food to eat, work to do and the tools with which to do it (even if they are not the most up-to-date and sophisticated). We are utterly dependent on God through the community for all we need.

Simplicity also calls for an acceptance of the bodies we have, with their particular frailties and demands, the obedient acceptance of any necessary treatment (eg it may even require the humble acceptance of a special or complicated diet. I recall hearing of a sister of one community who was ordered by her doctor to have a cooked breakfast each day. Imagine the simple acceptance needed to sit in a refectory eating your bacon and eggs under the noses of all your sisters, eating for their part bread and dripping), the gracious acceptance of help from others and the gift of their service, the patient acceptance of the diminishments of old age. Perhaps, above all, it means the humble acceptance of one's failures and a willingness to pick oneself up and go on.

It is freedom of choice that we offer to God in our poverty, expressed in small ways, yet cumulatively they can test our degree of given-ness in that other vow – obedience. For our simplicity means that we have no choice in, for example, the cell we are given, our place in refectory or chapel, the work we do, our superiors, or the sisters with whom we work. We accept the clothes provided and the menus planned, the decisions made. This is not mindless submission. It is the positive, voluntary offering of self-will and the promise to live in love, joy and contentment.

Simplicity brings a growing inner unity, that singleness of heart and purpose already mentioned. It brings an ever increasing and desperately needed freedom. Most of us are unaware of the extent to which we are bound since our ties are not always obvious great chains but numerous Lilliputian bonds that peg out our emotional life in a bondage like that of Gulliver. And as one sage put it, a bird, if held by so much as one thread, is not free. A simple lifestyle brings freedom from anxiety and the burden of great possessions, freedom from the consuming desire always to go bigger and better, to keep up with the Joneses and hanker after increasing luxuries. When Jesus said that it was easier for a rich man to go through the eye of a needle than to enter into the Kingdom of Heaven, he was not condemning the riches in themselves. Elsewhere in the Scriptures they are regarded as God's blessings and rewards. But so few who are rich, or perhaps more especially, who have 'become' rich, are able to be content and live in simplicity, coveting nothing, desiring nothing, anxious about nothing.

A group leader from Taize said,

> I think that more and more young people are becoming aware that having more does not make you happier in the end. I have never met happier people than I did in the poor neighbourhoods of Mexico and Africa. Not that I would want to be poor, but poor people sometimes know how to give a quality to their lives that I've never seen anywhere else. For me, they were an anticipation of the kind of Church I'd like to see. Really living beyond every hope.[9]

Simplicity does indeed bring joy and a freedom to travel light, but our own inner disintegration and insecurity can war against such freedom.

In the talk (which proved to be his final one) that Thomas Merton gave at the Conference of Abbots and Superiors at Bangkok, he told the story of

> a Buddhist abbot fleeing for his life from a Tibetan monastery before the advance of Communist troops. Another monk had joined him with a train of twenty five yaks loaded with 'essential' provisions. The abbot didn't wait with the yaks. While the other monk stayed with his 'necessities' and was quickly overtaken by those from

whom he was trying to flee, the abbot, leaving everything behind, swam across a river and at last reached India.[10]

How many yaks do we have trailing in our wake?

The contemplative life also leads to a deepening harmony with one's environment, a new relationship with creation both plant and animal. And, indeed, ought there not to be a real connection between our vow of poverty and the ecological movement?

One of the reasons why young people (and not only young ones) long to break out of the aesthetically ugly, overcrowded, cramped conditions of their life in the city or housing estate, is an innate, instinctive feeling of loss, a sense of having lost touch with their roots – the soil, the elemental forces, the animal creation. Urban life prevents them from experiencing directly the interdependence between men and the rest of creation. The lack of such experiential knowledge can lead in the long run to callousness and abuse of both animal and plant life. As a civilisation – often brash, sophisticated, calculating and aggressive – we have lost the simple wisdom and earthy knowledge of past ages. We have indeed lost touch with our roots, yet, "a man may only detach himself from nature in order to revert to it again, and, in hallowed contact with it, find his way to God".[11]

The stories of St Francis of Assisi and his relationship with animals have often been cheapened by sentimentality, obscuring at times what it was he was really saying about simplicity. Nevertheless, he exemplified a general truth in a particular way, namely, that through the greater simplicity into which prayer leads us we establish a new unity with the soil and with all living creatures. This, in turn, leads to an ever deepening concern for the right use of our natural resources, a proper reverence for life in all its aspects, wise conservation and an end to all exploitation and plunder.

It is not merely coincidental or only for self-support that religious communities have, all through the centuries, found value in gardening, farming, forestry, fruit growing, bee-keeping, and sheep rearing. At-one-ment with God means a growing at-one-ment with his creation. There is an ever deepening wonder at the mystery of life that throbs through all nature – certainly not experienced by the Religious alone, but increasingly integrated into his life of prayer. It would seem that he is, albeit in small ways, discovering the way back to that perfect communication with God and his creation that was lost at the Fall.

Ought not the Religious Life to be an eschatalogical sign of that time when redeemed humanity will enjoy a fearless co-inherence with all creation; the "wolf shall dwell with the lamb, and the leopard shall lie down with the kid . . ."[12]

The stories of saints and their animals are legion, even if St Francis is over-quoted as the classic example. Some speak of extraordinary affinities with the type of wild animal commonly feared by men – animals which usually precipitate fight or flight in man. Do animals detect the presence of reverence and delight in human beings? It would seem so.

What is the meaning of the old Christian tradition that the saints in the desert were not attacked by lions, savaged by wolves, or bitten by snakes? They didn't even have to pull thorns out of paws; the animals loved them anyway.[13]

The meaning lies in the growing harmony they found with creation through reverence, through an awareness of God in all things, "all creatures great and small."

Dostoevsky has articulated for us the attitude that seems to strengthen with deepening prayer.

Lord may I love all thy creation, the whole and every grain of sand in it. May I love every leaf, every ray of thy light. May I love the animals: thou has given them the rudiments of thought and joy untroubled. Let me not trouble it, let me not harrass them, let me not deprive them of their happiness, let me not work against thine intent. For I acknowledge unto thee that all is like an

185

ocean, all is flowing and blending, and that, to withhold any measure of love from anything in thy universe is to withhold that same measure from thee.[14]

Some people have far greater natural rapport with animals than others, but I would judge that prayer would give to anyone that sense of kinship with nature expressed by Fr Zossima, and with it an eye for natural beauty.

Some of our sisters have greener fingers than others, some have an exceptional way with animals. Sister Zoe was one. She so rarely seemed to be without some injured creature as a patient, that Mother Candida was heard to remark on one occasion that she realised she would have to accept Sister Zoe's veritable menagerie or lose her to the zoo. There are numerous and legendary stories about her coming into choir with a bird nestling in the wide sleeve of her habit, and certainly I remember her picking up an injured dove in the road as she was on her way to catch a bus. She popped it in her bag preferring that it should journey to Oxford and back than be left to the mercy of cats or traffic. Another sister had a reputation for being able to do anything with bees and, somewhat to my embarrassment, I seem myself to have a Pied Piper effect on cats. But apart from these examples, which are of no consequence in themselves except in so far as they are pointers to that reverence and harmony which we find growing in the prayer life, most of the community delights in the world of nature, in that part of it that we meet in our own convent garden – the hedgehogs, the many bird families, especially the swifts who announce their arrival each May by wheeling round the chapel with their queer high-pitched screams, and whom we greatly miss when they migrate at the end of summer.

Animals, fish, birds, reptiles, plants, trees . . . all the elements . . . are gathered up in our first Office of the day as we offer praise and thanksgiving to God. Indeed, in the Benedicite they are each called on specifically in turn to "praise him and magnify him forever," and it is always an additional joy when Lauds corresponds with the dawn

186

chorus and we literally have bird song to accompany our praises.

> We praise thee, O God, for thy glory displayed
> In all the creatures of the earth,
> In the snow, in the rain, in the wind, in the storm;
> In all of thy Creatures, both the hunters, and the hunted.
> For all things exist only as seen by thee, only as known by thee . . .
> They affirm thee in living; all things affirm thee in living;
> The bird in the air, both the hawk and the finch;
> The beast on the earth, both the wolf and the lamb;
> The worm in the soil and the worm in the belly . . .[15]

In a world of so much senseless brutality and needless cruelty, it seems right and proper that Christians in general should witness to a reverence for all life. Certainly it is of the essence of our own life. Man may have been given dominion over the animal creation, but it is our belief that this authority places a heavy responsibility on him to treat all creatures with dignity and a use proper to their nature. It is difficult to take a stand against exploitation, inhumane treatment of and experimentation upon animals, other than by respecting and reverencing those that come within the orbit of our own life and experience, though sisters have, from time to time, sought wider influence by signing petitions and writing to MPs protesting against some form of ill-treatment or misuse of animals.

As we pondered some of these things in our novitiate, we were conscious, sometimes a little troubled, that we seemed so privileged with our beautiful setting and views of the downs. Supposing the day came when we moved from a large, institutional plant to a diversity of community groups living in smaller houses in far less congenial surroundings? How would it affect our life? Is there essentially any difference between the Religious Life lived by those in a privileged environment such as ours, with trees, flowers, and plenty of green, growing things, and that of the Little Brothers of Jesus in their tenement block, the Taizé brothers in a Third World slum dwelling, or indeed our own sisters in Inner London with traffic roaring by and surrounded by high-rise towers? What does the cultivation of a love of animals, trees and plants have to do with people who live in concrete jungles with not a square foot of soil in which to grow anything?

Reverence belongs to all of God's creation even in the bleakest slum or the darkest place – though it may be the darkness of malice and hate rather than material poverty. Contact with the world of nature can help to encourage the growth of reverence – indeed creatures can be our teachers in this respect. But the learning doesn't stop there . . . or at least, it shouldn't. If it does, it has degenerated into sentimentality. Certainly let us have reverence for life in all its forms, but, the all-important thing, though sometimes the harder, is the growing reverence for other people in their uniqueness – for people above all, but also for property . . . especially that which is not our own; for work . . . particularly manual work where we can offer labour that is cherished with love and reverence. That is a quality sadly lacking today, when slipshod, sloppy work will do.

It is reverence that we hope and pray would spill over from our Religious Life into the life of any local community in which we became rooted – a reverence that carries with it a stillness, a gentleness and a caring.

Through such reverence we are able to meet Christ in our brother. Out of reverence flows the listening, compassion, service and love that is God meeting others in us and through us. Daily in the news we hear of the effects of irreverence – mugging, murder and rape, vandalism and violence, the devaluing of work so that it becomes a form of financial remuneration only, rather than an offering of service.

If by learning to co-operate with the rhythms of nature and by living in harmony with all creation, we develop an ever-deepening quality of reverence and restore some balance to life, then surely that can be carried into whatever situation we may find ourselves? Those Religious and laymen who are encouraging the growth of community life in the inner city areas, often witness to the healing and revitalising power of reverence, showing that life can be lived with a quality of hope when, materially speaking, the odds may seem against it.

One priest and his wife, who visited us, had declined the rather pleasant suburban house provided by their church, choosing rather to live in a tower block in the midst of their parishioners. Every block, every apartment, was exactly the same. One could swiftly get lost in the confusion of identical alleyways. Not a bush, a tree, or a hedge relieved the uniform grey of the concrete. The homes were drab and depressing, for there was nothing to encourage beauty. The young couple began by whitewashing all the walls of their flat, hanging a few carefully chosen paintings, placing a windowbox at the window and growing plants on a climbing frame. They transformed the dreary rather squalid flat into a place of beauty and restfulness. It was not long before window boxes appeared at other windows. Occupants were seen wielding paintbrushes. Suddenly ideas caught on. Beauty and living things were not, after all, completely out of reach. People began to take a new pride and interest in their homes.

By using natural decorations like an autumn leaf or an interestingly shaped piece of wood to beautify their home they encouraged others to use their eyes and to 'see', and thus to wonder. And in that wonder, people often took their first step in contemplation.

Our Lord comes to us again and again in material guise – in bread and wine, in water at baptism and oil of chrism, in wind and fire, in human personality, through the written and spoken word, through a leaf or a piece of wood. He came in flesh and still meets us in the flesh of his children and his creation.

When we receive him into our flesh, as we do at the Eucharist, unlike vessels being filled with water, which remain essentially the same, our actual flesh is changed. Growing holiness affects our physical bodies – though it would not show on a scan, nor could it be monitored. We are, however, being transfigured from glory to glory.

A former infirmarian of our community told me of an occasion after a sister had died when for some reason it was necessary just before the requiem to open the coffin. The doctor was present and as the lid was removed they gasped aloud. The body of the sister was radiant with such a translucent light, it completely transformed her body. We can't explain why this happens, we only know that there is evidence that sometimes it does in those who have lived lives of holiness and prayer.

This seemed like a parable of the kind of effect contemplation has on the individual and on the world; it lets in the light of God and transfigures all creation – human, animal, vegetable and material.

What does it mean to be a contemplative in the twentieth century? Basically, what it has always meant – to be an agent of transforming power.

12

CREATIVE CONSENT

"Do you think perhaps you should spend some time in one of the enclosed communities, to see if God is calling you to that way of life?" I was asked on five occasions by priests during my novitiate years. "It would seem to be the logical step for you," one said.

I had visited a number of other communities in the years between my first visit to Wantage and my arrival as an aspirant. Not that I had gone shopping around, my visits were usually for conferences or retreats. None of them had clicked with me in the way C.S.M.V. did. Although there is a sense in which all communities form one family, each branch of the family has its own special ethos, usually stemming from the original vision and charism of its founder. And often one knows when one has arrived 'home', though it is not altogether uncommon for people to transfer from one community to another, or to spend part of their novitiate in a community with a different lifestyle or emphasis. However, I didn't sense any strong call from God to test my vocation elsewhere.

"Are you sure you wouldn't be happier in a lay community where you could be more active?" I was asked by two or three sisters, in complete contrast to the priests.

Broadly speaking, I was being asked on the one hand if I shouldn't lead a more contemplative life, and on the other a more active one. God, I felt, had directed me to C.S.M.V.

which is a mixed community with its very wide range of vocations within the general vocation to the Religious Life. We, in our community, are not unique in living this kind of life with its tension between the active and contemplative aspects of our vocation. There are other such mixed communities.

Nor really is it a tension peculiar to religious communities. All Christians live with it to some extent. We all need our times apart, our periods of withdrawal and solitude, and our times of active engagement with and service to other people. It is a balance to be held – sometimes a very difficult and delicate balance, and the balance is not the same for everyone.

It is not easy for a community (and the larger the community, the more difficult it is) to hold that balance. A great deal of the onus of responsibility for this rests with the Reverend Mother and the Superiors she has appointed. The late Sister Janet C.S.M.V. refers to this in her biography, *Mother Maribel of Wantage*.

> Always within C.S.M.V. there had been the two inter-woven strands, the outward and the inward, the active and the monastic tradition. Mother Maribel's whole vocation drew her towards the second, even while recognising the needful place of the first. There were many who felt that she was pulling the Community too strongly inwards. Yet it was just because of her awareness of both the great opportunity and the danger of the Community's active involvement with the world . . . that she knew its need of a yet deeper involvement in God if it was to fulfil its vocation; and this was no easy thing, no soft option.[1]

The balance is difficult to achieve whether one thinks of it corporately or individually. Asceticism is not a very popular word. Literally it means training, but it is often grossly misunderstood and confused with a kind of miserable, unhealthy, world-rejecting, body-denying, kill joy attitude to life. Nothing could be further from the truth. Asceticism in Christian spirituality has to do with balance.

At the still point of the turning world
There the dance is . . .

said T. S. Eliot.[2]

The dance at the still point symbolises equilibrium.

Asceticism is a means of redressing the balance both within ourselves and in the society in which we live. Dr Victor Demant has pointed out that, "because of the Fall . . . a man becomes ec-centric" (ie drawn away from his centrality).

From our end of the community as novices, we could only dimly understand the enormous responsibility that lies with those in authority, and the constant vigilance needed, to safeguard a community from becoming "ec-centric", drawn away from its true vocation.

The desire for a right balance lies behind our taking of vows, and also behind our concern for a proper reverence for creation through a just and wise use of the earth's resources. We see this asceticism working through 'hidden' identification – suffering in prayer; through 'actual' identification – sharing of physical and political deprivations, as the sisters in our overseas provinces sometimes do – and through an outwardly protesting role, in which attempts are made to influence and possibly bring about change in the local community, and indeed in the wider society, if there seems an urgent need to redress some imbalance. For, far from being centres of quietism, as communities we are meant to be a violent challenge to the world.

Whatever our call, each individual, and the community as a whole, is trying to find this right balance between protest and passivity, stillness and movement, speech and silence, encounter and withdrawal. The balance will not always appear to be equally weighted for each sister and while some are frequently out on the frontier of the world, others are drawn into the fierce, spiritual combat of the solitary life. Between these two positions lies the whole spectrum of active-cum-contemplative vocations. And whilst we as novices knew that, if we persevered in the Religious Life, we too should have to find our own equilibrium within that spectrum, we were also busy discovering that there is often a false dichotomy driven between those two words, active and contemplative.

It was evident, too, that, in order to keep a corporate balance within the community as a whole, the individual balance might sometimes have to be a changing one according to the obedience asked of us. Each sister makes her own individual and unique response to God's call, but it is the sum of all the individual responses that leads to the corporate balance. However, sisters are not left to stumble along on their own until they hit upon the right balance. We all have access to wise counsellors, directors and confessors and are free to discuss our spiritual journey with them at any time. And any sister may ask to see the Mother of the community if she needs to share particular problems or wishes to sound out ideas.

That, however, does not mean that every sister is free to do her own thing or decide for herself what work she should do and how she should do it. Often our discussions in the novitiate came round to the subject of freedom and authority, and Sister Geraldine left us in no doubt as to what the future would hold. However much a Mother might listen to a sister and consider her suggestions very carefully and prayerfully, ultimately she must be able to ask of that sister obedience. If there are very good reasons why it is inadvisable for a sister to undertake a certain work, or go to a particular country, then it is her responsibility to make those hidden factors known. Nor is a sister denied a particular request simply because she has requested it. There are always reasons for a "No", but it is not always possible to give the reasons and not necessarily right to ask for them.

Once in a Novices' Study Weekend when we were discussing obedience, I ventured to suggest that it often sprang out of mature consultation. My fellow novices ragged me about this – perhaps it was just the way I had phrased it that amused them. In fact however that is mainly what happens. But sometimes it has to be a blind obedience without prior consultation. At that same study weekend, Sister Harriet Ruth gave a talk in which she spoke of "the priceless response of running to do God's will – sometimes without knowing the reason."

"There is a place, on occasions, for simply doing as one is asked without argument or questioning," Sister Geraldine said to us in more than one conference. "What a relief it is to any superior, when she has a sister who says a simple 'Yes' without a lot of fuss."

We knew that during our training period we should spend some time in two, at least, of our branch houses, and that we should also be given experience in a variety of departments of work. This was by way of a foretaste of what could be asked of us later, should we be professed in the community, for then we might be asked to serve in parish work or a neighbourhood ministry, on a cathedral staff or amongst students, in a healing ministry to alcoholics, the elderly, or the sick. We might be living on a local housing estate or in the centre of London, in the north or in the south, at home or overseas. We might be out in branch houses or at the convent. There, at the Mother House, we might be involved in the ministry to visitors, and all that that entails pastorally and domestically, the nursing of the elderly, the oversight of the garden, the cooking, the cleaning, the making of new clothes and mending of the old, the laundry, the printing press, the sacristy, the overall arrangement of music with the appointment of singers and readers for all services, the organ playing, the library, the tape library . . . and all the many jobs involved in ordinary administration and day to day running of a large institution. Nor of course, is it just the work of the convent plant, for the Mother House is the administrative centre for the whole community and the work of the bursar and secretarial staff covers needs far wider than those of the convent alone.

"I have never had a job in my whole community life," one sister said to me, "that I would have chosen to do, but I have always found joy in every job because it was asked of me and I did it."

I was reminded of the Psalmist whom Sister Harriet Ruth had quoted in her talk to us on obedience.

195

"I am content to do it, yea thy law is within my heart."[4]

Part of the gift of discernment is to know how to obey. The community has had, and still has, some very great saints. I was privileged to see the way one of them accepted an exceedingly hard change of work. Her example will stay with me to the end of my days.

She had been asked to leave a house where she was doing a job at which she was superb, and for which in her pre-community days she had won some top awards. She is a highly qualified and very gifted sister, but she was needed in another house not so much for her qualifications and natural gifts as for what she 'is', in herself, – for the spiritual gifts she brings as a great woman of prayer and a shining example of how fruitful the Religious Life can be if it is faithfully lived.

I had been with her in the first house and had seen her functioning very ably in her professional role. It happened that, at the time of her move, I was at the second house when she arrived. I knew something of what it must have been costing her. Obviously no other human being could have known the full extent of her suffering, and it must have been very considerable, but we could enter into it a little by empathy as she laid down for ever something very dear to her heart.

Never once, however, was there a hint of bitterness, regret or resentment. Never once did she allude to her pain or cast a cloud over the group of sisters in that house. When it came up naturally, in conversation, she spoke of the other house and her work there, but she didn't harp on about it. She gave herself utterly to her new life and the work of the house, threw herself without restraint in to all its activities and ministry, even though they were unfamiliar to her. The same discipline of prayer was there, the same thoroughness in everything she did. Only her laughter betrayed the depths of what she was feeling. It revealed at times an undercurrent of deep pain. I wept for her, but if she ever shed any tears herself (which I rather doubt) she only did so in private. Not only was she never downcast, she positively exuded joy.

196

Occasionally a square peg is fitted into a round hole, or there is a clash of personalities and a sister has to ask to leave a house, but apart from such exceptions, our obedience – if we were to take the Vow – would, we knew, require of us a readiness to accept any move anywhere at any time. It would also rule out the coveting of any particular work or office.

"There is absolutely no room for ambition of any sort in our life," Sister Andrea once said to us with great vehemence. I forget the occasion which called forth the remark but, she went on, "You've heard the saying, 'Anyone who wants to be the Reverend Mother deserves to be,' haven't you?" As we laughed she added, "And that goes for any office or responsibility."

The challenge that was being put to us was to be fully 'given', fully oneself and contented wherever one is.

"How would you feel if you were sent to such and such a house?" Camilla asked me one day, naming a house involved in work of which I was terrified.

"At this point I can't say how I would feel," I said. "I can only hope that if and when such a request came, I would be given the grace to obey."

It came.

In my second week at that house, however, I came upon these words which were meat and drink to me at the time:

It is not the place where you are that is the important thing. It is the intensity of your presence there. It is not the situation that counts. What counts is that you are fully alive in any situation. It is this that puts down roots and then flowers in your life. Availability: that is obedience. That and looking hard at the place where you are, instead of wanting to work wonders somewhere else.[5]

This particular aspect of obedience – the being willing to be moved around – is of course something we have to face in our mixed life which those in enclosed orders do not encounter in quite the same way. They do often have other houses, and then the question would arise, but more often their obedience necessitates a staying put, a stability.

Inevitably questions about authority and obedience rank very high in the minds of enquirers and aspirants, and indeed in any Novitiate worth its salt.

We know all too well the kind of obedience that is little more than an outward conformity covering a heap of gripes and grumbles. Probably many of us would have to admit to being guilty of that travesty of it at times.

"Resignation is the lowest degree of clinging to the will of God," wrote a Cistercian monk. "It lacks heat and drive; it leaves a sour after-taste of regret."[6]

I should imagine we were all pondering deeply the meaning of obedience and its outworking for us. I certainly was.

I knew that I would not be satisfied with an outward acceptance only. A total response would require the "Yes" to come from the inner depths and work its way up through all the levels of one's being until it surfaced in a complete acceptance. As far as I could see, if it didn't spring from some hidden, inner spring of love, it would just be sterile. Hence the need for the healing spoken of in a previous chapter, 'Skinned Alive', for if there has been a real integration of the different levels of one's being then the answering "Yes" can travel to the surface unhindered by blocks at any point. Like a swift arrow of desire it can respond with, "Lo, I come to do thy will, O God."[7] The freedom to make that response will often involve great trust, for the obedience may well call for a leap in the dark.

Many enquirers rightly question the meaning of this particular vow, as we had done. For the very last thing any of us had wanted was a form of obedience that blocked maturity and led to an infantile subservience or an abdication of adult responsibilities. Our concern was matched by that of Mother and Sister Geraldine. It could equally be said that the last thing a community wants, or ought to have, is a lot of immature women who, far from having renounced their wills, have renounced their adulthood.

198

Thomas Merton saw the dangers and speaking of life as a struggle to seek the truth, he said:

> The work of understanding involves not only dialectic but a long labour of acceptance, obedience, liberty and love. The temptation of monastic life is to evade this austere responsibility by falling back into passive indifference, thinly veiled resentment disguised as obedience and abandonment . . . The worst temptation, and that to which many monks succumb early in their lives, and by which they remain defeated, is simply to give up asking and seeking. To leave everything to the Superiors in this life and God in the next – a hope which may in fact be a veiled despair, a refusal to live. Resignation is not enough. God demands of us creative consent, in our deepest and most hidden self . . .[8]

"I've still got some very big question marks about community life," I had said to Sister Harriet Ruth when she visited me on that occasion when I was languishing in bed feeling at rock bottom. I said it to her again later when she had become Mother. Even now she still teases me about those question marks and I realise that they were defence mechanisms as well as genuine questions, for I was still afraid that I would not be able to give my 'creative consent' to absolutely anything asked of me.

'Would I' – if I were professed – 'despite some unhealed areas of my life, be able to give an unconditional "Yes", no matter how uncongenial the work I was asked to do, or the place to which I was asked to go?'

These were of course question marks about myself rather than about the community.

'Would I?' I had asked myself. But how can one know? In a sense one can't, although one is given something of a dummy run during one's novitiate by being sent out to branch houses. And in this, at any rate, there had to be immediate consent – no arguments, no fuss.

In part, it tests a novice's ability to be moved from one house to another. Far more, it gives experience of community life within a smaller group. Usually one had a few weeks as a postulant in a branch house, and later, as a novice, two spells in other houses of roughly 6–9 months and 9–12 months.

As a postulant I was to go to one of our houses that we had at the time for mentally handicapped women, some physically handicapped as well. I was petrified. Never in my life had I come into contact with handicapped people as a group.

In retrospect it seems far longer than three and a half weeks, for so much experience was crammed into that time. I had set out fearfully quite sure that I would never be able to cope, little dreaming, during that journey down into the country, that I was about to be introduced to a whole new and very beautiful world.

As the car turned into the drive, the residents ran out to greet me, accepting me with such warmth and childlike trust, all fear was overcome and I loved them at once. Even though they seemed to point up my own difficulties in trusting rather sharply there was an immediate bond. They gave me far more than I was ever able to give to them. Their simplicity touched me deeply, so too did their contentment with their life. They were loving, responsive, devout and very natural.

For example, Jean was very angry with God because her adored brother (and only relative) had been killed in an accident. I came upon her one day in the chapel standing in front of a large crucifix, rating the figure on the Cross very soundly indeed, wagging her finger like an irate schoolmistress and externalising her anger very volubly. Maybe we wouldn't all express it in that way, but how many of us are as honest as that, and can be truthful before God when we are angry with him? Her honesty extended to human beings too. On one occasion she asked the sister in charge of the meal if she could have a second helping of pudding.

"No Jean," said the sister. "You know you can't. You are on a diet." Jean went back to her place muttering darkly.

After a while a smile spread over her face. She left her

seat again, walked over to the sister and said, "Sister, I do *love* you."

"You don't really, do you Jean?" asked the sister in a teasing voice.

"No," replied Jean. "But I'm trying."

Worship was something into which they entered very naturally and with great reverence. They came to Mass on festival days, and 'Diction' (as they were wont to call Benediction) on Fridays. We also went to the parish church where woe betide a preacher if he asked a rhetorical question, for he would get a ready answer. They were great pray-ers – faithful, natural and above all simple. Rosemary had speech difficulties and found it very hard to get her tongue round words. Nevertheless, when Judy was to be confirmed she wanted to add her prayers to the others being offered.

"Our Father . . . Judy . . . Amen," she prayed in an urgent and staccato way, straight to the point and completely comprehensive.

One day the chaplain was celebrating in our own chapel and as he moved along the row administering communion he reached Georgina. As he came to put the Host into her mouth she suddenly looked up and said in her gruff voice, "Does Jesus love me?"

"Yes, of course he does," whispered the chaplain hoping to satisfy her.

It didn't.

"How do you know?" she demanded even more audibly.

"I'll tell you afterwards," he said and, with great presence of mind, placed the wafer on her tongue before she could raise any more theological objections.

They were tremendous fun. They responded to music, drama, dance, and art work in such a lively way – it opened up for me a new range of possibilities in non-verbal communication.

Whitsun was coming and we acted out the story of Pentecost in mime and movement. They sang, they danced, they waved coloured scarves, and prayed . . . and, at a high point of dramatic piquancy, stopped and had an argument.

Those who couldn't move banged on percussion instruments. Everyone was involved in some way including the sisters, and I'm not sure that I have ever experienced anywhere else quite such a marvellous mixture of devotion, gaiety, reverence, fun and sheer enjoyment combined with deadly seriousness.

Yes – they certainly taught me a lot, and opened my eyes.

That was a superb introduction to branch house life. The sisters were kindness itself and were themselves such fun too. It seemed to be infectious. It was a place of great laughter, and, despite the inevitable tensions and frustrations, great peace . . . at least, so it seemed to me in my short stay there.

When the time came to leave, I felt very sad, and wished I were free to ask to come back. As I went to the dining room to wave goodbye to Georgina, Jean, Rosemary, Judy and all the others, they assured me that they would be praying for me. I was to be clothed two weeks later, and the knowledge that I should be upheld by their prayers, springing as they did from such holiness and purity of heart, was a tremendous encouragement.

That was the first test of 'going out' and God had filled it with rich things. Why should I fear again? Yet, I did.

In the second test, he was just as faithful, of course. I didn't return to the first house but went to another where we also had the care of mentally handicapped women. They were not quite so severely handicapped as the others, but, like them, they were loving, accepting, and very trusting. They took me to their hearts and I took them to mine. I loved them, loved the house, the garden and especially the chapel, loved the sisters, loved the devoted band of helpers who came in each day, loved the way in which we were able to share in local church life. It was a very happy and creative time.

My problem now was not whether or not I could adapt to branch house life, but whether I could throw myself wholeheartedly into the life and yet remain sufficiently detached. After all, in six months I should have to be uprooted to return to the convent. It was here that one of my greatest and most painful tests was thrown into sharp relief. For it meant the replaying of the tapes of a very unsettled and root-less early childhood. The question it raised was clear. Would the replay lead to healing of the memories, or would it prove too much? If I were to be elected to profession, would I be handicapped in this area?

In the meantime, I enjoyed life enormously. Many times I thought, 'If anyone had told me that one day I should be doing this kind of work – and loving it – I would have been astounded.'

Again, the residents were enormous fun. Sometimes their handicap made them violent or aggressive, but in the main they had a great capacity for spreading happiness and laughter wherever they went. They were well-known and loved in the town as they walked back and forth to their Day Centre, or went on their afternoon shopping expeditions. More than one driver stopping to let them cross the road must have been taken aback, perhaps with delight, to find himself rewarded by a deep curtsey from Betty in the middle of a zebra crossing.

There were the Sunday afternoon walks in the country, Sunday evening swimming parties (a local sports centre made the beginners' pool available to us) and then back to the invariable Sunday evening meal of boiled eggs and toast and one of the highlights of the week – a talking supper in the sisters' refectory. Conversation was always lively, discussion often heated. Always there was plenty of laughter.

We were a great mixture of ages ranging from a sister in her thirties to sisters in their eighties, but every one seemed young in heart. One sister of eighty-two began every day with a cold bath – winter and summer alike – and when we went walking together she strode out so eagerly I was always hard put to keep up with her. She ran the garden with another sister in her late eighties. The sacristan was also in her eighties, the infirmarian in her seventies. There were others in their middle years, but when a group of young Americans came to teach us something about sacred dance, they all joined in. That might sound ludicrous, but believe me, it was an inspiration. For body language doesn't lie, and what those older sisters were, and the years of devotion and prayer that had been the pivotal point of their lives, all came out in their movements. As the newest and rawest recruit to the life, it was humbling to be amongst these giants.

As I had foreseen, it was a great wrench to leave the house, but between them the residents and sisters had taught me invaluable lessons about the meaning of simplicity and trust, and the faithful, hidden, deep prayer which is the mainspring of our life together and the fruit of the love affair with God that the Religious Life is.

Twice then, so far, I had experienced unexpected joy and enrichment by doing what, in my ignorance, I would not have chosen to do. Twice I had gone out "not knowing whither . . ." and had received untold blessings.

Twice since then I have been sent to branch houses doing very different work. In both I have been extremely happy and have come away wiser and richer. Each time I have gone fearfully. Each time God has dealt with those fears. But I know there may be times, probably will be times, in the future when it will not only be hard to say the initial "Yes", but even harder to go on saying the daily "Yes". When the testing comes it will not be beyond what I am able – the Scriptures assure us of that. And I shall have behind me a great wealth of example upon which to draw – given me by those who have lived the life with such integrity and fidelity over many years.

The Psalmist said, "No good thing will he withhold from those that lead a godly (and, he might well have added, an obedient) life."[9]

Our Mother, speaking to the community, once reminded us that, "love is the fulfilling of the law," and added, "So we look for givenness, generosity, what used to be called being R.F.A., ready for anything, and there *are* sisters who R.F.A."

"Behold the handmaid of the Lord, be it unto me according to your Word,"[10] is the way Mary responded in obedience. Her words are worn on every community cross; they are repeated every day, several times a day.

I had learned much in my years in community, but I also brought with me an experience which God may well have been using to prepare the way for a vow of obedience.

For thirteen years as a younger person, I had belonged to a group that sought to lead a dedicated life of prayer and service, and I owe it an incalculable debt. We had regular weekly meetings and annual conferences and a quality of training to which we all look back with gratitude acknowledging it to be superb – both in Biblical teaching and in the fundamentals of Christian doctrine. Nobody could be a casual member of the group for it had a demanding discipline and Rule of Life and, as its motto, the words, "Ready to do whatsoever my Lord the King shall appoint."[11] The small badge given to us, in a special ceremony preceding a communion service, had a map of the world engraved on it, symbolising our readiness to go anywhere in the service of our Lord.

The real crunch came when one saw the other side of the badge – the 'hidden' part of that symbol of dedication. Engraved on the back was a cross, and on the arms of the cross the one word, "Whatsoever".

13

CHANGES

"For anyone joining our Community these days," Sister Geraldine said to us in one of her spiritual conferences, "it is a bit like jumping on a moving bus."

It was an apt description, for there was much that was already changing in our community as in all religious communities, and there were even more changes to come. Some of the Roman Catholic communities had undergone very radical, even drastic, changes as a result of Vatican II and its *aggiornamento* (up-dating of policy and practice). In some orders, habits disappeared, large institutional houses gave way to smaller groups, beliefs about authority and its exercise were re-assessed, and the Office revised, reduced – and translated into the vernacular.

The changes in Anglican communities were perhaps not so swift or obvious. Nevertheless there were noticeable developments, some almost forced upon communities by changing circumstances and reduced numbers. These changes were not an attempt to 'get with it' in the vain hope of being understood. But the Religious Life stands as a sign within the Church, and if it is hopelessly out of touch with contemporary needs both in the Church and in the world, then it becomes an ornament rather than a sign.

Some of the deeper changes affecting our life within C.S.M.V. did not impinge on us very directly in our earliest days in the novitiate. In an indirect way, they did. There

206

was an atmosphere of change, sometimes of unrest and uncertainty, which we could not help but pick up.

Along with many communities, our ratio of old to young sisters was changing. Time and again old sisters would engage us in conversation and in the course of it say, "Of course, it's all so different now. When I was in the Novitiate, there were forty novices. There were so many of us, we didn't often see our Novice Mistress – perhaps once every three or four weeks."

This kind of remark, made so often by so many sisters, hints at two of the areas of change.

It was true that in the earlier days of the community, there were many more novices. It would seem to be the historical pattern of most orders – small beginnings, then a boom period with aspirants flocking in, then a gradual recession. This had been true of C.S.M.V.

It stands to reason that the amount of work that could be undertaken by the girls of St Joseph's,* or by a veritable army of novices cannot be covered by half a dozen. Yet the convent building was just as large, and there were nearly the same number of mouths to feed. They were, on the whole, just older mouths. Whereas it had always been our custom to leave certain jobs to novices, now they had to be shared by sisters too. Some of the seniority pattern broke down therefore and the different division of labour brought novices and sisters into a closer working relationship and levelled out the old hierarchical systems.

This was good and healthy, but there was still need to reduce the workload if other developments, particularly in novitiate training, were to take place.

Various items of equipment were introduced to ease strains in the domestic scene. It was hard for some of the older sisters to accept mechanisation where work had always been done by hand, carefully and lovingly. But realism was essential. The infirmary wing was being reconstructed when I arrived at Wantage. New and up-to-date equipment was being installed so that the nursing could be

*(The reformatory for girls once housed at the convent in St Joseph's Wing.)

brought into line with more recent developments in the field of geriatric care. And also so that the reduced staff of nursing sisters could do a good job and still live the Religious Life with the same commitments to prayer and reading as any other sister.

The domestic work had to be done, and could be done, with the help of some machinery, thus reducing the time involved, and with the employment of secular staff. For at the same time as numbers in the Novitiate were becoming fewer, there was an increasing desire to give sisters more space. More space in a day, more space in the week, so that they shouldn't feel under continual pressure to fill every waking moment with work of some sort. When I had first arrived as an aspirant, and throughout my time as a postulant, we had worked every day. Now Sister Madeleine was encouraging sisters, at the convent at least, to try and get a half day a week away from their departments of work – a time when they could perhaps follow some hobby, do some study, or get out for a walk – and go to bed early. This was blissful. The simple break in routine made a half day seem far longer than it was in actual minutes and hours. It meant one could stop, relax, do nothing and not feel guilty. Mainly sisters used the time very profitably but it was entirely up to them how they spent it. Later, the half day became a whole day wherever it was possible or desirable. Not every sister can get a complete day away from her work. Much depends on the nature of it. But in normal circumstances it should be possible to build it in. For it was increasingly being recognised that perhaps one of our contributions in the contemporary world where so many are unemployed, or half employed, is an understanding of leisure and the right use of it.

Lest there should be any misunderstanding, however, let it be stressed that this did not mean a half-day holiday from the Religious Life – only from departmental work. For, there is a real sense in which the Religious is never off duty. Prayer, both corporate and individual, continues – not as a work to be done but as a life to be lived.

The old sisters, as they reminisced, continually made the

point that has been cited earlier. "There were so many of us, we didn't see our Novice Mistress very often."

Not only is the period of novitiate training considerably longer than it used to be in the days when those old sisters were novices, but there is perhaps a greater emphasis placed upon teaching and individual pastoral care – both of which require time. There have always been classes, but methods of teaching in community have changed along with the changes in education in the world. No longer would novices receive something in the nature of a weekly lecture to which they listened and took notes without the possibility of questions. Nowadays classes are more akin to seminars, or at any rate there is free participation in discussion. For us, it was certainly one of the ways by which we got to know each other – that mutual exchange in discussion, which, not infrequently, could be heated. At first, I felt somewhat isolated in classes and very conscious that I came from a different stable from most of the others. 'Did they really mean what they were saying?' I sometimes used to wonder. 'Or even *know* what they were saying? Or is it just the in-jargon?'

No. They knew all right. I was the odd man out and, at one point, grew quite nervous about contributing. I ventured to tell Camilla as we sat in the orchard one day. "Would it not be better if I just listened in silence on these occasions?" I asked her. "Oh no," she replied. "You may be more 'trad' than most of us, but we need people in the group who know what they believe and have firm Biblical roots. We look to you as a kind of rock that we can safely bash." I often felt more like a quivering jelly than a rock, but I could see what she meant.

Our education then in the novitiate was given formally through our classes in Biblical Studies, Liturgy, Roots and Origins of the Religious Life and the Spiritual Conferences which covered such subjects as the vows, silence, solitude, enclosure, prayer, penance, freedom, leisure etc.

Apart from the formal teaching, there was a great deal of incidental teaching and the most common channel for that came through our individual sessions with Sister Geraldine.

Usually we saw her each week, less often in especially busy periods, more often in times of personal crisis.

It was very different indeed from the pattern of the larger Novitiates, and not always easy for older sisters to understand. Some however reckoned that the traumas which they had faced after profession as they deepened in self-knowledge, were now being met head on by many during their novitiate, partly because the period of training was longer and adapted to individual needs, and partly because the pastoral help necessary to face this part of one's growth was more readily available with smaller numbers of novices. Added to which, novitiate training was benefitting greatly from modern psychological insights. There was a growing appreciation of the need not only for growth in the Religious Life but also of ordinary human development and maturity – and there can be no blue print for that. Growth is never forced, but the right conditions and encouragement are given for it. For although people come into community these days from a very unstable world, they often have great depth of insight about themselves and are ripe for pastoral help and direction.

Patterns of work were changing in the wider field of the community's life, too. In the early days of the resurgence of Religious Life in the Anglican Church (in the middle of the last century) there had been a great need for women to serve in educational, nursing, reform and social work in a way only made possible in those days by a habit or a Salvation Army uniform. Many coming into communities at the time did so because they were fired by the ideal not only of leading a life of prayer, but also of serving their fellow men. In the history of our community we have had schools, a Home Office reformatory, mother and baby homes, a rehabilitation centre for alcoholics and drug addicts, homes for the mentally handicapped, homes for the socially inadequate, homes for the elderly, as well as a variety of parish and mission works, in this country and overseas.

In more recent years two things have happened. The Welfare State has provided for some of these needs and it has seemed right to discontinue works rather than duplicate them. Then too, professional qualifications are required now in a way they were not years ago. For example, it is not now enough simply to hold a degree in order to teach. Yet, in the past, quite a number of sisters taught in our schools on the strength of their degrees, but without a teaching certificate. None in the community was specifically qualified in the care of the mentally handicapped, whereas training is now desirable if not essential. Hence, we have withdrawn from some of these active works (but by no means all of them) and closed some of the houses we once had. In place of them, smaller houses have been opened attached to cathedrals or engaged in team and neighbourhood ministries. The energies of sisters are being diverted to what seems to be the crying need of our day – the need for teaching on prayer and spirituality, on how to use silence to relax the body, on the place of the arts, movement and dance in worship. Sisters preach and teach, conduct 'quiet days' and retreats, speak at conferences, lead seminars and study groups, engage in healing, prayer therapy and counselling ministries, serve on a variety of diocesan and church committees, and assist regularly in parishes.

However, it is not only, or even chiefly, these avenues of service that bring enquiries to our doors, for nowadays it is perfectly possible for a Christian to be involved in social reform, care, counselling etc without necessarily joining a religious community. Indeed, it could be argued that there are state and church agencies far better qualified in these fields with resources and expertise beyond anything we could offer. So, it is not what communities do that is the pull to would-be aspirants. Increasingly, it would seem that they come seeking an experience of valid and genuine community and a life of disciplined, contemplative prayer, deeper than anything they may have known before. Not that such prayer is only to be found within the Religious Life, but for them (and here is where the personal sense of God's call and obedience to it is the absolute touchstone) it seems the most valid offering of their lives that they can make both to

God and to the world. They believe that by responding to God's call to follow him along this mysterious path, they will mature into the "measure of the stature of the fulness of Christ."[1] In current terminology, he or she wants to 'be' – to be as God intended him to be before the Fall when he began to acquire all his masks, his illusions, his protective 'fig leaves' . . . when he ceased to be the Proper Man. Here, in community life, he believes he will discover the truth about himself and his world and hopes to live in that truth in simplicity and joy. The pathway to it will, of course, be through suffering. He is under no illusions about that. But none of us can know in advance the ways in which we shall be touched by it, nor the depths of pain we shall be asked to plumb. It is part of the mercy of God that we don't. Chiefly it is a search for God in restored simplicity and 'free speech' as the early fathers used to express it. At Eden that free speech ($\pi\alpha\rho\rho\eta\sigma\iota\alpha$) – the unbroken, unhindered, perfect communion with God – was destroyed by man's disobedience which led him into falsity and shame, whereas, previously, he had stood before God in the simple, unashamed nakedness of his being, now he needed to hide behind masks.

That free speech, translated in the New Testament as "boldness"[2] to approach God, is offered back to us through Christ, through the new and living way he has opened to us. However, such perfect communion can only be restored if we are real and free from the need to posture, play-act and cover up. Hence the man who is truly seeking God will most surely find him, and will also find himself in the process.

Besides the possible change in the expectations of aspirants, there were more practical changes taking place at the convent. Never shall I forget the day when I walked into my cell and found a blue, seersucker counterpane on my bed. It gave me a great shock, and somehow, looked out of place. It was a pretty pastel blue but, believe it or not, I quite resented its presence.

'Oh well,' I thought, 'I suppose my white bedspread has gone to be laundered. It will reappear in a few days.'

I missed it. That white spread with its large red cross had

212

come to mean a great deal to me. It was an inescapable visual reminder of the close links between sleep and death, dying and rising. I blushed to think how I had blurted out to Mother Candida at the end of my first week at the convent that it was "like sleeping in an ambulance, with those things on our beds."

I waited, but it did not reappear. After nearly a week, I marched in to Sister Geraldine and demanded to know what had happened to them. She roared with laughter. "I have been wondering when you would react," she said, remembering my initial horror.

"Aren't we ever going to get them back?" I pleaded.

"No, I don't think you will see them again," she replied. "I believe Sister Madeleine has replaced them all with these lighter bedspreads that can be washed more easily."

I walked away slowly. It made sense, and yet I felt a great pang of regret that such a rich symbol had been sacrificed.

The more surprising thing about all this, of course, was the realisation that quite imperceptibly I had changed. This was far more significant than the bedspreads. I, who had reacted violently against the austerity and seeming ugliness of my cell on that first night, was now upset at the introduction of coloured, washable bedspreads.

The bedspreads were as nothing compared with the next bombshell. The Novitiate was to move! Our novitiate room and study with our own cloister into chapel and beautiful little secluded garden had, for generations, been the novitiate enclosure. We even had our own entrance and cloakroom. Sisters didn't come into this enclosure without invitation or permission. It enabled novices to let off steam from time to time without disrupting the peace of the convent. It helped them to grow together as a group. It also meant a degree of separation from the professed sisters. But with the smaller numbers in the novitiate now we found ourselves with two very large rooms to be shared between a dozen or less people.

Now it was to change – not just because the amount of space we had was disproportionate to the size of the group, but because there were to be structural changes throughout the convent. If the buildings were not to fall down around our ears there was much that needed doing on the outside, and in order to meet with present day fire regulations there were going to have to be major changes inside. As soon as the infirmary wing was completed, another wing would be tackled, and then another . . . There lay ahead of us years of noise, dust, re-routing, knocking down walls here, opening up doorways there. The builders, decorators, plumbers, carpenters and joiners were to be with us for an indefinite length of time, it seemed; but they were marvellous. They bore with our strange ways, respected our silence (never did we have to endure transistors by the hour) and were models of cheerfulness and patience.

The old wooden floorboards in our cells, so beautifully polished and lovingly cared for over years, also constituted a considerable fire hazard and were replaced by industrial felt – quick to hoover and durable enough to outlast the life times of any of us in the present community. Dark brown paintwork was replaced by white; fire doors appeared, dark cupboards disappeared. More adequate washing facilities were installed.

It began to look rather posh . . . or so it seemed to some. There was disquiet. Were we becoming too comfortable and plush? Was this in keeping with the vow of poverty?

Many of the changes had been forced upon us by law. But in other cases they were the result of the building committee's attempts to cut down our expenditure, to make labour-saving economies which would reduce wages, time-saving measures which would enable sisters to live humanly instead of like drudges, and sensible conservation of human and electrical energy. It was austerity in a new guise. All of which was important if another vision was to be implemented.

Plans were afoot to convert the west wing into a guest wing. The rooms would be enlarged or adapted for visitors to make retreats, or spend periods of rest. It would have its own quiet room and sitting room, alcoves for reading and utility rooms for getting breakfasts, teas and occasional drinks. In this way whole groups wanting to confer, or retreat together, could be accommodated whilst the life of the convent continued as usual.

With all these changes going on around us, the real test for many was, "How far were our disciplines based upon the externals, and how far were they inward and authentic? To what extent would our inner structures be rocked by outward changes?"

When the Novitiate moved to a new part of the convent, we ceased to be separate and enclosed. We no longer had our own study room, but now shared the sisters' library. We lost our novices' cloakroom and entrance. Gone was our own separate cloister. We went into the sisters' community room far more frequently and shared their facilities. The change came about by accident perhaps, more than by design, but the result was a far greater mingling of sisters and novices, and an easier and more natural exchange between one another. We still had our own room which served as a bolt-hole and a venue for classes, but gradually we were being absorbed into the larger community which was a great enrichment – to us, anyway, but I believe for the sisters too.

Still the changes continued in the buildings and each week a new hole or door would appear, a familiar landmark would disappear. It was hard on the old sisters who tended to become confused, and sisters from branch houses sometimes had to ask the way around their own home.

Even so, such changes did not affect us as greatly as the changes in the community life itself. People came. People left. Sisters died. Chaplains changed. Postulants were clothed and novices professed.

Now Mother Candida was to retire. It was not a total shock for she was midway through her second term of office and had been far from well after one of her visitations to our Indian province. The community places a huge burden of responsibility on its Reverend Mother General which inevitably takes its toll in nervous, mental and physical energy. Mother Candida felt the time had come to hand over the reins to another, possibly younger, sister.

I had just gone to my first branch house when the

215

announcement was made. All the machinery for the election of a new Mother General began to be put in motion but, as novices are not members of Chapter, we did not have any part in the nominating, nor in the two rounds of voting that take place before the final election is made. It is a long business, for enough time has to be allowed for voting papers to travel to and from the Indian and African provinces and, in all, there is a triple traffic of these.

Throughout these waiting months, I had no idea what was happening. I don't think the sisters in my house talked of it much – certainly not in my presence. I had the feeling there was a great deal of praying being done, a lot of waiting upon God. Finally I wrote a somewhat desperate letter to Sister Geraldine. "I can't stand the uncertainty," I wrote. "Are you free to tell me anything of what is happening?"

Greatly surprised, she wrote back saying she had assumed I had been kept informed from my end. She herself had certainly kept the novices up to date with news. In actual fact, it was full marks to the sisters at my branch house for their discretion.

The final vote was taken. In a matter of days we received the result. Sister Harriet Ruth had been elected our new Mother.

As Mother Candida's Assistant she had become very well known and loved so it was not a surprising decision. I rejoiced that our new Mother was someone I had already found I could talk to very easily, who had on several occasions listened to my outpourings and given wise advice and counsel. I still had vivid memories of her kindness to me when I was ill. As novices, she had taken our singing classes, so there had been ample opportunity to discover her tremendous sense of humour, and the way she valued everybody's contribution no matter how inadequate it might seem to them to be. We also knew the top priority she placed on obedience.

'What changes will there be under our new Mother?' we wondered. There were, of course, no immediate and radical changes. She was far too wise for that. In theory, when one Mother retires all her 'appointments' go into liquida-

216

tion with her – ie the Assistant General, all the Superiors of the houses, the Novice Mistress, Oblates' Mistress, Associates' Mistress, Infirmarian etc officially cease to hold those positions. In this case, the only immediate change that had to take place was in the position of Assistant General now left vacant by Sister Harriet Ruth's election. Mother chose Sister Andrea.

The day of the Installation Mass dawned. During the course of this Mass, the new Mother makes promises in response to questions put to her by the Bishop and is then conducted to her stall – easily recognised by its large shepherd's crook, made for one of our former Mothers by a Berkshire shepherd. At the end of the Mass, the community comes one by one to stand before their new Mother and, placing their hands between hers, each one promises obedience. It is one of those ancient customs still observed by many communities, and I am thankful that at least that is one which has not changed in ours.

We waited. Life continued much as usual. We assumed that Mother had re-appointed those whom Mother Candida had left in positions of responsibility. Not that I think any of us had expected a general post in the first week.

The weeks went by and stretched into months. Mother seemed to be listening carefully to what people were saying, her finger well and truly on the pulse of the community's life.

In the meantime, more parts of the building vanished, or new rooms appeared. More upheavals occurred every week, more dirt, dust and noise. A hymn from my school days often came to mind, "Everything changes but God changes not . . ."

One day after Vespers, Mother called the Novitiate together and told us that she was asking Sister Geraldine to become Superior of our house in London.

"Sister has done five years as Novice Mistress," said Mother, "and that's a long stint for anyone in such a demanding office. She has given herself unsparingly to you all and now it is time we gave her a little rest from it and used her gifts in another house. Of course this will be a great shock to you, and it will be hard to adjust to a new situation. I am asking Sister Freda to take over as Novice Mistress, but not immediately. Sister Geraldine will still be with you for a few more months. However, I need to tell the community tomorrow, so I felt it right that you should know first."

We were, of course, stunned by the unexpectedness of the announcement. None of us could find anything to say – not that it was necessary anyway. Mother made one or two more remarks and then rose to leave. She was gentle but very business-like. It was obvious that we were upset by the news but, as she so rightly said as she moved to the door, "Remember, you came to community for God, not Sister Geraldine."

I found it very hard to face the fact that Sister Geraldine, who had stood alongside me in all those early days of trauma, who had been guru, mentor and guide introducing me to untold treasures within the Office and liturgy, was not to see me through to profession. She had been an anchor in some very stormy seas; she had fostered my vocation, trying to give it the right conditions for growth and I had come to trust her.

It was not that Sister Freda might not be able to do all these things superbly – but we didn't know her. Most of us had met her only very briefly during a furlough stay at the convent.

How selfish can one get? My first thoughts were not of how exhausted Sister Geraldine must be after five years in this exacting role. Nor was I giving much thought to the needs of the London house. I was struggling with a most acute disappointment. Sister Geraldine was not going to be there for my last lap in the novitiate.

Yet, Sister Geraldine would have been the first to endorse what Mother had said. We were in the community for God, not for any human being or groups of human beings, however supportive they might be and however dearly we might love them. Here we were, facing perhaps the toughest test of detachment a novice can face. There are very few sisters in the community who have not known

218

this experience from the inside. Most have had one or more changes of Novice Mistress. One learns to trust, but then one has to learn to let go – not of course of the relationship, but of any element of clinging in it.

At least we had a little while left to adjust to the news and possibly round off any unfinished agenda begun with Sister Geraldine. I felt very sorry for those novices in branch houses. But typically, Mother had written personally to each of them, and Sister Geraldine had added a note of her own.

More fire doors appeared; more familiar sights vanished. Two branch houses closed, one moved from Surrey to Hertfordshire, two houses opened.

It had been one of the precepts of our Founder, that the community should be ready to undertake whatever work seemed urgent at any given time in its history. "Whatsoever he saith unto you, do it,"[3] Mary had said to the servants of Cana, and we applied the words to our own life. Our vision for a guest wing in the convent was now reality. A stream of visitors seeking refreshment, teaching on prayer, and spiritual replenishment started to pour in. Parish and Diocesan groups arrived for retreats and conferences. Oblates and Associates came for their study weeks, social weekends and retreats, and we were now able to get to know many more of them, appreciate their tremendous contribution to the life of the community and value them as members of it.

Poor Sister Andrea couldn't hope to meet the flood of requests that poured in for sisters to preach, speak and conduct quiet days. She had her work cut out to deploy the forces as best she could but it was and is impossible to say "Yes" to every one. More than ever we became conscious of the insatiable spiritual hunger that there is today (and not only in the Church) for teaching in the field of prayer and spirituality. I guess there has always been a need, but has it ever been more pressing? Throughout the history of monasticism people have looked to religious communities as resource centres, places of teaching, healing and spiritual direction.

From the ever growing number of calls upon us it was

evident that this was still so – that people continued to look in our direction for such a ministry. Yet, before any form of service, they want to know that we are people of prayer.

A young priest working in a tough and difficult parish told me that he always wore his cassock as he moved about the city, "And I don't find it puts people off," he said. "If anything it makes for quick identification and easy contacts." It didn't stop him having a drink with the men in the pub. "But," he added, "they don't appreciate me simply because of that. In a curious way, they want to know, even those who do not claim to be Christians, that they have a man of God in their midst who gets down on his knees and prays."

In whatever way the outward service of our community might change according to the needs of the day, we could be sure that the one thing that would be unchanging, as long as we existed as a religious community, would be the primary place of prayer. There might come liturgical changes and revision of the Office, new translations of the Psalter and different tables of readings but the chief work would still be prayer – faithful, persistent and unceasing. That is our only justification.

Sometimes on entering chapel, I would be filled with awe, 'This is where it all happens,' I would think. 'This is the nerve centre,' and would be reminded of the way Fr Hugh Benson pictures a saintly nun, in the eyes of the world unimportant and unknown, praying in a convent chapel. Yet from that obscure chapel are radiating currents of spiritual power which have influence far beyond the chapel walls.

This black figure knelt at the centre of reality and force and with movements of her will and lips controlled spiritual destinies for eternity. There ran out from this peaceful Chapel lines of spiritual power that lost themselves in the distance, bewildering in their profusion and terrible in the intensity of their hidden power.[4]

This is the vital network in which we are all caught up – those on the threshold of the life, and those bed-ridden on the infirmary wing, those on the frontiers of spiritual warfare through their vocation to the solitary life, and those (like most of our Oblates) in the thick of things in secular life. From that one centre flow out many and changing ministries; that stability makes possible the flexibility and adaptability to meet the changing demands made upon us as a community.

We might indeed be "jumping on to a moving bus," as Sister Geraldine had put it, but it was going in a very hopeful and exciting direction.

14

TO BE OR NOT TO BE?

It was one thing I had not expected to face, once in the habit. Yet, even before I opened it, I think I knew what the bulky envelope contained. As I slit it open I told myself not to be so absurdly imaginative – yet my feminine instincts were right.

As students we had been very good friends, meeting regularly at lectures and working together on intercollegiate committees. I had admired and loved him – but we were not in love. He was engaged to a charming doctor, and when our respective courses ended I left for Zaire and he married. Neither of us had been in touch since, until the day when he phoned – right out of the blue.

He had gone to considerable trouble to track me down for he was as ignorant of my present whereabouts as I was of his. The last place he had thought to find me was in a convent.

Could he come and discuss a project on which he was working, he asked. He needed to co-opt one or two more people into a working party. Mother and Sister Geraldine agreed and so he travelled down to Wantage to thrash out ideas and draft details.

It was one of those friendships where the passing of years makes little difference. One picks up almost as though there has been no break in the contact. I met him at the station – he hadn't changed all that much outwardly. Immediately there was the same ease we had always known, the same freedom to be ourselves.

I had gleaned occasional snippets of news via mutual

friends over the course of the years, but I had not known, and could not have guessed, that his life had been touched by tragedy when his wife had been killed in an accident, and that for several years he had been a widower struggling to bring up a young family. I was stunned as he told me about it. In fact, I found it so distressing I was glad we were not going to start work immediately.

Getting down to the project was just like old times with the same friendly working basis. When it was completed he left, and I assumed that was that. Having parted, our ways might not cross again for a very long time . . . if ever. But once he had gone, I began to wonder. Instinctively I knew that something had changed in our relationship, but the work had been so absorbing that I hadn't been consciously aware of it at the time. Now, however, the red light warning signals were flashing, for I had to confess that my own inner turmoil was more than deep compassion for his own terrible loss.

He phoned several times and suggested coming to stay again, but I firmly discouraged that. Feeling that I might even yet be having no more than a romantic fantasy trip, I went to Sister Geraldine, and, in acute embarrassment, laid my cards on the table. All along it had been my policy to be as open as possible with her and my superiors. How else would they be able to discern whether or not I had a vocation?

I told her how matters stood but added, "Even if his affections have been awakened, he is hardly likely to make them known to me as a novice of a religious community."

But he did. And now I had proof of how he felt, for he was asking me to marry him.

I pocketed the bulging envelope and, feeling rather like Hezekiah, went to chapel to "spread it before the Lord".[1]

Naturally he had asked that we should meet again and have time to get to know more of each other 'as we are now'.

Sister Geraldine explained carefully why that wasn't on.

"But, unless we can meet, it's a bit like shadow boxing," he wrote, when I told him.

It was a desperate situation, and I felt completely torn

right down the middle. I realised that if I wanted to be free to explore the possibility of marriage I should have to leave the community – I couldn't be testing two vocations at once. The choice then was either to stay put and turn down the proposal, or leave and take the marriage path.

The worst part of the next few weeks was the utter loneliness. No one could choose for me. I had written and asked him to give me time to consider my answer. The decision could only be mine, and even any advice or discussion would have been inappropriate. Only Sister Geraldine, Mother and Sister Andrea knew what I was facing, but obviously none of them wanted to influence my decision. The space I was given whilst I worked things out felt horribly like withdrawal at a moment of need. Yet there was no other way.

Whatever I decided, it would require a step of very great faith with no guarantees or certainties as yet. If I left, there was the possibility that it wouldn't after all be right to marry. We might both have changed too much, and might not be able to cope with the adaptation it would need.

On the other hand, if I continued to test my vocation in the novitiate there was absolutely no guarantee at all at this point (indeed at times there seemed very little likelihood) that I should eventually be elected to make my profession in the community and take life vows. I was still inclined to believe that my feebleness in domestic matters would actually mean curtains for me as a sister. So many times I had mused rather bitterly on the fact that there seemed little room for those of artistic temperament or academic training in the Religious Life.

In that I was completely wrong. I look round now and see sisters who are bursting with artistic and creative energy as well as scholarly wisdom. But that was how it seemed to me then, and it was against that backcloth of uncertainty that I had to make my decision.

I may have done some crazy things in the past, but I have never been a gambler. Now it appeared that I was about to take the biggest gamble of my life.

It was, of course, scarcely a gamble. With the three

sisters who shared my secret praying with me that the Holy Spirit would guide, one could hardly liken it to a game of chance – even if it felt, for the time being, like groping in the dark.

I tried to switch off from thinking about it, consciously at any rate. The strain was affecting my work and I had come in for some sharp rebukes, made all the harder to bear because I couldn't explain why I was all in pieces and miserable.

My world suddenly seemed to have turned upside down. It had a kind of *Alice in Wonderland* quality about it. Why was it that now, of all times, all the things I had once longed for – love, a home, security, children . . . yes, and perhaps even a dog again, were being offered to me?

Time dragged on and I knew I must give an answer. It was cruel to keep him waiting. My love for him was not in question but I still wasn't sure if it was God's will for me to withdraw from the novitiate. Never had a Lent been more dark or penitential.

It was at Terce one day that my answer became clear. There was nothing spectacular about the Office itself that day, but in our psalm cycle, we happened to come to psalm 73. When we reached the twenty-fifth verse, I knew which way the decision would go.

"Whom have I in heaven but thee?" we sang,
"And there is none upon earth
that I desire in comparison with thee."

That moment brought to an end my agonising.

"There is none on earth that I desire in comparison with thee . . ." I got no further. The choir continued singing the psalm.

Tears streamed down my face, and, in the silence of my heart, my desires folded back into 'one pleat'.

"Lord I would follow you with an undivided heart . . ." I prayed. The light was still beckoning me on.

Marriage was not, after all, to be my vocation. God calls some to love him, serve him, give themselves wholly to him through loving union with a marriage partner. He asks of others a more solitary path that enables them to love more widely, to be more available. I was to be wife and mother to none in order to be a sister to all.

The time had come to go to my next branch house. This would be for a longer spell than before – for about a year. It was a particularly poignant stage in my novitiate life for, in leaving for Oxford, where I was to be sent, I would be saying "Goodbye" to Sister Geraldine. The "few more months" that Mother had spoken of, when she broke the news to us about the change of Novice Mistress, were nearly up, and in four weeks' time, Sister Geraldine would herself be taking up new work as Superior of a branch house. How thankful I was, however, that she had still been my Novice Mistress as I had faced the particular choice of marriage or the Religious Life. It was not that I doubted that Sister Freda would be most loving and understanding, but I simply didn't know her. It had been painful enough to share it all with someone who knew me well and whom I had come to love and trust. It would have been infinitely harder with almost a complete stranger.

I shall never forget my last morning before leaving for Oxford. It turned out to be a brilliantly sunny day, crisp and bracing but warm in the sunshine. There had been one of those unseasonable falls of snow that sometimes come in the spring.

"What are you doing now?" said Sister Geraldine coming into the novitiate halfway through the morning. Typically I was catching up with last minute letters, but nothing really urgent.

"Let's go for a walk," she said.

Off we went to walk by the river with its flotilla of Canada geese, and enjoy the spring flowers bravely opening out to the sun despite the snow. Everything sparkled and looked extra beautiful. Frost-lined cobwebs gave an ethereal quality to the countryside. We walked briskly and reminisced happily. Despite all the trauma of my training so far, there had been a very great deal of joy too and much cause for thanksgiving. Dag Hammarskjold's words best express what was uppermost in our minds that morning. "For all that has been – Thanks! To all that shall be – Yes."[2]

On the way back we stopped to say goodbye to an engaging and sociable horse who loved passers-by to talk to him. I think he considered every sister his friend. As I stroked his nose, Sister Geraldine drew from her pocket two sugar lumps (wrapped in British Airways wrappings). "I thought you might like to give him these," she said, looking so guilty that it might have been cannabis she had smuggled out of the airport. "I saved them from my coffee when we went to meet Sister Beryl at the airport."

Our friendly horse crunched them eagerly, and I was very touched at Sister Geraldine's thought. Such a simple thing really, and yet, to be revelling in the beauty of nature together and even sharing my passion for animals seemed a very tender and fitting way to be ending our time together as novice and Novice Mistress.

We laughed and chatted gaily all the way back to the convent and when, after dinner, I was driven off, it was not with tears and sadness, but with a curious joy – that the work which we had begun together, God had allowed us to finish, and now a new chapter was about to start.

"I hope you cycle," Sister Caroline, my new Superior, said when I arrived. "You really need a bicycle around Oxford."

As in my other branch houses, I was very happy at this new one. It took a while to adjust to the new routine, and after twenty years on four wheels, I was pretty wobbly on the bicycle at first. But I soon got the victory.

I was at home in more ways than one. To begin with, I was back in the kitchen. By this time I was becoming fairly familiar with the cooking scene. Getting meals for fifteen was less taxing than cooking for eighty or ninety, and I greatly enjoyed the challenge of getting the 'whole' meal on the table and seeing the operation through from start to finish, ie doing the shopping, planning and cooking both courses, and having them dished up and ready to serve by the time the bell went for Sext. Sometimes it was a case of 'beat the clock' but mainly it was a smooth routine, with plenty of silence . . . and, I have to confess, I enjoyed working on my own.

"There are a number of contacts we should like you to follow up, and things we thought you could take on," said Sister Caroline, and soon I found myself out and about meeting some of the college chaplains and joining in the work of some of the Christian societies in Oxford.

There were our own students at the house, too, for we had fourteen living with us. It was important to get to know them, and to receive the visitors who came regularly to our Sunday teas and often during the week too. After all the careful protection that I had had from too many visitors and distractions, here I was, exposed to them on all sides. This then was the test as to whether or not the years of seclusion at the convent had produced the right kind of inner discipline and enclosure.

Time seemed to pass very quickly with days that brought a very mixed diet of shopping, cooking, chaplains' groups, student meetings, workshops and speaking engagements . . . and yet there was much space and time for prayer. There were all the beauties of nature to nourish contemplation – the parks and Port Meadow for walks, squirrels in the garden and nightingales on the Banbury road.

Interesting places to see, and interesting people to meet, reading in the Bodleian, worshipping at the University church, weekly meetings in one of the colleges, chapel flowers to be arranged, and yet, with all that, perhaps because of all that, I grew more and more lonely. I missed my fellow novices. I missed Sister Geraldine. I missed the convent. It was however, far more than merely missing the presence of people. God was, I think, providing opportunities for learning how to convert loneliness into solitude.

There is something of a paradox in branch house life. In one sense, being a smaller group of seven sisters, we were thrown together more closely than in the larger convent group. But in another sense, simply because we were a small group, we had to stand apart.

Stand together yet not too near together,
For the pillars of the temple stand apart,

And the oak tree and the cypress,
Grow not in each other's shadow[3]
They could aptly apply to our life.

The need for a right reticence and solitude of heart had often been stressed in novitiate conferences.

"Don't be so eager to share that your inner strength becomes dissipated," warned Sister Geraldine.

Just as there is a need to guard one's own enclosure, so there is great need to respect the alone-ness and privacy of another. Life in this smaller group might be a way to greater alone-ness, but it came, at times, in the guise of loneliness. Nevertheless, it was a growing point and certainly something to have to face before making any final decision about profession.

> The mystery of love is that it protects and respects the alone-ness of the other and creates the free space where he can convert his loneliness into a solitude that can be shared. In this solitude we can strengthen each other by mutual respect, by careful consideration of each other's individuality, by an obedient distance from each other's privacy and by a reverent understanding of the sacredness of the human heart.[4]

How often have we not given thanks to God, in community – especially as novices – for the discretion of our sisters; the questions that are not asked, the eyes that don't pry or search the face for emotional weather forecasts, the distance that is kept – not because they don't care, but because they care enough.

Life at our Oxford house had taken me back to a similar world to the one I had left three and a half years before. Yet it was different. Now I was in it but not of it. I was a fringe member of this society.

Two things happened. I found I entered it from a different standpoint, and learned to do so without pain. It didn't awaken longings for the past – in fact, there seemed to be a considerable degree of freedom and certainly of enjoyment. As the months went by I was able to analyse this new freedom. It had to do with what I can only describe as the anonymity of our life. I was 'out there' on those particular frontiers of student life, not as one with a professional reputation to uphold, not in a competitive situation, not looking for promotion or success, but in a habit, in a new role that didn't link me to any past, and above all, as a representative of our community. The arm of the community reaches out into many areas of the world's life and I was just part of a fingernail on the end of one of its fingers. Increasingly I became aware of that arm – that continual link with the rest of the body of the community. Almost without realising it, I was discovering where my roots now were. The seedling had begun to take.

Some of us from the house happened to be the people who were called to be out front quite a lot, but behind us and holding us at home were our older sisters, not quite so able to get out and about. They faithfully backed our endeavours with their prayers. And what generous and loving support it was. Concern and care were shown before any venture; interest, sympathy and rejoicing afterwards. That the support was sometimes given at cost was very clear to me, and I often wondered if I could, or would, have matched their graciousness, had the roles been reversed.

One of the University chaplains asked me one day, "Are you really planning to take final vows?"

"I wish I knew," I said. "I still don't feel certain, and I have yet to be elected by the community."

It was strange that there was still uncertainty after having had to face the decision whether to stay or leave several times, and each time resolving to carry on. Each time I was haunted by the thought that if I gave up, I might in fact be turning my back on the pearl of great price. Something, or Someone, was still drawing me on down that tunnel.

Even so, I was waking up regularly in a cold sweat of fear because I couldn't bring myself to the point of commitment by asking to be professed.

"Would you consider working in the University chaplaincy?" he asked. "We need more women to help with pastoral and counselling work. You would have far greater freedom here if you were not tied to the structures of your Religious Life."

I think that suggestion pointed up a truth of which I had been only dimly aware. "Far greater freedom," he had said. How mistaken. Of course, I could have had a far more flexible timetable, probably sitting up till all hours drinking coffee and discussing. I could have had my own home from which to operate, and possibly the few for whom the habit is rather inhibiting would have accepted me more readily in secular clothes. I seriously think the numbers of students feeling that way would have been few, for in the main people find a safety in the habit. It makes a clear statement about one's position and priorities, and people know where they are. It also gives a confidence that there will be a seal on anything shared. But, "far greater freedom". No! I personally would not have been anything like so free. It was the strength of the corporate, disciplined life of prayer that made possible the public ministry. There was the knowledge that when meetings or other engagements required one or more of us to miss an Office, the rest of the community in that house said it for us and held us in their prayers. There was the nourishment of personal prayer and solitude, and the submission involved in communal living where one's own desires and idiosyncracies are sandpapered, tempered and tried by the rest of the group.

As a Religious, I could be made available by my community, or withdrawn, from any sphere of service, at any time. Hence the need to sit loose to any particular work. I knew I was only at Oxford for about a year, so the dangers of getting too attached to the life there were not as great as they might have been had there been no *terminus ad quem*. Even though, when the time came to leave, it was a wrench and I was sad to go, I think I can honestly say that it remained a free-floating life – that is to say, there was a freedom to come and go, to be needed or not needed without worrying about it, and liberty from the awful bondage of having to make a good impression. For the service given was that of C.S.M.V. and not of an individual sister.

231

This was a searching but very good and necessary test. I had been back, as it were, to the life where more than anywhere I might have rushed to put on old masks. And yet, in truth, God was continuing his work of 'skinning', often very painfully but not without wise support from those more advanced in the Religious Life.

The second significant thing that happened again concerned my older sisters. By the latter part of my time at Oxford we were a group of six. Three of us in particular were actively engaged in work in and around Oxford. The other three had some outside contacts but more usually were at home. They were superb at looking after guests and talking to our students, and maintained a steady continuity and rhythm in the house.

We all met together at recreation each day, and once a week we spent a longer period in community discussion. Little did those sisters realise at the time that those sessions were to be one of my chief clues about my vocation. In the old days of community life there had been the Chapter of Faults, when sisters admitted to failures and breaches of the Rule. Our discussions, at Oxford, were a replacement or extension of that old Chapter. We were not concerned so much about more trivial and minor defects but about matters of personal relationships in our life together.

To me it was a revelation that we could reach such depths of open-ness and honesty, that sisters could be so free to "speak the truth in love", that we could be completely real with one another and air the things that were dragging us down as a group or fracturing our corporate life. We gave ourselves an hour for these discussions and nearly always needed it in full. All this was very often costly – especially for those sisters who had not grown up in a generation used to this kind of sharing.

It was, for me at any rate, an immensely healing thing. I was but a novice, yet no one put limits on my freedom to share in the group. I spoke with a liberty equal to that of any professed sister. We sometimes touched on deep and painful areas, sometimes we attacked one another (verbally), we apologised, we confessed to fears and failings, we shared joys, and dared even to reveal our insecurities. Often one felt desperately exposed and vulnerable, but I never left those meetings without a deep sense of acceptance and love.

Somehow, although very costly, it seemed to make for far greater reality in our relationships when sins that affected the whole group were not only confessed privately but, if we wished, publicly before that same group. If it took a lot of courage to do this, as indeed it did, it was worth it just to know the wonder of being brought into the arena of forgiveness, acceptance and love that was incarnated through one's sisters.

Usually by the time our discussion ended, the period of afternoon silence would be beginning. Frequently a group of us would return to the kitchen to finish any clearing up and prepare for the next meal, working alongside one another in a deep, harmonious silence. The love between us on those occasions would be almost tangible.

We were by no means a perfect society, and the students who lived with us were well aware of it. We sometimes irritated one another, were thoughtless towards each other, inconvenienced one another, and indeed had flaming rows. But underneath the occasional surface turbulence, we loved one another, forebore with one another and forgave one another. That is what redeemed the situation.

All through my novitiate I had known the pull to prayer, and equally all the way through I had had doubts as to whether I could live out that life of prayer in community. That had been one of those 'question marks'. Throughout those years I had seen great holiness in different sisters, received much love and understanding, but the awful niggling doubt was whether or not my longing and seeking for God was to include, or be conducted through, a lifelong commitment to a community.

This had been the last conscious block and now, by the love and witness of this group of sisters, it was being removed. My commitment to this group, this very imperfect group, was of such depth that I needed no further proof.

People spoke of the peace they found in our house. Few

could have guessed at the hard work which lay behind it, the underlying stresses and strains out of which that peace grew.

That, to me, was the hopeful sign that a religious community (like a happy family) can be to the world. Here were ordinary, fallible human beings creating peace not by avoiding rows but by working through them, not by fitting in to a perfect mould but by being themselves and loving, forgiving and accepting themselves and one another.

Sister Freda had been installed as the new Novice Mistress for nearly nine months now, and it was time for her to visit my branch house. It is customary for a Novice Mistress to see the novice *in situ* towards the end of her period at a branch house.

I told her how much I felt I belonged to the group of sisters at Oxford, how I loved being with them and what a lot they had taught me. Why I couldn't be more clear cut and certain about my choice at that point, I don't know. In retrospect, I am ashamed that I continued to dally and hold back for so long.

"I'm still not sure about profession," I told her. Maybe, by that time, I had become so accustomed to sitting on the fence, I couldn't bring myself to jump off.

"Don't worry," Sister Freda said, not seeming particularly concerned by my indecision. "I expect you'll wake up one morning and just know the answer."

I doubted it. It couldn't be that simple, I was quite sure.

We sat by the river and talked for a long time. Although we had written to one another, we had met only twice before, and I was amazed how freely I was able to talk.

She was right – in the end, it was that simple. Yet behind the simple resolution lay this deeply moving, searching and demanding experience of the corporate life.

I often look round now at the older sisters who have meant so much to me and surprise myself at the depth of love I feel for each one. But always there is a very tender and special love for those sisters who were in that group with me at Oxford, especially in those crucial final months. They will probably never know just how instrumental they were, under God, in helping me to say my final "Yes".

15

WHAT DO YOU DESIRE?

Exactly twelve months from the day of arriving at Oxford, I made my final decision. Time was running out. I had asked for an extension of my stay at the house, and it had been refused. I was due back at the convent in a week or two, and still I was waking up at night sweating with fear. Somehow, it seemed that God was putting on the pressure to get me off that fence on which I persisted in sitting, and to do so before I left Oxford.

Again the turning point came at Terce . . . or rather in the silence after Terce. A large crucifix hung down in front of a full length, floor-to-ceiling, frosted-glass window behind the altar. I gazed up at the figure on the Cross, silhouetted against the light. I had often gazed in this way before, for something in the line of that figure with its combination of tension, intense suffering, relaxation and submission, moved me deeply. On this occasion, however, it did more than move me, it spoke to me.

I was in retreat, and had lingered on in chapel after the other sisters had left. The voice, inward and yet as clear as any audible voice, said, "Why are you keeping me waiting?"

It was almost as though someone had given me a sideswipe. Before I could spell out my 'question marks' to the Lord and wait for him to tell me how reasonable they were, the voice continued, "Answer me. Have you ever known greater joy than you've found in this life?"

Riveted in my place by the unexpectedness of this, I considered the question. It honestly hadn't occurred to me before, with quite such force, that this life not only promised joy, but in very great measure had begun to yield it. Already I had received an earnest of things to come.

It isn't that finding personal joy is the chief and only criterion of whether or not one is doing the right thing. It is discerning the will of God and doing it that is all important, but I went back to a day over two years ago when I was feeling particularly miserable. Sister Geraldine had been ministering words of comfort when suddenly she broke off and said: "You know, it really is the most joyful life, if it is the right vocation."

She was certainly a very good advertisement for the joyfulness of it, standing there looking almost sickeningly radiant with health and happiness.

In my soggy state, I couldn't take it. 'You've got to be kidding!' I thought.

She was right, though. Absolutely right. For joy is to be distinguished from happiness which may after all be fleeting. Joy is like a deep underground river and it flows when one is in the path of God's choosing, even though that path may involve pain. For, are we not following a Lord who "for the joy that was set before him, endured the cross"?[1]

Certainly we are called to a very deep joy in the Religious Life, a life in which love surprises us round every corner. Here, now, the voice was challenging me, "Have you ever known a deeper joy?"

No, I hadn't. Despite all the pain of the ongoing self-discovery, all the adjustments to living in community – and an all-female community at that – despite the seeming losses, I had never known a greater unity and peace in myself, never felt freer in relationships or service.

"What are you waiting for?" the inner voice persisted. I lowered my eyes till they came to rest on the altar frontal that Sister Frances had made. With colours rather like a Gauguin painting, they depicted the movement from darkness to light, and seemed to symbolise my own journey.

I could keep him waiting no longer. Without more ado, I

gave my inner assent. It was as simple as that. Sister Freda had been right. I had woken up on this particular morning and knew my answer.

It was entirely undramatic, unemotional and ordinary. I doubt if any of the other sisters in the house would have guessed, by any outward sign, that between breakfast and dinner, about the most momentous decision of my life had been made.

A great enveloping peace descended from that moment on. The final doubts seemed to have been swept away completely and the energy that all the sitting-on-the-fence had taken, was now released for better purposes.

"I think you should get a short break before returning to the convent," said Sister Frances, who was now the Superior. "Is there anywhere you could go for a night or two to get some complete rest?"

There most certainly was. The friend who now looked after Pompey was due to go away. Her house would be empty and, of course, Pompey would welcome company.

After the decision making, I valued the solitude, and it was blissful to have time and space for reading, sleeping, catching up on letters, taking stock and contemplating – it was a time full of a great and overflowing peace. Pompey enjoyed it too. On my return, I packed my things, said my farewells and, with a great pang inside at the parting, left for the convent.

The three months that elapsed after returning from Oxford provided a period of re-orientation, of adjustment to the larger group of sisters and absorption into the novitiate group again. Nothing weakened my resolve – indeed I now had only one desire and that was to make a total commitment through profession.

I sat down one evening to write to Mother asking to be considered for election. Every novice sister, when she reaches this point of certainty, has to make application in writing. A request of such importance cannot be given verbally, or conveyed to the community by the Novice Mistress or any other acting intermediary.

Once such a letter has been received by the Reverend

Mother, the machinery for an election is put into motion. Before a sister can make her profession, the community is asked to vote on whether or not it considers this to be the will of God. Since our community is so large, it is no longer the practice that every sister votes. In some cases, there may be sisters (eg those overseas) who have never met the novice. So the community delegates its responsibility, and a representative group of sisters, together with the Reverend Mother, her Assistant and the Novice Mistress, form what is known as an Elective Chapter. Through written reports from the sisters, from their own knowledge of her, and through much prayer, the Chapter has to try and discern the will of God and the mind of the community. The novice sister is invited to meet the Chapter and together they examine her life in community so far, and she has an opportunity to tell them in her own words why she feels God is calling her to take this step. After further time for discussion and prayer, the members of the Chapter vote and, usually after Vespers on the same day, the votes are counted. A two-thirds majority is required, and if the novice sister is elected, the date of her profession day is then announced.

I could not help recalling, as I solemnly placed my application in Mother's post box, the horror I had felt for Bronwen and Celia when they were asking for election – the fear their stripping, their long profession retreat and the profession itself had evoked in me. I began to understand now why they had been able to go through it all with a great and deep calm.

In a way, once one has reached the point of making one's own decision and asking for election, there is nothing more to be done. It is up to the community, under God, to ratify that decision or not. The period of waiting is something of a limbo experience. One is already moving out of the noviti- ate. This happens almost as soon as one has made one's own mind up about profession. Without perhaps anything being said, the other novices detect a change and there is a gradual casting off.

Others had spoken to me of this curious feeling before

their Elective Chapter and I hadn't really understood it till now. Nor had I been wholly convinced when they claimed that they really didn't mind which way the election went. They were equally prepared for Yes or No.

"Surely you'll be devastated if you are not elected?" I said to Helen when she spoke of this detachment to me.

"No," she replied. "One really does reach a point of not minding. Of course I should be sad in one way to leave the community, but if God makes it clear through the voting that he does not want me here, then I will be ready to leave."

This too I began to understand from the inside now, paradoxical though it may seem when one has asked to be professed in the community one has come to love deeply. It was a fear-less time in the next few weeks as I waited. I had no plans for returning to secular life, but I wasn't worried. My future was in God's hands, and more than ever before in my experience I was content to leave it there.

The day of the Elective Chapter arrived at last – a beautiful, sunny day. In the convent there was a prayerful stillness and God's peace seemed to pervade everything. Before being called in to meet the Chapter, I walked round the garden taking in the scent of the flowers, the acrobatics of a fly catcher feeding its young by a willow tree, the deep green of some moss on a tiled roof. The cows grazing near our hermitage hut lifted their heads as I approached them, and fixed me with great soft brown eyes, quietly ruminating in their rhythmic, unhurried way. Even the creatures themselves were spreading peace today.

When I was called in to meet the Chapter, the warmth and understanding of the sisters overwhelmed me. This was not, in any sense, an interview or an examination. Everyone was waiting upon God, concerned only that the right decision should be made. It was in its deepest sense a meeting – a mutual seeking of the mind of God, and was not at all the frightening experience I had once dreaded it would be.

There were fifteen sisters, any of whom were free to ask questions or raise points for discussion. I can recall most of the questions but, even more, I remember the remarkable degree of freedom I felt as we talked. What a difference from the last time I had sat before some of these sisters, at my second year review, feeling almost transfixed with terror.

The votes were counted the following day at dinner time. There was a strange dream-like quality as I waited in a little side chapel to be called to the vestry to hear the result. It was the same chapel in which I had waited before my clothing. Then my heart had been pounding and my thoughts full of morbid reflections on execution. Now I found it hard to concentrate on the reason why I was there. My attention seemed totally held by the beautiful reds in the stained-glass window over the altar.

When Sister Freda arrived and beckoned me to follow her, she was smiling. That told me the news, even before the chaplain made the official announcement. I had been elected.

Mother and her Assistant were there in the vestry besides the chaplain and Sister Freda. Everyone was smiling and after I had knelt to receive a blessing, Mother slipped away to put a notice up to tell the waiting community the result.

It was celebration all round throughout the rest of the day. Most of the details are rather hazy, but I remember the great happiness, the warmth of the community's greeting, the embraces and the laughter. No longer was I on the perimeter but welcomed right in. This was not just the Community of St Mary the Virgin, it was 'my' Community; I was to be a member of this family for the rest of my life.

However, my natural family was also biting its finger nails waiting to hear the good news.

"Give them a ring when you've had your dinner," said Sister Freda. And I did. Joy and gladness went back and forth along the telephone wires as I shared the good news.

My initial decision to enter a convent had not been altogether easy for them to accept, but now . . . now that they knew that there was no turning back they rejoiced with me and for me, and I knew that I had their blessing and complete support.

There was much to be done before the profession which had been fixed for seven weeks ahead. Days would be full with my ordinary work plus profession classes, constitution classes, visits to the habit room to be measured for my profession habit, a black veil to make (and I am no great shakes at sewing), the final settling of all my temporal affairs with the selling of the house, disposal of the remaining personal belongings, and the closing of my bank account etc. When it came to sorting things out, I had forgotten how much was stored away in the loft at my family home. In fact it was a shock, because it made me realise just how fearful I had been when I entered and how little I had really believed I should stick it out.

It is strange what hurts most when it comes to ridding oneself of belongings. Of course Pompey and my car had gone before. At this stage it was photographs that presented a conflict. I suppose because they represent one's past (in my case, childhood, school and college days, holidays, Africa, staff groups, special friends and places of significance), parting with them is a very vivid and symbolic reminder that one is making a complete break and starting afresh. Not that it is a rejection of one's past, but a break in which the past is integrated into the present and future without the need to capture it on paper. The same applied to the correspondence and notebooks that hadn't been destroyed in the first purge. They had to go now. Another bonfire was lit, and burned steadily for a long time with a sacrificial blaze. Sister Freda roared with laughter when I handed in twenty-five empty files. "The contents are now dust and ash," I told her.

If some things hurt, others were a great joy and I longed to be free to travel light. I can remember the delight I felt when I received my final statement from the bank with a row of noughts in the credit column, accompanied by a most warm and understanding letter from my bank manager who, far from telling me in polite terms that I was a mad fool, wished me well and said how much he admired the conviction that was making me take this step.

Besides the inner preparation, there were a good many

practical arrangements to be made. Invitations had to be sent to my family and the few friends who would be able to attend the profession service. Documents had to be signed, a will made (a nice, simple affair, now that I owned nothing), measurements taken for the gold ring I should wear permanently from profession on.

Then there would be the pre-profession stripping. Oh yes – even after my own sorting out and burning, there would be the official stripping just before the profession retreat began.

"God loveth a cheerful giver,"[2] Sister Andrea reminded me as we began.

But it is difficult to be cheerful and fearful at the same time, and despite my desire to travel light, there was still a good deal of fear lurking around. The things I laid out for her inspection were all, in my view, essentials, and it was going to take time and a greater degree of security to separate the real essentials from clutter. There have been a good many more bonfires since; more files emptied, more notes destroyed.

With so many matters to be dealt with before the great event, I practically fell in to my profession retreat in exhaustion. There were to be ten days of retreat before the profession, and four after.

Once more, Sister Madeline had made a room available in a quiet part of the convent, and Sister Freda advised me to get plenty of sleep on the first day of the retreat since she wasn't going to begin the retreat addresses till the following day. These were to be given in the quiet room at the top of the house on the guest wing, which has a magnificent view of the downs. I was to spend a great deal of my retreat up there.

I had been looking forward keenly to the retreat. The memory of the wonderful week before my clothing was still fresh. But every retreat is different, and one has to receive what God wills to give.

It was not long before the old enemy, fear, crept back in full force – fear as to whether or not I could go anywhere I was asked to go. It was not just the fear of being asked to do work which might be unfamiliar or daunting, but also fear that other people were making, or indeed had made, decisions about my future and I knew nothing of them. Somewhere in the community, a Superior knew that I was coming to her house and I didn't know myself, and wouldn't know till I was told by Mother at my profession tea party. Others in authority knew too. The fear mounted steadily to absurd proportions.

We each have our own individual battles and I knew this one had not bothered some of my fellow novices as they had approached profession. They had seemed quite relaxed about it. For me, however, once I got into silence, it loomed large on my horizon as a great bogey. Obviously, I still hadn't completely let go the reins on my own life . . . the old spirit of independence was raising its head once more. Yet as we come to profession, we have to make an open offer of our lives.

Sensing my distress though not knowing its cause, Sister Freda came to see me one evening and I explained about the fear. We talked and prayed, and as we did so the fear which had held me in its vice-like grip went. The great peace that had descended at my election returned and I no longer worried about the future.

Blessing upon blessing followed after that but over these I draw a veil, for we all have those sacred areas in our lives where we are on holy ground . . . and these are very personal to us.

> When all thy mercies, O my God,
>   My rising soul surveys,
> Transported with the view, I'm lost
>   In wonder, love and praise.[3]

So, wrote Joseph Addison.

Inevitably my 'rising soul' was doing a good deal of surveying. Thanksgiving was predominant in this time of retreat – thanksgiving for all the mercies of God over the past four years.

The words mercy and olive have a common derivation in

243

New Testament Greek, and the olive with its oil was not only valued as a relish but as a source of healing. Certainly the mercy of God to me had included much healing in my time in community – healing of the memories and indeed healing of the body, for I was in far better physical shape than when I had entered the novitiate. There was thanksgiving for all the discoveries of the riches of the liturgy and Office, thanksgiving for this community which had proved itself such a loving family, thanksgiving for all the wisdom and learning that had been so generously shared; but, above all, thanksgiving for, and wonder at, this call of God to serve him in the Religious Life. As my profession day approached and I grew increasingly excited, I knew that there was nothing else I would rather do, nowhere else that I would rather be, than here giving myself to him in this way and in this community.

"With the drawing of this Love and the voice of this Calling,"[4] I had made my choice, and everything in me looked forward to the moment when it would be sealed for the rest of my life in this world. Yet the wonder of it was that because it was God's voice and his love the initiative was his. It had been his choice first and he had brought my choosing into line with his.

"Sister Kirsty, what do you desire?" the Bishop would ask me publicly at the profession.

The answer would be given in the prescribed words of the profession service, but in a nutshell they are summed up by the Psalmist. "Thou O Lord God, art the thing that I long for."[5]

The joy, the thanksgiving, the love were all fresh and vital at that moment. It was springtime in my community life. As T. S. Eliot said: "Love must be made real in act, as desire unites with desired,"[6] and the test would be in the sustaining of this love and thanksgiving through thick and thin, year after year.

The vocation, the choosing to follow this way of life, would have to be renewed each day.

The vocation can evaporate even in a consecrated person unless it is re-chosen. The constant renewal and continuous re-choosing is often done 'implicitly' by the conscientious observance of rule, prayer life and community love. But more and more . . . it must become explicit, deliberate and conscious. Vocation is not a state . . . a once for all profession. It is a condition for the growth of a personality, consecrated and set apart for the people of God.[7]

Yet at the time of profession one is straining forward eagerly and one's sisters, recalling their own joy and first flush of enthusiasm, seem to spill over with love for the one just setting out on her professed life, and enter into her holy exuberance with her.

Their ways of sharing the joy were beautiful. As I went into chapel for Vespers on the eve of the profession, my breath was quite taken away. Sister Philippa had excelled herself with her floral decorations. At the shrine in the ante-chapel, a wreath of small white rosebuds had been twined round the heads of our Lady and the Holy Child in a most ingenious way. Another magnificent arrangement of predominantly pink and white flowers practically filled one corner of the sanctuary. 'What a marvellous gift she has,' I thought. The singing practices, the rehearsals, the polishing and cleaning were over. Excitement was building up. Some of the guests were already arriving and were staying overnight. The profession cake had been iced, the novitiate decorated. All was in readiness. I felt excited, nervous, and yet deeply at peace.

That evening I sat in the quiet room gazing out at the velvety greenness of the downs in the evening sun. House martins swooped in and out of the eaves where they had nested, and I heard the racket of their young as they clamoured for food.

'This time tomorrow,' I thought, 'I shall be a professed sister. By this time tomorrow, I shall know where I am to be sent.'

No, it really hadn't worried me, and still wasn't worrying

me, since that evening when the demon of fear had been cast out.

I looked at the naked third finger on my right hand. 'By this time tomorrow, that finger will never again be without a ring symbolising my covenant with God and the community. By this time tomorrow I shall be vowed for life in poverty, chastity and obedience.'

Perhaps on such a night one could be forgiven for not living in the present moment, not concentrating on the now, the today, but looking ahead to tomorrow. For tomorrow was going to be a very full and demanding day. It would start with a breakfast tray in my cell – blessed thought. Then would come the profession service followed by the community's greeting. Eventually I would join my visitors and family for coffee. As at my clothing, I knew the time with visitors would be frustratingly brief. Yet some of them were making long journeys to be there. Naomi, I knew, would be starting out at 4.30 am in order to arrive in time for our 9.15 am service. When the visitors had left, my family and I would drive over to Oxford where the sisters there were entertaining us to a celebration lunch. It seemed very fitting to be going back to that house, and to those sisters, to whom I owed such a debt, and sharing part of the day with them. In the afternoon there would be the cutting of the profession cake in the refectory, followed by a tea party in Mother's room. At Vespers I would sit in my new stall as a sister – still wearing the special profession posy. Then would come a visit to all the sisters in the infirmary wing, some of whom would have shared in the service over the relay system, but would naturally want to see their newly professed sister in the flesh. After that . . . supper, Compline and bed. And with the beginning of the Greater Silence, I should return to retreat for a further four days.

Amazingly on that night before the profession, I slept very well and woke refreshed, bursting with joy, and eagerly awaiting my breakfast tray that would herald the day's celebrations.

Camilla arrived with it – nearly as excited as I was – and stayed for a few minutes to chat. Again there was an envelope on the tray. I braced myself this time knowing that the love the card bore would knock me sideways. Even so, I was unprepared for what was to come – words chosen by Sister Freda which she knew would mean a very great deal to me, superimposed on a drawing of the altar at our Oxford house with Sister Frances' frontal, and the long frosted windows in front of which hung the crucifix – 'my' crucifix. My fellow novice who had designed this card could not have known the special significance of that crucifix to me, for I had told only one person of its part in my decision making.

It was all too much, and I wept that God should be providing these confirming touches, even at this eleventh hour, and through my profession card.

Breakfast over, I bathed and put on my new clothes. Punctually, Sister Freda arrived to pin the posy on to my scapular and assure herself that I was all right and hadn't forgotten anything.

I took a last look round at my cell. 'The next time I come in here,' I thought, 'a whole new thing will have happened to me.'

The novitiate was beautiful – decorated with white flowers and the words of the special text chosen by Sister Freda as the 'intention' for the profession. My candle stood in readiness. If there was any last minute feverish activity in the convent, any greetings being exchanged with sisters arriving from branch houses, I was totally unaware of it. It was all stillness here, as Sister Freda and I knelt in prayer. All nervousness seemed to evaporate. I was aware only of a heart overflowing with gratitude and joy.

Promptly at 9.00 am, the other novices filed in and knelt in a semi-circle with me. As the chapel bell rang, Mother arrived to begin the preliminary ceremony which takes place in the novitiate before the entry of the Sister Elect into chapel.

"The Lord is my light and my salvation; whom then shall I fear"[7] we began. Hadn't it been the Lord my light who had drawn me on towards himself through all the darkness in these preparatory years? Wasn't it that glimpse that he had given me of himself as light, that had held me through all the vicissitudes of my four years as a novice.

"Whom then shall I fear"[8] Whom indeed? For he had banished so much fear already, and he who had begun that good work would bring it to completion,[9] of that I was confident.

We continued the versicles and responses – all taken from the Psalms.

"Thou shalt guide me with thy counsel: and after that receive me with glory,"[10] said Sister Freda.

And we all replied, "Whom have I in heaven but thee: and there is none upon earth that I desire in comparison of thee."[11]

There it was – the verse that had clinched for me that other choice, and focused for me my longing for the Heavenly Bridegroom.

"Father, by your Spirit," prayed Sister Freda, "you have inspired our sister with the desire to follow Christ completely. Given her perseverance in what she has begun. When he comes in glory may he welcome her into the joy of his Kingdom, where he is Lord for ever and ever. Amen."

We rose to our feet and Mother lit the candle. Crossing the room to me, in what is one of the most moving parts of the service, she presented it to me formally. It was, symbolically, the candle of my clothing still alight. Very soon now, at the moment of presentation to the Bishop, the choir would sing: "Behold the Bridegroom! Go out to meet him," and the candle would signify my lamp "trimmed and ready". Gazing at it, I prayed that the flame of my love would always burn surely and steadily within the "sheltering glass of a holy desire".

Eagerly, I followed Mother and Sister Freda out of the room. Clutching my candle very firmly, I passed through the novitiate door for the last time as a novice, into the cloister, to join the waiting acolytes and banner bearers who were in readiness to lead the procession to chapel.

The precentrix started the respond, "My beloved speaks and says to me . . ."

And we all took it up, singing: "Arise my love, my fair one, and come away."[12]

We began to move forward slowly and with great dignity.

Mother and Sister Freda were ahead of me. My fellow novices came in twos behind.

"His banner over me is love," proclaimed the banner in front.

The cloister stretched ahead like a tunnel, but in the distance the lights of chapel were blazing, and he who is my Light and my Salvation waited to keep faith with me.

REFERENCES

3

LIFE TOGETHER

1 *English Hymnal* No 135, verse 1 and verse 5.
2 Quoted on p 80 *Hasidism and Modern Man*. Martin Buber. Harper Torch Books, Harper and Row, U.S. 1958.
3 *Till We Have Faces*. C. S. Lewis – quotation from review by Harry Blamires.
4 1 Corinthians 4:10.
5 p 283 Laude (Lauda LXXXIV) Jacopone da Todi. Underhill. J. M. Dent, 1919.
6 Suggested by E. Herman p 177. *Meaning and Value of Mysticism*. J. Clarke. 1922.
7 Chapter 17. *Fire of Love*. Richard Rolle. Penguin, 1972.

4

ADJUSTMENTS

1 p 68 *Sign of Jonas*. Thomas Merton. Sheldon Press. 1976.
2 p 65 *Mother Maribel of Wantage*. Sister Janet C.S.M.V. St Mary's Press. 1972. (Quotation from letters originally circulated to the Community.)
3 John 6:12.

4 Verse 4 Hymn No 184 *Ancient and Modern* [Revised] 'Dear Lord and Father of Mankind'. John Greenleaf Whittier.
5 Mark 10:30.
6 p 81 *Hasidism and Modern Man*. Martin Buber. Harper Torch Books. U.S. 1958.
7 p 81 *The Mystery of the Holy Innocents*. Charles Peguy. Harvill Press. 1956.
8 Recorded on p xix of Introduction to *Letters from the Desert*. Carlo Carretto. Darton Longman & Todd. 1970.
9 Recorded on p xix–xx Introduction to *Letters from the Desert*. Carlo Carretto. Darton, Longman & Todd. 1970.

Quotations from the Exultet taken from *Holy Week*, A People's Edition. Church Literature Association. 1972.

6

WILL IT BE ALLOWED?

1 *Crossroads* – a popular ITV serial which has to date run for some 20 years.
2 From *Le Cenacle a son Message*. Paul Vernion. Paris. 1950.

7

THE COMMON DENOMINATOR

1 *Against All Reason: Religious Life in the Modern World*. Geoffrey Moorhouse. Weidenfeld and Nicolson. 1969.
2 A Reader in the Anglican Church is a lay person licensed to conduct religious services.
3 Matthew 6:19.
4 p 112 *The Struggle with God*. Paul Evdokimov. Paulist Press. 1966.
5 Psalm 45:10, 11.

6 Luke 1:38.
7 Song of Songs 2:4.

The passages from Psalm 45 in the Respond and Introit are
taken from the *Book of Psalms*. William Collins. 1977. Copyright
David Frost, Andrew MacIntosh, John Emerton.

8

THE SHELTERING GLASS

1 Philippians 3:13, 14.
2 Matthew 10:37.
3 Quoted by A. M. Allchin p 33 in *Religious Communities in the World of Today*. SPCK. 1970.
4 p 34 *Religious Communities in the World of Today*. A. M. Allchin. SPCK. 1970.
5 Luke 12:50.
6 John 6:67.
7 Psalm 132:5 (Coverdale).
8 Psalm 59:9 (as translated by St John of the Cross p 50 Book 1 Chapter 10, *The Ascent of Mount Carmel*. Burns & Oates. 1947).
9 p 38 *School for Prayer*. Anthony Bloom. Darton, Longman & Todd. 1970. (Quoting Alexis Carroll in *Man the Unknown*.)
10 John 4:29.
11 Article in *The Times*. Maria Boulding. November 1980.
12 p 88 *Markings*. Dag Hammarskjold. Faber. 1960.
13 John 3:16.
14 Hebrews 13:14.
15 Clothing prayer of C.S.M.V. (unrevised).
16 Exodus 13:21.
17 *Mother Jane Margaret*. Sister Janet C.S.M.V. St Mary's Press. 1974.

SKINNED ALIVE

1 Song of Songs 3:2.
2 *Why am I Afraid to Tell You Who I Am?* John Powell. Fontana. 1975.
3 John 3:4.
4 John 8:32.
5 Story originally published in Readers' Digest (date untraceable). Reproduced from memory.
6 p 103 Meditation 3:3 *On Contemplating God*. William of St Thierry Cistercian Study Series. Irish University Press. 1972.
7 p 27 *Merton's Palace of Nowhere*. James Finley. Ave Maria Press. 1979.
8 From *The Velveteen Rabbit*. M. Williams Bianco. By permission of Heinemann Ltd, London. 1970.

10

A NEW SONG IN MY MOUTH

1 Psalm 73:16, 17 (Coverdale).
2 p 3 *Plainchant for Everyone*. Mary Berry. RSCM. 1979.
3 Chap 2 pp 59/60 *Life Together*. Dietrich Bonhoeffer. SCMP. 1954.
4 p 30 *Meditations*. Ladislaus Boros. Search Press. 1973.
5 p 87 *The Rose-garden Game*. Eithne Wilkins. Gollancz. 1969.
6 p 110 *Markings*. Dag Hammarskjold. Faber. 1966.
7 p101 *The Spirit of the Liturgy*. Romano Guardino. Sheed & Ward. 1930.
8 Isaiah 29:13.
9 Matthew 6:21.

11

THE SIMPLE VISION

1 Chapter 1. p 1 *Confessions of St Augustine*. Howard Press. 1969.
2 Mysterium tremendum et fascinans. cf *Idea of the Holy*, Rudolf Otto. OUP. 1968. And p 215 *Twentieth Century Religious Thought*. J. Macquarrie. SCMP. 1971.
3 pp 88, 89 *Taize*. Rex Brico. Collins. 1978.
4 In a lecture at Trinity Institute, New York, in January 1971. As quoted Chap 1 p 12. *Paths in Spirituality*. J. Macquarrie SCM. 1972.
5 Matthew 12:43–45.
6 Psalm 132:5 (Coverdale).
7 Article 'For Christ's Sake', *Playboy*, Jan. 1970. As quoted Chap 1 p 3 *Paths in Spirituality*. J. Macquarrie. SCMP. 1972.
8 Gandhi, quoted p 107, *Return to the Source*. Lanza Del Vasto. Rider & Co (Hutchinson). 1971.
9 p 90. *Taize*. Rex Brico. Collins. 1978.
10 p 97. *Thomas Merton*. James Forest. CTS. 1980.
11 p 162. *Hasidism and Modern Man*. Martin Buber. Harper Torch Books, NY. 1958.
12 Isaiah 11:6.
13 p 42. *Travelling In*. Monica Furlong. Hodder. 1971.
14 The Conversations and Exhortations of Father Zossima' Book VI:3 *Brothers Karamazov*. Dostoevsky. Heinemann. 1912.
15 *Murder in the Cathedral*. T. S. Eliot. Faber. 1938.

12

CREATIVE CONSENT

1 p 65 *Mother Maribel of Wantage*. Sister Janet C.S.M.V. St Mary's Press. 1972.
2 'Burnt Norton', *The Four Quartets*. T. S. Eliot. Faber. 1944.
3 p 42 *Christian Spirituality Today*. A. M. Ramsey. Faith Press.

1961. (chap 5. 'Asceticism in the Modern World'. V. A. Demant.)
4 Psalm 40:8.
5 p 53 *Michel Quoist: a biography*. Neville Cryer. Hodder. 1977.
6 p 83 *The Hermitage Within*. A Cistercian Monk. DLT. 1977.
7 Psalm 40:7, 8.
8 p 166 *Conjectures of a Guilty Bystander*. Thomas Merton. ed. Naomi Burton. Sheldon Press. 1957.
9 Psalm 84:11.
10 Luke 1:38.
11 2 Sam. 15:15.

13

CHANGES

1 Ephesians 4:13.
2 Hebrews 10:19.
3 John 2:5.
4 p 124 *The Light Invisible*. Robert Benson. Isbister & Co Ltd. 1903.

14

TO BE OR NOT TO BE

1 2 Kings 19:14.
2 p 87 *Markings*. Dag Hammarskjold. 1964 Edition. Faber. 1964.
3 *The Prophet* Kahlil Gibran. Heinemann. 1926.
4 p 44 *Reaching Out*. Henri Nouwen. Collins. 1976.

15

WHAT DO YOU DESIRE?

1 Hebrews 12:2.
2 2 Corinthians 9:7.
3 'When All Thy Mercies, O My God'. Hymns Ancient & Modern. No. 177, verse 1.
4 'Little Gidding V.' T. S. Eliot. Faber.
5 Psalm 71:5.
6 Choruses from 'The Rock II'. T. S. Eliot. Faber.
7 p 19 *Consecration and Vows: Psychological Aspects*. E. F. O'Doherty. Gill and MacMillan. 1971.
8 Psalm 27:1.
9 Philippians 1:6.
10 Psalm 73:24 (Coverdale).
11 Psalm 73:25 (Coverdale).
12 Song of Songs 2:13.
13 Song of Songs 2:4.